Wine Wars

Wine Wars

The Curse of the Blue Nun,
the Miracle of Two Buck Chuck,
and the Revenge
of the Terroirists

MIKE VESETH

ROWMAN & LITTLEFIELD PUBLISHERS, INC.
Lanham • Boulder • New York • Toronto • Plymouth, UK

Published by Rowman & Littlefield Publishers, Inc.
A wholly owned subsidiary of The Rowman & Littlefield Publishing Group, Inc.
4501 Forbes Boulevard, Suite 200, Lanham, Maryland 20706
http://www.rowmanlittlefield.com
Estover Road, Plymouth PL6 7PY, United Kingdom
Distributed by National Book Network

British Library Cataloguing in Publication Information Available

The hardback edition of this book was previously cataloged by the Library of Congress as
follows:

Veseth, Michael.
 Wine wars : the curse of the blue nun, the miracle of two buck chuck, and the revenge
of the terroirists / Mike Veseth.
    p. cm.
 Includes bibliographical references and index.
 1. Wine industry. 2. Globalization—Economic aspects. I. Title. II. Title: Curse of the
blue nun, the miracle of two buck chuck, and the revenge of the terroirists.
 HD9370.5.V47 2011
 338.4'76632—dc22

                                                                    2010050585

ISBN 978-0-7425-6819-8 (cloth : alk. paper)
ISBN 978-0-7425-6820-4 (pbk. : alk. paper)
ISBN 978-0-7425-6821-1 (electronic)

∞™ The paper used in this publication meets the minimum requirements of
American National Standard for Information Sciences—Permanence of Paper for
Printed Library Materials, ANSI/NISO Z39.48-1992.

Printed in the United States of America

Contents

Flight Three: Revenge of the Terroirists

Prelude
GRAPE EXPECTATIONS?

1

A Tale of Two Glasses

It was the best of wines, it was the worst of wines (apologies to fans of Charles Dickens). The global wineglass it seems is both quite empty and full to the brim.

We live today in the best of times for wine if we evaluate the situation objectively as economists like me are trained to do. Never before has so much good wine been made and so many wine choices offered up to consumers. For someone who loves wine, the glass is very full indeed; it is hard to imagine better days than these. The global markets deliver a world of wine to your door. Drink up!

And yet many enthusiasts are anxious about the future of wine. The good news we find in our wineglasses and on the supermarket shelves is often accompanied by disturbing rumors, feelings, and forecasts.

It is the worst of times, too, you see—especially if you are a maker of cheap wine in France, Italy, or Spain, the largest wine-producing countries. Everything about wine is wrong for you. Consumption is falling, squeezing your market share, and import competition has increased. You find yourself making the wrong wine in the wrong style from the wrong grapes at the wrong price and trying to sell it in the wrong markets. You are betrayed at every turn by the markets that once treated you so well, and now betrayed as well by the European Union, which once bought up your surplus wine lake and now tells you coldly to "grub up" your worthless vines. You hold an empty glass, or so it must seem.

Times are troubling in Australia, too, where a wine boom has been followed by a wine bust as consumers around the world have seemingly turned away from the muscular Aussie wines they enjoyed so much just a few years ago. Recession, falling consumption, rising antidrinking lobbies, water shortages, global warming, and even raging brush fires all threaten the livelihoods of winegrowers and producers in many parts of the globe.

It is the worst of times for consumers, too, or so it is said, if they seek that special taste of a place that wine geeks like me call *terroir*. The wine in your half-empty glass is free of any technical flaw, but so what? Does it have a soul? Does it express any particular place or any producer's distinct vision of what wine should be? This is the age of McWine, I have heard people say: wine that is all the same. When everything is the same, then it is all nothing! And what's worse than that?

These are good times and bad ones, too, for the world of wine—what a contradiction! What about the future? Will wine's tale of two glasses have a happy ending? Or will our (excuse the pun) "grape expectations" be crushed? I'm an optimist about the future of wine, but as an economist I am trained to pay close attention to the "dismal" side of any situation. I wrote this book to try to find out just how empty or full the global glass really is and how the world of wine is likely to change.

The first thing to understand about wine is that it is many things, not just one, both in terms of wine itself and the economic forces that drive the wine industry, so the story of the future of wine will necessarily be a complicated one. Although hundreds of particular factors will come into play as the wine world evolves, three big forces will almost certainly shape the overall pattern: globalization, Two Buck Chuck, and the revenge of the *terroirists*. Globalization and Two Buck Chuck are economic push forces that are transforming the world of wine. The revenge of the terroirists is all about pushing back, but with a twist because global climate change is going to force us to change the way we think about terroir.

GLOBALIZATION: REDRAWING THE WORLD WINE MAP

Globalization comes first. It isn't something new, as we will see, but it is a powerful force that is becoming even stronger. It is quite literally redrawing the world wine map, pushing it out from the Old World where most of the earth's wine is still produced to many New Worlds where both production and consumption are on the rise.

Wine has become a global or nearly global phenomenon, produced in a growing number of countries and widely consumed (except where religious edict forbids it). Most wine, however, is surprisingly local, produced and consumed in the same country and often the same region. There is enough wine traded internationally, however, to provide wine consumers with the impression of complete globalization.

Ironically, the most global wines live at the top and bottom of the "wine wall," my name for the various real and virtual spaces where wine enthusiasts (as demand) confront the vast and often confusing supply of available wine. The top shelf holds Champagne, of course, and iconic wines that can sell for hundreds and even thousands of dollars. These wines travel the world, reaching collectors, investors, connoisseurs, and upwardly mobile wine snob wannabes wherever they live. Asia is a hot market for these wines just now, but really they end up everywhere.

The bottom shelf of the wine wall holds inexpensive generic wines that can sell for as little as two dollars in the United States. In the European Union you can get a liter of this wine for a single euro coin (VAT included). Some of these wines are packaged in traditional 750 ml bottles, but most of them come in other sorts of packages—1.5 liter bottles, foil-lined cardboard tubes that look like exaggerated juice packs, and 3 and 5 liter "casks" of wine, cardboard boxes containing special plastic bags. You get to the wine through a spigot, not by pulling a cork, with these "box" or bag-in-box wines.

Whereas status and prestige pull iconic wines to the four corners of the globe, cost concerns drive the generic wine trade. Cost is key on the bottom of the wine wall and there is always cheaper wine somewhere in the world. With the advent of efficient bulk wine shipping (huge bags of wine in huge ocean shipping containers) even relatively small differences in price can unleash tidal waves of wine. Thus cheap wine in China (some of it even labeled "Chinese wine") makes a long journey from Chile while the Pinot Noir sold by a California-based brand might come from the South of France, Northern Italy, Chile, or somewhere else. It's a small world after all down there on the bottom shelf.

The vast majority of wines made today are neither top-shelf trophies nor bottom-bin bulk. These midwall wines, generally consumed closer to home than you might expect, are numerous enough to create a kaleidoscopic if slightly misleading image of wine globalization, especially if you live in Great

Britain or the United States, the two most important markets for global wine today. (Germany, as we will see, is the third great international market, but Germans prefer their wine cheap and cheerful—they lap up that euro-a-liter stuff—so they are best seen as an important but special case.)

If globalization simply meant that more of the world's people are drinking wine and more of the earth's surface is covered with vine, well it wouldn't be very controversial. But it doesn't; money and power are at stake. Money, of course, because vanity vineyards aside, people make wine to make a living. They may seek personal fulfillment or artistic achievement, of course, but they also need to pay the bills. It's hard to completely avoid the bottom line. So globalization is not an abstract concept to winemakers, it is a steely sharp double-edged sword: the prospect of new demand comes with the threat of new competition.

Money is an understandable issue, but power? Yes. The battle for the future of wine is all about power—whose idea of wine will dominate and whose tastes and interests will prevail. You don't have to take my word for it—you can see power politics at work for yourself the next time you go to purchase wine.

The wine wall has many political divisions, each with its own internal power structure. The French wine part of the wall, for example, is organized according to French geography, with Rhone here, Bordeaux there, and Burgundy somewhere else. Power resides (or is meant to reside) with producers in this part of the wine world, and the wine wall makes it clear. But if you move over to any of the New World shelves (California, for example, or Chile or Australia) you'll find a different political organization, dominated by branded varietal wines like Yellow Tail Shiraz or Mondavi Woodbridge Chardonnay.

Globalization has brought these political systems into direct conflict. It's like the Cold War all over, only that it isn't just capitalism versus communism—it's more important than that. It's the soul of wine that is at stake. Who will call the shots in the wine market of the future? Who will set the price? Whose palate will prevail? To paraphrase the Chairman on *Iron Chef,* whose idea of wine will reign supreme?

TWO BUCK CHUCK: WINNING THE CONFIDENCE GAME

Many fear that power and taste will shift from the Old World to the New and *vin de terroir* (wine from the earth) will be replaced with *vin du marché* (market wine)—wine designed by marketing executives and engineered to appeal to least common denominator palates shaped by long exposure to vast quantities of fizzy, sweet, ice-cold Diet Coke.

This is the world, wine snobs say, of Two Buck Chuck—the simple, cheap wine sold in the United States at Trader Joe's supermarkets. Every country has its Two Buck Chuck (sometimes at prices significantly below two dollars!) and every wine snob worries that the global market has unleashed a race to the bottom, where taste and terroir are endangered species and Chuck and his even cheaper cousins will someday rule.

Two Buck Chuck (or TBC for short) is a phenomenon; Trader Joe's sells hundreds of thousands of cases of this low-cost wine each year. TBC is a classic element of the tale of two wines. It has drawn thousands of consumers to the wine wall, introducing them to wine as an affordable quotidian pleasure, but by focusing their attention on the bottom shelf has it encouraged an epidemic of arrested development? TBC has raised the floor on bulk wine in terms of quality, but has it simultaneously lowered the sensory or aesthetic ceiling?

The story of Two Buck Chuck as it is usually told is all about price, quantity, and quality—the economist's familiar playground—but there is more to it than that. The miracle of TBC is not that millions of bottles can be produced at low cost—that's surprisingly easy to do—it is that consumers are willing to buy it! You see, wine is a mystery to most consumers. They have little confidence in their ability to tell what's in the bottle as they stare at the wine wall or puzzle over a restaurant wine list. Some of them are adventurous and treat it as a treasure hunt game, but far too many buy the same thing over and over again (that arrested development problem again) or, worse, walk away in frustration buying nothing at all.

Just cut the price if you want to sell wine—that's what Econ 101 teaches us. Ah, but there is a problem. Insecure wine buyers often read price as a proxy for quality. They are afraid to pay too little for a bottle of wine because they are worried that it will be horrible. Paying more, they believe (falsely, as a general rule), guarantees a better product—but they are also afraid to pay too much. No wonder so many people don't purchase any wine at all! So selling cheap wine is trickier than you might think.

The miracle of Two Buck Chuck is that it has given millions of Americans the confidence they once lacked as they try to stare down the wine wall and make a purchase. The wine business is really a confidence game, if you get my drift, and the future of wine, and the money and power that it brings, will be influenced by how the game is played and who plays it.

THE REVENGE OF THE TERROIRISTS

For many people, globalization and Two Buck Chuck are wholly positive forces—more wine, better wine (or at least fewer bottles that are really, really bad): wine that is easier to understand, purchase, and drink. What could be better? But not everyone shares these happy thoughts. The terroirists sure don't.

Terroirists are people who see the new global wine map and shudder. Terroirists seek to preserve and protect an idea of wine that is more natural, more connected to the earth, more deeply embedded in culture. It would be easy to say that this is an Old World vision of wine, but nothing in wine is ever really as simply as Old versus New. Many of the forces that terroirists oppose most vehemently were invented in France, the Queen of Old World Wine.

Do you oppose simple, maybe even stupid wines that exist only because marketing campaigns can sell them? Then you may oppose Yellow Tail or Two Buck Chuck, but you must first confront Beajoulais Nouveau, France's most successful *vin du marché*. Are you against wine that is highly processed and manipulated, wine that is almost manufactured? Then it is understandable that you may dislike many New World wines, since there are often fewer restrictions on winemaking techniques, but you should hold your greatest contempt for Champagne, a wine that is made underground (not in the vineyard), processed, blended, and sold for huge sums by French luxury goods conglomerates.

The Old World is home to both terroirists and the wines, winemakers, corporations, and critics they oppose. And the New World is too. It's hard to find Old World winemakers who are more committed to the idea of terroir than, say, Randall Grahm of Bonny Doon or John Williams of Frog's Leap. In truth, you won't learn much about terroirism by looking at a physical map—mental maps or moral ones have more to say. But the physical map will tell you something, if you stare at it long enough. *Terroir*—the idea that wine is deeply rooted in a particular place—is now a moving target.

The problem is global climate change. Now, outside my window I know lots of people who are climate change doubters and think that Al Gore's contribution to world peace (he shared the Nobel Prize in 2007) is overrated.

But I've never met anyone in the wine business who has the slightest doubt that climate is changing. The world is getting hotter and the weather more variable and extreme (which means, ironically, that some places are getting cooler, too). Global climate change makes set notions of wine terroir pretty problematic. Interestingly, it both undermines the terroirists' case and makes it stronger.

So the future of wine is up in the air. How can we tell how the battle for the soul of wine will be resolved? The answer, I propose, will be found by taking a *sideways* approach. Wine enthusiasts are trained to tip their glasses so that they can see how the color changes at the far edges. That's one way to know how a wine has developed and how it may change in the future. In the same way I want to tip the wine world sideways at the end of this book and look at its edges, the places where the change may be greatest: that means looking at China and how the forces of globalization, Two Buck Chuck, and the revenge of the terroirists are shaping that huge potential wine market.

HOW I STUMBLED INTO THE *WINE WARS*

People often ask me how I became a wine economist, an economist who studies the global wine markets. The answer is rooted in a particular time and place. Sue and I were still newlyweds, taking a low-budget vacation in the Napa Valley back in the day when that was still possible. We were headed north on the Silverado Trail late on our last day, pointed toward our economy motel in Santa Rosa, when we decided to stop for one last tasting.

The winery name was very familiar and I had high hopes for our tasting. If I had known more about wine back then I would have recognized this as one of the wineries that kicked French butt in the 1976 Judgment of Paris wine tasting. We pulled off the road and went in to find just the winemaker and a cellar rat at work. No fancy tasting room back then, just boards and barrels to form a makeshift bar. They stopped what they were doing and brought out a couple of glasses. If I knew more about wine back then, I would have been in awe of the guy pouring the wine, but I was pretty much in the dark. So we tasted and talked.

I started asking my amateur questions about the wine, but pretty soon the conversation turned around. The winemaker found out that I was an economics professor. Suddenly he was very interested in talking with me. What's going to happen to interest rates? Inflation? Tax reform? He had a lot of concerns about the economy because his prestigious winery was also a business and what was happening out there in the financial markets (especially to interest rates and bank credit, as I remember) had a big impact on what he could or would do in the cellar. Wineries, especially those that specialize in fine red wines, have a lot of financial issues.

Besides the initial investment in vineyards, winery facility, equipment, and so forth, there is also the fact that each year's production ages for two or three years, quietly soaking up implicit or explicit interest cost as it waits to be released from barrel to bottle to marketplace. The wine changes as it ages, but the economy changes, too. It's impossible to know at crush what things will be like when the first bottle is sold. As Bill Hatcher (of Oregon's A to Z Wineworks) likes to say, from an economic standpoint the only person who is crazier than a winemaker is his or her banker.

Wine economics is a serious concern. Few winemakers are completely insulated from the business side and sometimes the economy can have a huge effect on what winemakers get to make (if they have the resources to stick with their vision) or have to make (if they don't).

And so a famous winemaker taught me to think about wine in economic terms and to consider that supply and demand sometimes matter as much as climate and soil when it comes to what's in my wineglass. I should have known. Fully a third of the ferociously difficult Master of Wine exam (the MW designation that appears after the names of many famous wine experts) deals with business and economic issues.

ADAM SMITH, WINE ECONOMIST?

I wasn't the first wine economist and I'm certainly not the only one (there is in fact an organization called the American Association of Wine Economists that meets each year to read academic papers and somehow manages to consume a truckload of wine). Adam Smith, the Father of Economics, was also probably the Father of Wine Economics. The foundation of Smith's wine economics is laid out early in *The Wealth of Nations*,[1] where he wrote about the value of vineyard lands and how Old Vineyards are threatened by the expansion of wine production to new areas. He talked about the winegrape's unusual sensitivity to growing conditions (that's *terroir* talk, my friend) and how much money buyers were willing to pay for the most distinctive wines.

I am reminded of Adam Smith every year when I help my friends Mike and Karen Wade bottle their vintage at Fielding Hills Winery in Washington State. They operate an eight hundred case winery from a tiny building near their home, overlooking the Columbia River. They make award-winning reds—Cabernet Sauvignon, Merlot, Syrah, Cabernet Franc, and a blend called Tribute.

The bottling process reminds me of Adam Smith's famous pin factory example of the division of labor. Smith explained that a dozen men could make enormously more pins by dividing production into a series of specialized tasks. I get to experience the same process each year bottling Fielding Hills wine.

One person (1) brings in pallets that hold cases of empty wine bottles. A second person (2) removes the bottles from the cases onto a table so that another worker (3) can invert them over a nitrogen supply, which removes any oxygen. The bottles are then (4) filled with wine on a specialized six-bottle machine, then corked (5). A foil cover (the capsule) is then placed over the cork top (6) and secured firmly (7) using a surprisingly nasty electric device (that was my job). Then the bottles are wiped down (workers 8 and 9) before going through a label operation (10), being loaded back into boxes (11) that are sealed and stacked (12) and then moved out on the pallets they came in on.

It took a group of a dozen volunteers about six hours to bottle two hundred cases of Cabernet Sauvignon one May afternoon. One thing I learned from this exercise is that although eight hundred cases of wine is a tiny operation by the scale of global wine business today, it is still a very significant investment of time and energy—and all I did was run one machine! I thought we would never come to the end of those two hundred cases (2,400 individual bottles) of Cabernet!

Although my interest in wine and economics merged about thirty years ago, it sat on its lees for a long time, as I waited for an opportunity to link my personal passion with my professional research agenda. The two naturally converged a few years ago when I began writing what turned out to be a four-volume series on the global economy. My 2005 book *Globaloney: Unraveling the Myths of Globalization* included a chapter called "Globalization versus *Terroir*" that was my first attempt to write about wine economics for a general audience. *Globaloney* argued that complex global processes shouldn't be reduced to a few simple images. Globalization and food is more than just McDonald's, for example, and globalization of wine isn't just McWine.

The wine chapter in *Globaloney* gave me confidence that I had more to say about money, wine, and globalization. So I launched a website called *The Wine Economist* (WineEconomist.com) where I could work out my ideas in public, make connections, and develop a wine "voice." After several years and nearly two hundred thousand words of blog posts, *The Wine Economist* has evolved into this book. I've written about dozens of interesting topics on the web, but nothing interests me more than the question of how economic factors will shape the future of wine—how the wine wars will turn out.

In a way, this journey has brought me back to that dark cellar on the Silverado Trail in Napa Valley, the great wines we sampled that day and the questions that were debated there. I've learned much more about wine and wine economics, and I appreciate now more than ever the many challenges that the world of wine faces. But I remain an optimist, as you will see. I still have grape expectations!

TASTING NOTES

The publication of this paperback edition of *Wine Wars* provides an opportunity for me to reflect very briefly on how the battlefield has shifted in the year and a half since the book originally appeared. In the spirit of wine culture, I'm calling these occasional updates "Tasting Notes."

Going from Bad to Worse: Things got worse before they got better for Australian wine. In addition to all the woes I listed on page 4, add one more: Dutch Disease. Dutch Disease is an economic plague that occurs when one sector of the economy experiences a surge of exports that drives up the exchange rates, making all the other sectors less competitive abroad. The name comes from what happened to the Netherlands when oil was discovered in the North Sea. Australia's natural resource exports to China drove up the Aussie dollar's international value, making it even harder for them to sell wine abroad. Poor Australia: so "down under" that the only way is up!

Think Big: Two Buck Chuck, the Charles Shaw brand wine sold exclusively in the United States at Trader Joe's stores (and featured in the subtitle of this book), celebrated its tenth anniversary in February 2012. Americans have purchased over 50 million cases or 600 million bottles of the wine since it was introduced in 2002.

2

Old Bottles, New Wine

Founded shortly after the invention of the corkscrew, Berry Bros. & Rudd (BBR), the London fine wine house, celebrated its 310th anniversary in 2008 with the release of a booklet called the *Future of Wine Report* written by four of their top wine buyers, Alun Griffiths MW, Jasper Morris MW, Simon Field MW, and David Berry Green.[1] The MW means that Griffiths, Morris, and Field are Masters of Wine, the top international wine certification. Green is the eighth generation of the Berry family to work the wine trade. Presumably, when it comes to wine, these guys know their stuff. The report makes pretty good reading if you are interested in what wine and wine markets might look like in 2058 and beyond.

Let me break the news to you gently: the future doesn't look so good. Pretty much everything you think you know about wine is going to change and you probably aren't going to like it. Here's my executive summary of the sour news.

The geography of wine is changing, shifting north and east. China will be the world's largest producer of volume wines in fifty years, according to the study, and will make some fine wines that will rival the great French Chateaux. Meanwhile global warming will heat up today's great vineyards and make them unsuitable for fine winegrapes. Vineyards and winemakers will have to move north (and south) toward the polar extremes to survive.

The best Champagnes (or sparkling wines, if we respect the European Union's label regulations) will be made in England or perhaps even Norway as French Champagne vineyards heat up. Australia, the great global wine success story of the 1990s, will be dried out and largely useless for wine, although small quantities of boutique wine will still be made in cooler, damper spots like Tasmania. Napa Valley will shift north, to British Columbia. Ice wine? Well, I don't know. Alaska, maybe.

The identity of wine will change, as well. The way we think about wine today depends upon where it is from. If it is New World wine (from South America, Australia, New Zealand, South Africa, or the United States) its identity comes from the grapes it's made from: Chardonnay, Merlot, Shiraz. If it comes from the Old World (France, Italy, Germany, Spain), the designation is more often geographical: Côtes du Rhône, Rioja, Chianti.

In the future, according to the Berry Bros. report, popularly priced wines will be branded products like beer, cola, or laundry soap. Instead of Bud Light you'll be buying Bud White (and Bud Red, too). Wine will be pretty much dumbed down—standardized, homogenized, McDonaldized—to appeal to an unsophisticated mass market. These consumers won't know or care where it comes from, what kind of grape juice is in the bottle, or if it is even made from grapes. The wine aisle of your supermarket will look more like the beer case. I expect that there will be "microwines" that are like today's "microbrew" beers for upscale customers with more discriminating tastes.

Global wine conglomerates will blend wines for cost and consistency, not character or terroir, and sell them as lines of branded products to appeal to different market segments. Science will help this process. Genetically modified test-tube grapes will be used to create Franken-wines with dialed in taste profiles. You can expect "Lite" wines that taste great but are less filling. I don't think that vitamin-fortified wines or caffeinated wines are out of the question, once wine's identity as a natural product has been shed.

Do you like the rituals of wine? The dusty bottle. Cutting the foil and pulling the cork? Well, you can pretty much forget about all this, too. Corks will all but disappear, but they won't be replaced by screw caps as you might think. We won't need corks or bottle caps because we won't need bottles, period. Bottles are too heavy and hard to recycle and these factors will weigh heavily against them in the greener and more environmentally stretched world of the future. Wine will come in cardboard packaging and you'll just have to pop open the spigot to get at the contents. A lot of wine will be sold in those bag-in-box containers that the Australians call "casks," with most of the rest "bottled" in Tetra Pak–type containers that look like a cross between a milk carton and a kid's juice box. You'll still be able to decant the wine, I suppose, if you are desperate to preserve ritual, but that's about all you'll have left.

High transportation costs will change how wine is moved internationally. French and Italian wines will be loaded into massive food-grade plastic bladders and shipped to the United States in big climate-controlled 20-foot ocean containers, where they'll be "decanted" at rail yard processing plants into millions of juice boxes. It's already happening today, you just aren't aware of it. Many wine snobs who would never stoop to "box wine" have been drinking box wine for years—it's just that the box is a 20-foot ocean shipping container and the bag inside it holds thousands of liters. Who knows, perhaps we will even see huge wine tankers to rival today's oil tankers.

What will happen to price? The Berry Bros. report doesn't have anything to say about the cost of supermarket wines, which is probably wise. Rising demand (especially in China and India) and higher environmental costs will probably overwhelm efficiencies due to industrial production, more efficient distribution, and genetically modified (GMO) grapes, pushing prices higher. But it is hard to know how much.

The report is confident, however, about the price trend for fine wines. It is headed up. Way up. The supply of the finest wines is limited by nature (unique geography) and law (protective legislation). As the market for trophy wines expands, the price of the very best wines, which are already very high, will rise to truly stratospheric levels. The Berry Bros. experts project that Chateau Lafite-Rothschild, which was priced at £9,200 a case at the 2005 release, will cost perhaps £10 million in fifty years.

With scarce wines worth so much, fraud will be a big problem so greater effort will be required to assure authenticity. The report suggests that microchips will be embedded in bottles or corks, but I'm thinking that DNA tests will be the answer.

The report's final prediction is my favorite. Corked wine will be a thing of the past, we are told, and not just because corks will virtually disappear. Honey bees are the answer. Recent studies show that honey bees have very sensitive sniffers and so perhaps they can be trained (or genetically designed) to detect sensory faults in wine just as some dogs are schooled today to sniff out illegal drugs. Wine merchants and sommeliers will use these talented honey bees to identify and eliminate bad wines before they ever touch your glass.

I admire the experts at Berry Bros. & Rudd for making such bold predictions, but I'm not convinced that the future for wine is going to be quite so grim. Economists like to say that forecasting is difficult—especially about the future. So while the honey bee, Mondavi Lite, cardboard cask scenario is certainly possible (except perhaps for the honey bee part), it clearly isn't locked in.

No one can know for sure what the future of wine holds, but we can be sure of one thing—when it comes around we will be surprised. The future of wine will bear only a superficial resemblance to its present state. You will still be able to find wines in bottles with corks and fancy labels, of that I am sure. But almost everything else about wine is an open question. How do I know this? Not because I can see the future. It's because I have seen the past.

PAST IS PROLOGUE: REVOLUTION ON THE WINE WALL

Imagine what the wine wall—the wine department of your local supermarket or wine store—must have looked like fifty years ago. If you lived in the United States then chances are the wine wall was pretty small—maybe a single narrow supermarket shelf—and kind of grim. Not a place where a wine enthusiast could work up much passion. If you lived in Great Britain, well the supermarket wine wall basically didn't exist at the start of the 1960s. Wine, if you wanted to buy any, was something you found in specialist drinks shops. Government regulations strictly separated wine and food sales in Britain in those days, as they still do in twelve U.S. states today. The convenient global market for good quality wine that we take for granted today did not yet exist fifty years ago.

What do you suppose was on offer in the 1960s on a representative American wine wall? There was probably some Port and Sherry up on the top shelf and then perhaps a few rather pretentious French labels from obscure domains and chateaux. Italian wines? Maybe—Soave, Chianti in a raffia-wrapped flask. Australian wine? No. New Zealand? No. Spain? Probably not, except for the Sherry. Chile, Argentina? No. No. Germany? Regrettably, yes. Blue Nun.

Down toward the bottom of the shelf, if you were in the United States, you'd find the jug wines like Gallo or Italian Swiss Colony. The wines were identified by style, not grape. No Pinot Noir, Chardonnay, or Riesling. It was Burgundy, Chablis, and Rhine wine—Old World names that had nothing in common, not even the grape varieties used, with the New World brands that paid tribute to them and took a free ride on their reputations. Quality domestic wines were hard to find. Bad ones, however, were everywhere.

Somewhere on the rack, for example, I'll bet that you'd find sweet, strong wines like Thunderbird, a headache in a bottle, cheap as can be and fortified up to the legal alcohol limit, nearly 18 percent. It sold quickly to people who wanted a fast buzz. The wine market and the wino market were only inches apart. Thunderbird, a Gallo brand fortified wine, competed head-to-head with Wild Irish Rose; the strong selling (and smelling?) wine was the commercial foundation of the corporation that is today Constellation Brands, the second-largest wine company in the world.

You could tell the good wines from the cheap ones easily, cork (good) versus screw cap (bad), but really there weren't very many really good choices except in big city specialty shops. It was hard to get good wine in the heartland because its movement and sale were so tightly regulated by state and local authorities. (A wine lover in Washington State, I am told, was actually jailed for having a cellar full of wine he had illegally smuggled in from California.)

The sorry state of the supermarket wine wall in 1960 reflected very well the condition of the world of wine. A thin layer of spectacularly good wines floated like cream on a cloudy sea of red and white plonk.

THE PRESENT AS AN UNLIKELY FUTURE

Standing in the wine aisle fifty years ago, staring down that bottle of Thunderbird or jug of Gallo Hearty Burgundy, what would you have thought about the future of wine? Certainly the present, as we know it today, represents an unlikely future when viewed from the past.

I don't think anyone back in the 1960s would have predicted that the wine world would unfold as it has.[2] Wine in the 1960s was centered in the Old World—Europe, Italy, and France accounted for 48 percent of all the wine produced in the world and more than 50 percent of consumption. No other country came even close. Spain produced 10 percent of the global total, Argentina 7 percent, and North Africa (mainly Algeria and Morocco) 6.5 percent.

What about New World producers? Hardly on the map. The United States accounted for less than 3 percent of global wine output. South Africa's production, a mere 1.5 percent, was small but still about two and a half times the meager Australian total.

The reason Old World dominated wine production is simple: it also dominated consumption. France enjoyed (and I think that's the right term) the highest average wine consumption in the world: 122 liters per capita. Italy followed with 107 liters. Portugal (100), Argentina (84), and Spain (61) trailed behind. Wine culture in the New World just didn't compare. Per capita consumption in the United States was just 3.6 liters, less than Australia (5.3) but more than Great Britain (2.1 liters).

A map of the global wine trade in the 1960s would have an unexpected look. Most wine was consumed close to the source, so international trade was pretty thin. Exports of quality wine from France were important, accounting for 14 percent of global wine trade. But the biggest wine flow was actually *into* France not out of it—tank loads of cheap, dark North African red that fortified thin French products and filled the bottles and pitchers that workingmen drained and refilled and drained again.

The dirty little secret of the 1950s and 1960s was that France's wine of the people was really Algerian at heart. More than half—can you imagine it!—of the global wine trade in the early 1960s was from North Africa to France. And although much of this trade was illicit in the sense that many wine drinkers never knew what their glass of wine really contained, it is clear that some buyers welcomed the boost that Algerian wine gave to the French product. The French writer Hilaire Belloc advised the British readers of *Gourmet* magazine in 1961 (via a posthumous article edited by Evelyn Waugh) to purchase their wine from one Théophile Guillon of Nantes. "Make Guillon blend your wine with Algerian," he recommended. "They hate doing it because they think it vulgar, but it is a most sound rule. . . . It adds body and makes the wine last." A proportion of 25–30 percent Algerian was recommended. "The mixture of Algerian wine and water (often sold in England as St.-Emilion) is to be deplored."[3] Yes, probably on several counts.

If you were writing a report called The Future of Wine in 1961 you might have looked at these trends and forecast them to continue or perhaps accelerate, as would seem logical. There would be no reason to think that the wine aisle would change much in the United States or Great Britain. Wine would continue to be an Old World phenomenon except in places like Argentina, where Old World ways had been transplanted to New World soil. You would have been confident in your prediction. And you would have been wrong. The past fifty years have witnessed dramatic changes in the world of wine.

REDRAWING THE WORLD WINE MAP

I have a small collection of "vintage" (that means out of date) wine atlases, magazines, and guides. They aren't much use when I want advice about what to buy to drink with dinner tonight, but they provide a pretty good window on the past—what wine was and how it has changed. Here's what you see when you crack open a few dusty volumes.

Wines of the World, edited by André L. Simon, provides a fading snapshot on the world of wine in the early 1960s.[4] The 700 pages of text (with maps and color photos) were a welcome companion for the sophisticated wine enthusiast of the day. The world of wine was very narrow—much narrower than we think of it today—and Simon's guide is organized accordingly. Wine was many things here—history, culture, taste—and Europe was the center of the world.

We begin in France, of course, and emerge 140 pages later with a thorough understanding of French wine and manners. It is the largest single section of the book and very complete, reflecting France's preeminent status in the world of fine wine at the time. North Africa (Algeria, Tunisia, and Morocco) comes next with 10 pages, which is not a lot given Algeria's status as a top-five wine-producing nation at this time. Simon reports there were over eight hundred thousand acres of Algerian grapevines in 1959 and over 375 million gallons produced.[5] Not much more to say, however—it all goes to France, where it disappears behind sealed corks with some other name on the label. Other Old World wine countries—Italy, Germany, Portugal, Spain, and the rest—take us to page 600, where we enter relatively uncharted territory of New World wine.

Australia and New Zealand own lots of territory on the wine wall today, but they did not really merit serious attention in the 1960s. Australia was to Britain a bit as Algeria was to France—the supplier of cheap wines for people who couldn't afford (or didn't appreciate) the good stuff. "It is unfortunate that Australian wines have been so cheap for so long," Simon notes. "It makes it more difficult to market the better wines which necessarily cost a

little more."[6] More than half the bottles Australia produced contained fortified wine which is not necessarily the sign of high quality. The most popular
red table wine was marketed as "Burgundy" or "Claret," according to Simon,
implying that they were made with Pinot Noir or Cabernet Sauvignon grapes
respectively. Shiraz, however, was the most-planted black grape, suggesting
that the contents of these Australian bottles did not perfectly match the profiles of their French counterparts.

South Africa, Argentina, and Chile receive cursory attention (with Chilean
wines singled out for praise). The final 25 pages of the book were set aside for
the United States and here we learn about America's three great wine-growing
regions: California, naturally; New York; and Ohio. Oregon, known today for
its lovely Pinot Noir wines, was understandably missing. No wine was made
there until the 1970s. Washington State, the second-largest U.S. producer
today, was snubbed, too, but perhaps with some reason. Although wines have
been made commercially in Washington for more than a hundred years, the
industry was stuck in a rut in the 1960s, cranking out sweet fortified wines
behind state laws that limited competition from France, Italy, Spain . . . and
even California.

THE JUDGMENT OF PARIS

The wine world was already vastly changed by the mid-1970s. The huge
wave that sloshed red wine from northern Africa to southern Europe was
drying up due to Algeria's contentious but successful push for independence
from France. Strong "Algerian" wine was still being made and used to fortify
weaker French efforts, but it came from France now, from the Languedoc,
made by francophone refugees called the *pieds noir* who fled Africa to return
to the motherland, bringing their winemaking skills with them. Their efforts
ultimately would contribute to the vast lake of surplus wine that still plagues
the European Union today.

Although world wine production was still centered in Europe, the center of
gravity of wine drinking was beginning the shift that continues today. France
and Italy together consumed more than half the world's wine in the early
1960s—an astonishing quantity. This figure fell to a bit more than a third by
the mid-1970s on its way down to the current level of 25 percent. The Old
World—the world that had dominated André Simon's book just a few years
ago—was undergoing fundamental structural change.

Change was everywhere, but because I'm an American I find the story of change in my part of the world most interesting and instructive. Wine was beginning to come into its own in the United States, driven in part by the passion and ambition of people like Robert Mondavi. Mondavi believed that California could make wines as good as the Europeans and, backed by funding from a Washington State beer-making family, he opened his distinctive Napa Valley winery in 1966. His success started a gold rush. Things changed, but more slowly than you would think.

Unexpected names appeared in a 1966 California wine report in *Gourmet* magazine.[7] On arriving in San Francisco the wine authority did not travel north toward Napa, where the Mondavi project was getting under way, but rather south to the center of California fine wine. There he sampled the wines of Almaden, once a leading maker, now reduced to a bottom-shelf wine wall role. Paul Masson and Inglenook, which have suffered similar fates, are also featured in the report.

Hugh Johnson, the eminent British wine writer, visited California a few years later in 1970 and said he was impressed. He tried to persuade skeptical Americans (especially, I suspect, Eastern elites) that their homegrown wines were good enough to drink.[8] "It seems curious that I, a visitor from Europe, should be telling Americans about the unrecognized glories of some of their country's produce," he wrote. His eyes were opened, he said, by the very first glass . . . of Gallo Chablis (poured from a half-gallon jug). He praised the Gallo Vin Rosé and Hearty Burgundy, too, as "clean, fresh and in perfect condition" in contrast to French wines, which were so highly variable—filled with peaks and depressing troughs compared to the consistent American goods. Johnson visited other winemakers, Mondavi, Mirassou, and Louis Martini among them, but it was that clean, inexpensive Gallo Chablis that lingered in his memory.

There certainly was fine wine being made in California in the 1970s. The question was, would anyone buy it? So winemakers hedged their bets for the most part, making wines they thought would find a market to finance more sophisticated projects. A set of 1975 reviews of Ridge Vineyards' offerings suggest both how far California wines had come and how far they still had to go.[9] Ridge today is known for complex red wines, especially Zinfandels. The 1971 Monte Bello Cabernet Sauvignon was singled out for praise despite its high price ($10 per bottle). The Zinfandels are praised of course, but also, unexpectedly, was a White Zinfandel. "Ridge's red Zinfandels are especially famous," the review explains. "This white variety shows good promise . . . ; use it as you would Chardonnay." Three stars (compared to four for the Monte Bello) and a good value at $4.

A Ridge White Zin? White Zinfandel (the red Zin grape made in a rosé style) is known today as the least common denominator wine, the vinous equivalent of Kool-Aid. To think that Ridge would make one, however good it might have been, is an indication that the market for sophisticated wines was not yet strong enough to support even a relatively small high-quality operation.[10]

California wines, it seems, were both cursed and blessed by low expectations. So overwhelming did the force of reputation bear down that little was expected from American wine and small victories like the Gallo Chablis were celebrated nervously and a bit too much. No wonder the 1976 Judgment of Paris came as a surprise.

To celebrate the bicentennial of American independence, a Paris-based British wine merchant organized a comparative tasting of leading French and American wines. George Taber, then a *Time* magazine correspondent in Paris, recorded the event for posterity.[11] A recent film, *Bottle Shock*, may be more fiction than fact in the details, but it amusingly passes on the shocking result to today's audience.

The judges were French experts and the French wines were first rate. Fortunately, the American labels were not Gallo, Almaden, and Paul Masson, although that would have been interesting, too. Instead Steven Spurrier (now a leading wine authority) rounded up California Chardonnays from Chateau Montelena, Chalone, and Freemark Abbey; and Cabernet from Stag's Leap Wine Cellars, Ridge Vineyards, Clos Du Val, and Heitz Cellars among others.

Given the low expectations it would have been surprising if the California wines simply held their own in this exalted company. In fact, however, the French judges were stunned to find, when the bottles were revealed, that they had awarded top marks to two California wines. Suddenly, and to everyone's surprise, California was on the map. Nothing was proven at the 1976 Paris tasting, but much was revealed about both the wines on the table and the winds of change that were sweeping around the world.

IT'S [NOT] A SMALL WORLD AFTER ALL

Italy's Slow Food movement set out to identify the most important wines of the entire world in the early 1990s, sending reviewers to the four corners of the globe. Their ambitious report, published as *Guida ai Vini del Mondo* in 1992, rated five thousand wines from 1,900 makers.[12] It is the next stop on our survey of the wine wall's recent evolution.

The breakdown of the wines and wineries reflects quite well the small world of wine at the time. France accounted for more than a third (673) of the wineries rated, with Italy (366), Spain (198), and Germany (187) lagging far behind. A respectable 152 wineries from the United States were rated, reflecting the elevated status of California wines post Judgment of Paris. Australia (80) and South Africa (40) headed the list of lesser players.

Wine enthusiasts love wine rankings of all sorts, and Slow Food responded rather boldly, I think, with a Top 150 world wine list. Fifteen U.S. wines made the cut (14 from California and 1 Washington State Merlot). The vast majority, however, came from France (52 wines), Italy (26), Germany (18), and Spain (14). Australia (8 wines), South Africa (5) and Chile and New Zealand (3 wines each) rounded out the New World side of the list along with Old World stalwarts Austria (4) and Portugal (3). Many of the producer names that appear on the Slow Food 150 would also likely show up on any similar list today reflecting the self-reinforcing tendency of such rankings. No one would be shocked to see names like Penfolds Grange (Australia), Château Pétrus (France), Gaja (Italy), Vega Sicilia (Spain), or Shafer (United States) on an elite wine league table today.

Slow Food gives us a pretty clear picture of the wine world of the early 1990s from the European perspective. Was the view the same from the United States? *Wine Spectator* magazine's annual Top 100 list, first published in 1988, shows how much things have changed.[13]

France and Italy accounted for 60 of the Top 100 wines in the first *Wine Spectator* (*WS*) ranking in 1988. The U.S. contribution (34 wines) was surprisingly small for an American publication, and, perhaps in an attempt to even the score, *WS* reversed the ratio in 1989—33 wines from France and Italy and 61 from the United States. Although the particular wines and place of origin varied from year to year in the 1990s, the dominance of these three wine-producing countries persisted. In 1992, the year that Slow Food's 150 was released, France and Italy accounted for 53 of the *WS* 100 wines along with 36 from the United States. That doesn't leave much room on a Top 100 list for the rest of the wine world.

While the globalization of wine (the subject of the first flight of chapters) is not a really new phenomenon, it is as you experience it at your wine wall, on restaurant wine lists, and in guides and magazines. Only in the last ten years has an appreciation that wine is a big world after all really sunk in. *Wine Spectator*'s Top 100 list, for example, has in recent years been divided into roughly equal thirds with France and Italy making up one tranche, the United States the second, and the ROW (rest of world) the third. About a dozen countries typically appear on the *WS* 100 list today, up from five or six in the early years.

The comfortable traditions of wine haven't changed very much since the 1960s, but just about everything else has. Wine is different now. There are more choices from more places at more price points. Wine is better now, at least supermarket wine is, and cheaper, too, for the quality you get. Wine's social role has changed, too, especially in the New World, where it has become as much a lifestyle expression as a beverage. At the same time, however, concern that wine is being commercialized and homogenized—McDonaldized, in short—continues to be voiced.

The supermarket wine wall today could not look more different from the dismal product patch of the 1960s, don't you agree? It is, as I'll explain in the coming chapters, the semi-glorious creation of globalization, which has broadened the world of wine; the Two Buck Chuck effect, which has deepened its commercial core and shifted power within it; and the revenge of the terroirists, who seek to preserve and protect a particular idea of wine and its meaning. These are three forces that have created today's wine world and I think they will continue to shape its future.

The future of wine? Who knows? But it won't hurt to do some research to try to figure out where wine is going. In fact, I think it will be fun! You've got to pull lots of corks to get any answers in the world of wine. To try to get a feel for the future, let's look more closely at the present. This will require a short trip to one of your favorite places, the familiar wine aisle of your supermarket. Grab your wineglass and follow me.

Flight One
GLOBALIZATION— BLESSING OR CURSE?

3

The DaVino Code

The Metropolitan Market on Proctor Street in Tacoma, Washington, is a typical upscale American supermarket. It has all the upscale basics: a delicatessen and a fish monger, fresh seasonal local produce, a coffee bar and gelato stand. You can buy cat food, corn flakes, and laundry soap at competitive prices or, for $6.99, you can take home a quarter of a 1.9 kilogram loaf of Polâine whole grain sourdough bread, flown in fresh from Paris every Thursday. It is the kind of store that is increasingly common in American cities, patronized by people like me, who take their culinary cues from celebrity chefs on the Food Network. It is to foodies what Home Depot is to the DIY set: an adult toy store where imaginations can run wild.

You probably have a store like the Met in your town and, since you are reading this book, you probably go there frequently so that you can check out the wine wall. I'd like you to go there now (or if that's not convenient, to imagine that you are there) because this chapter requires your participation. I don't really want to *tell* you what the wine world looks like, although that's easy enough to do. I want you to see for yourself—and to be surprised.

I'm sending you to the supermarket because that's where the battle for the future of wine is being waged. It isn't the only battlefield; the idea of wine is contested wherever and whenever wine is bought and sold. Restaurants and bars. Wine shops and auction floors. Tasting rooms and cellar doors. Shoot, I've even bought wine in the middle of the night, directly from the maker, from the back of a pickup truck on a dark city street. (Don't ask.)

But the supermarket is the central stage of this story and that's where we need to begin. And to understand what's going on there we will need to inspect it closely, looking for the key to its secret code.

THE GRAPE WALL OF WINE

So let's walk the wine wall together. I want you to get a personal sense of the world of wine that global markets bring to your door every day. So first, please just stand back and try to get a sense of the scale of the place. There are probably at least forty linear feet of wine bins, boxes, shelves, and racks stocked from toe to tip with bottles, jugs, and boxes of wine. There are more than fifteen hundred different wines on display at the Met—fifteen hundred different answers to the question, what should I drink tonight? It's like searching for a needle in a haystack.

The wine wall is really the Grape Wall (pardon the pun) of the upscale supermarket empire. But wait there is more . . . more wine; and more wine choices are scattered around the store—in the cooler, by the bakery, and around the meat, fish, and produce displays.

How does the wine wall compare with other product venues in the store? There are clearly more choices for wine than for any other type of product, don't you think? Look around. Beer? Lots of choices, but nothing like wine. Milk? Not even close. Breakfast cereals take up a lot of room and there are sure a lot of them to choose from, but the variety can't compare to wine. What seemed to be an overwhelming variety of gourmet cheeses is nothing compared to the wine selection.

Your upscale supermarket brings the world to your doorstep, it's true, and showers you with choice. The wine wall is its crowning achievement. No wonder people spend so much time staring at it, trying to make sense of the choices.

Fifteen hundred wines is a lot, but it is not an exceptionally large collection for a retail store. The Tacoma Boys farm store a few miles away has a lot of space to fill in its big barn-size facility, so it can afford to give more room to wine. It stocks more than three thousand different wines. Your store may have fewer wines or more, but in any case it sure has a lot of them.

You've stared at this wine wall dozens of time—did you really appreciate the embarrassment of riches here, at least compared with the rest of the store? Now that you have a quantitative sense of this abundance, I would like you to walk through the wine aisle a couple of times to get a more qualitative feeling for what's going on.

First, try to get a sense of the types of wines on offer. Yes, I know—red and white. But there are really many more types of wines here than you think. Red and white table wine, for sure, and also sparkling wines, dessert wines, and several types of sherries and ports. You will find wine in bottles, half-bottles, double-bottle "magnums," 1 liter Tetra Pak containers, and 3 and 5 liter boxes. The alcohol content of these wines range from zero to nearly 20 percent and prices are as low as a couple of bucks per bottle to, well, the sky's the limit depending upon your store's clientele. I once saw a $100 bottle of Champagne on the shelf of a grocery store in a blue-collar neighborhood. Anything can happen here.

THE WORLD WINE WALL

Since this section of the book is about globalization, where does the wine come from? Assuming that your supermarket is in the United States, you will certainly find California wine. A lot of these wines will be Gallo products (Gallo is the world's largest winemaker), although they won't all say Gallo on the label. More will be made by Constellation Brands, although none of them will be called Constellation wine. I'll explain about the big winemakers and their "brand portfolios" in a later chapter.

You should also be able to find products from Washington State, the number two U.S. producer. Many of these wines will be Ste. Michelle Wine Estates products, although they won't necessarily say this on the label, either, because Ste. Michelle also has many brands (such as Columbia Crest) in its stable.

Keep looking for U.S. wines. Wine is made and sold commercially in all fifty states, so you may well find wine from other parts of the United States on the shelf. Oregon, New York, and Michigan have important wine industries and Ohio and Missouri were once the leading wine regions. If you dig around in the sparkling wines section you might find a New Mexico wine. Gruet, owned by the French Champagne family of the same name, is an important producer of American sparkling wine.

Now find the Old World wine section. You should see wines from France, Italy, Germany, Portugal, Spain, and maybe Hungary, Greece, and Austria. Madeira, a wine from the Portuguese island off the Moroccan coast, is frequently seen on this section of the wine wall.

Now find the New World section of the wall. These are wines from Australia, South Africa, New Zealand, Chile, Argentina, and maybe Canada, especially if there is a dessert wine section. Canada is famous for its sweet and expensive ice wines, although it makes good table wine as well. Some of these countries are not new to wine (wine has been produced in South Africa, for example, for over 350 years); they are simply new in grabbing our attention having been left off the wall for many years because of its focus on France, Italy, and Thunderbird. Now they are back and with a vengeance.

The only continent not well represented on your wine wall is Asia, unless you count Sake (rice wine). Japan has an emerging grapewine industry and its wines can be found at larger Asian grocery stores along with products from Thailand and India. It is only a matter of time until "Made in China" labels will show up on the wine wall as they have done already nearly everyplace else.

I predict that your upscale supermarket or wine shop will have wines from at least ten different countries and possibly as many as fifteen, which is amazing when you think of it. What is the next most "global" part of your grocery store? Fruits and vegetables? Maybe. Cheese? Possibly. The deli? Could be. Modern superstores are wonders of globalization, but there is no single product that routinely features more different international choices than wine.

All markets are local, even when they are global like wine, so your wine wall may feature some unusual labels based on local demand. Many immigrant families have settled in my part of town, for example, so some local stores carry specialty products including wine to bring them a sense of home. That's why I can frequently find wines from Romania, Bulgaria, Georgia, and Moldova in the market. These are all major wine-producing countries (Georgia is the "cradle of wine," they say) that are trying to break into the world wine market. Occasionally I find wines from Lebanon, Israel, and Croatia.

VINO EXCEPTIONALISM

This much choice demands organization, so look closely at how the wine wall is arranged and compare it to other parts of the store. Is wine arranged like the beer, cereal, and snack aisles, by producer? Lots of aisles in the store rent shelf space to manufacturers, who array their products together in competition with other suppliers. Thus Kellogg's Corn Flakes are in the Kellogg's section, not in some grouping of everyone's corn flakes. Ditto for Post cereals. It would make it easier to compare price if all the corn flakes were on the same shelf instead of being scattered in different brand sections, but that's not the system. Kellogg's paid for this shelf and it doesn't want any Post or General Mills products there.

Now, I have seen some wine walls organized this way—with all the Mondavi wines here (part of the Constellation Brands territory) and all the Turning Leaf wines there (in Gallo-ville)—but that's not how it works at my supermarket. State law stands in the way. Supermarkets make money renting shelf space to manufacturers, who then put all their products together on their "property" like hotels on a Monopoly board, but wine suppliers aren't allowed to pay for space in my state because their product contains alcohol. Alcoholic beverage sales are highly regulated in my state (as in most others). Distributors can't pay their way onto the shelves here, so they can't lease shelf acreage and must fight for position bottle by bottle.

Chances are that your wine wall is organized more like the General Assembly of the United Nations than the pasta or breakfast cereal section of the store. The American wines will be seated here, in one section, and arrayed according to the vocabulary of American wine, which is based on branded grape varietal wines. This is the language used by New World wine: brand/grape/region as in Mondavi/Cabernet Sauvignon from Napa Valley or Dancing Bull/Zinfandel from California.

The New World wine section is seated separately from the American wines, but the label identifiers use the same brand/variety/region system. You'll find Yellow Tail/Shiraz from southeastern Australia, Monkey Bay/Sauvignon Blanc from Marlborough, New Zealand, and Santa Rita/Cabernet Sauvignon from the Maipo Valley, Chile. Apart from relatively trivial translation issues (Syrah = Shiraz), it is pretty easy to move back and forth among the various New World wine producers, which is without doubt a fact that has helped all of them increase global sales. Brand/variety/region is the lingua franca of the wine world today just as English is the common tongue of the World Wide Web.

LOST IN TRANSLATION

It would simplify your wine wall choice if every wine were to identify itself according to a common classification system like brand/variety/region. This would be the vinous equivalent of a universal language—Esperanto for wine lovers. It would make choosing wine and understanding it much simpler than it is today.

And so, of course, nothing of the kind exists. Old World and New World speak different languages, both literally (how good is your German?) and figuratively in terms of product identification systems. The vocabulary of Old World wine is based on geography and there are hundreds and hundreds of wine-producing regions and locales: Chablis, Bordeaux, Burgundy, Beaujolais, for example. The wines of the regions are each based upon a dominant grape variety or designated blend (Chardonnay, Cabernet Sauvignon and Merlot, Pinot Noir, and Gamay, respectively), but the wines are identified by their place of origin rather than grape type because the geographical designation is a sort of brand.

Brands come in many forms. In the New World we are accustomed to private or corporate brands (Robert Mondavi, Yellow Tail, Cloudy Bay). The businesses that own these brands have an interest in maintaining consistent quality and the brand is a way to communicate this to customers. In the Old World, appellations (official geographic designations) serve the same purpose, although they are collective brands ("owned" by the winemakers in the region) rather than private brands. Geographic designations define, more or less as the case may be, what is in the bottle.

Old World geographical "brands" like Chianti and Beaujolais therefore advertise the quality of wines made by many different producers in a given region using the same basic grape inputs in the same way that New World brands like Mondavi and Columbia Crest identify the quality of wines by a single producer, sometimes but not always from a particular region and often using many different grape varieties.

A look at the Italian zone of your wine wall will illustrate the point. Many of the wines you find here are Chianti, which is both a style of wine and a geographic designation. Chianti wines must come from a particular geographic area in Tuscany and be made according to a particular recipe. In Chianti's case, the traditional recipe was set almost two hundred years ago by Baron Ricasoli and required the use of Sangiovese, Canaiolo, Trebbiano, and Malvasia grape varieties (Trebbiano and Malvasia are white grapes, unusual for a red wine). Until this recipe was revised a few years ago, winemakers could not legally use other grape varieties (or grapes from outside the Chianti zone) and call their wine Chianti. There are several subzones within Chianti (Chianti Classico is the most famous) and the wines come in differing quality levels such as Superiore and Reserva. Chianti is a brand (and a valuable brand to producers in this region), but a complicated one that requires some study to master.

Old World brands are like foreign languages—powerful communication tools, once you have mastered them, but lofty barriers to entry for the uninformed. One reason the wine wall often seems much narrower than it really is (weren't you surprised to learn how many wines your supermarket stocks?) is that significant portions of it are terra incognita.

THE DAVINO CODE

Once you have learned the Old World language of wine it is a tremendously useful tool, since the differences between and among geographical areas and their wine traditions allows for subtle but important differences in wine to be expressed and appreciated. The problem is that the price of admission—the time and expense of mastering the hundreds of valley and village labels for each Old World nation—is very high and so discourages consumers. For the uninitiated the language of European wine labels is an indecipherable code—not the *Da Vinci Code*, but the DaVino Code.

One reason New World wines have become so popular, even in the Old World, is that you don't need to break the DaVino Code to understand them. There is still a lot to know—Who are the best winemakers? What are the best vineyards? Which year is most reliable?—but the New World lingo is a much more transparent entry point to the world of wine.

A lot hides behind those European labels, if you don't understand them, including most importantly the real diversity of the world of wine. I frequently hear that wine is being dumbed down and homogenized, and I think this is because New World wine labels make wine seem very simple while the Old World labels are lost in translation.

The best way to begin to see this is to pick up some unfamiliar bottles from the Old World shelf and read the back label. Many will tell you only the maker and importer names, but some at least will provide more information. What you will see if you persevere is a world of grapes and grape varieties that you possibly never knew existed.

Rioja wines from Spain, for example, are blends of Tempranillo, Garnacha, Mazuelo, and Graciano grapes. Bardolina and Valpolicella from Northern Italy are blends of Corvina, Rondinella, and Molinara grapes. The wines of Chinon, in the Loire Valley of France, are Cabernet Franc (or Breton, as it is known in the region).

If you spend enough time reading the back labels of the hundreds of bottles of wines in your supermarket you will soon accumulate material to fill a book about the tremendous diversity of wine that is available to us today. You don't have to write the book, however, because it has already been done and by several different authorities. Jancis Robinson, the British wine critic, is author of one of the best: *Wines, Grapes & Vines: The Wine Drinker's Guide to Grape Varieties*, which has been continuously in print with frequent updates since 1986.

And so you can see that the wine wall is a very confusing space if you don't understand its secret code. Some of its territory is ruled by private brands that compete with one another to tell their story in the grape varieties that went into each bottle. The New World vocabulary is simple and clear and heavily marketed by the brand owners. The Old World of wine, on the other hand, is a kind of turf war among wine appellations. The appellation is the brand and the product it defines is embedded in its name. Pinot Noir and Sauvignon Blanc are known by these names on the New World parts of the wall (California, Chile, or New Zealand, for example) but will be classified as Burgundy and Sancerre respectively in French Old World territory.

TREASURE HUNT

Now it is time for a little treasure hunting practice to help you appreciate the wine wall's complexity. Suppose that you'd like a smoky, spicy red wine to go with dinner—a Syrah! What choices do you have? Well, first you'll need to understand that Syrah also has an alias, Shiraz, which is used in Australia, South Africa, and occasionally in the United States (to suggest an Aussie style of Syrah). So you will need to go to these parts of the wine wall to see what's on offer. Get a cart and start filling it with the Syrah wines you've found.

Syrah is called Syrah on the labels of wine from the United States, New Zealand, and Chile, just to name a few countries that produce wine from this grape, so you will need to visit each of these wine wall territories in turn.[1] When you have finished (and by now you ought to have dozens and dozens of bottles in your basket with prices ranging from very low to quite high) you will still have missed the most famous Syrah wines of them all—those from France. For these great wines you must look for names associated with the northern Rhône region—Hermitage, if you can find it, along with Crozes-Hermitage, Cornas, and St. Joseph.

Don't get northern Rhone confused with the wines down the river, however. Wines of the southern Rhone feature the Grenache grape, although they aren't called Grenache, of course. These wines can be great, too, but they are different. Chateauneuf du Pape is based on Grenache, which is confusingly also called Garnacha in Spain, where it originated.

Now that you have a proper big pile of Syrah in your shopping cart, you still face the biggest choice, which one? Obviously they come from many different places, reflecting different climates and styles, and are made for different markets according to different practices and philosophies.

You need to be a geographer (to chart the wine wall's curious map) and a linguist (to translate from Old World to New) if you are going to understand the future of wine. But that won't be enough. You'll also need to be a geologist who can read through the hidden strata that divide the wine wall into key market zones because price is the final part of the DaVino Code puzzle.

BEND DOWN, REACH UP

Ask any wine distributor or retailer and you will find that price is the critical factor in retail wine sales. Although wine enthusiasts like to think of themselves in complicated ways—favoring red versus white, Old World versus New World, Merlot versus Pinot Noir, fruit bomb versus oak-aged reserve—the dirty little secret of wine retailing is that price is the key to most wine buying decisions. When push comes to shove, buyers are really looking for an $8 wine or a $10 wine and make their purchases within a relatively narrow price range, regardless of other factors.

The wine wall in your grocery store is probably organized this way. Yes, I know there is a New World section and an Old World section and even a jug or box-wine spot, but look within each wine display and you'll see a clear price stratification effect. Here's how it usually works.

The wines you have come to buy are probably on the shelf just below your natural eye level, so that you can find them easily, but you cannot help but see those special occasion wines just above them (and the higher priced wines above them on the top shelf). Why not step up a notch? Cheaper wines are down below, near the floor, so that you have to stoop down to choose them. The physical act of taking the wine from the shelf mirrors the psychological choice you make—reach up for better (more expensive) wines, stoop down for the cheaper products. The principle will be the same in upscale supermarkets and discount stores but the choices (what price wine will be at the bottom, middle, and top) will differ as you might expect.

Studies suggest that people establish a wine price comfort zone (and corresponding wine shelf) and stay there, moving up a row for special occasions and down a shelf for parties and other higher-volume purchases. A lot of factors drive this behavior, including fear. I have some $8 wine friends who are afraid to start drinking $12 wines for fear that they will be able to taste the difference—and have to upgrade their wine budgets.

One local supermarket has taken this principle to its logical extreme. It is a discount store that counts a lot of low income and retired people among its customers. The wine aisle is not organized as you might expect—by country of origin or wine varietal. Its logic is simple and clear. This rack has wines that cost $3 and less. The next rack has $3–$5 wines. And so on up to the $15-plus wine rack. Large signs efficiently guide buyers directly to their target zone. Do they sell a lot of wine? You bet they do!

NAVIGATING THE WINE WALL

Navigating the wine wall is thus a fairly complicated task. You need to reach up for what you hope is quality, bend down for low prices, speak many languages, and know how to translate German geography into Australian slang!

The take away message of this chapter is that globalization has brought us an embarrassment of riches when it comes to wine. We have more choices from more places at more price points than can be imagined. And we want more. No Future of Wine report from the past would ever have been so bold as to predict the wine wall that we take for granted today.

But wine is changing in part because of the DaVino Code problem. A world of global wine demands a global language of wine and that language, for good or bad, is the New World vocabulary of brand/variety/region. As new buyers seek out wine labels they can understand, they will be drawn toward wines that identify themselves this way (and, if recent experience is any indicator, have cute animals on the label). The rise of these new brands will be stiff competition for a myriad of old, complicated geographic brands. What will they have to do to compete?

But before we think about that question we need to consider a more basic one. How did all this wine get here in the first place? It will take two chapters to answer this question and you'll need to leave the supermarket and come with me. We are going to two unlikely corners of the world of wine: New Zealand and London.

4

Missionaries, Migrants, and Market Reforms

The wine in my glass tonight is from New Zealand—it's a Sauvignon Blanc from Marlborough on the South Island. It's a very good wine, fragrant, fruity with a nice acid bite, but not a particularly rare wine. You can find it and other New Zealand wines in restaurants, wine shops, and supermarkets everywhere. You should probably pour yourself a glass to sip while you read this chapter.

What are the odds that a *New Zealand* wine would end up here? New Zealand is a former British colony, inhabited, according to popular stereotype, by fun-loving, beer-drinking rugby players, not sauvignon-sipping socialites. Why would Kiwis make wine like this when they are so unlikely to drink it?

And, if they do make nice wine, how in the world does it end up here? New Zealand is a long way from anywhere, really. And its wine production is teeny tiny, just three-tenths of 1 percent of world wine output. New Zealand is listed at around number twenty-five on the global wine production league table; it makes less wine than Brazil, Uruguay, or Mexico, for comparison, but more than Japan, Turkey, or Azerbaijan. Gallo makes more than eight times as much wine in its own cellars each year as do all of the New Zealand producers put together. (Although New Zealand produces just a trickle of wine when measured by volume, it is the tenth-largest wine exporter by value, a much higher rank: a status it achieves by virtue of the fact that much of the wine it produces is exported, not consumed at home, and that it earns a very high average price per bottle exported.)

New Zealand is just a drop in the global wine bucket. No doubt about it, the odds against finding a New Zealand wine in your glass or on the supermarket wine wall would seem to be spectacularly long. And yet here it is—and abundantly so. On a visit to Richmond, Virginia, to give a talk, I went with my wife's parents, Mike and Gert Trbovich, to try to find New Zealand wine at a typical suburban Kroger store. We counted thirty-six different Kiwi bottlings! So how did it happen?

The short answer is globalization—the process that delivers so many products from unexpected places to your doorstep each day. But it wasn't easy. It took an accident of geography and three waves of globalization to bring New Zealand wine to your table.

AN ACCIDENT OF GEOGRAPHY

The conventional wisdom is that global products like wine are made everywhere, sold everywhere, and consumed everywhere. Globalization covers the earth like a coat of paint whether we're talking about wine, hamburgers, or reality TV programs. We imagine that globalization works like this, but we know it isn't so. Even McDonald's isn't really global, although it is an oft-used symbol of globalization.[1] It has stores in only about 120 of the 200 or so recognized nations of the world today. McDonald's restaurants spring up when a country achieves a moderate standard of living and adopts a legal system that protects private property and encourages markets. About 40 percent of countries have unfriendly economic and political environments; Big Macs just won't grow there.

Wine is even more dependent upon the environment of course because it is an agricultural product. *Vitis vinifera* grapes—the ones that make the wines we love—are even more finicky than Ronald McDonald. They grow best within two relatively narrow bands that circle the earth between latitudes 30 and 50 degrees north and south. The northern ribbon of wine is the most familiar. Thirty degrees of latitude marks the southern wine boundary in the Old World, for example—Morocco, Algeria, Israel. It's too warm for winegrapes below this line, although high altitude (which brings temperatures down) can sometimes compensate for low latitude. Fifty degrees is about the northern limit—Germany's Mosel vineyards, for example. It is very difficult to ripen winegrapes farther north than this (and cold winters can damage the vines) although exceptions can be made. Winegrapes love to perch on steep hillsides in northern climes; the slanted aspect acts like a solar panel to collect more heat in the summer and helps cold air slide down and away in the winter.

If you follow the 30–50 degree wine belt around the Northern Hemisphere you see that it embraces the main vineyard areas of Europe and North America and wraps around to pick up Chinese and Japanese wine regions, too. Wine is consumed north or south of this band, but little is made.[2]

The northern wine belt covers a lot of area and includes about 85 percent of the wine made in the world. Why so much? Because it includes France, Italy, and Spain, which together make almost half the world's wine. But the map reveals an even better reason.

The 30–50 wine belt in the north includes a lot of land, much of it suitable for vines. The southern wine belt, on the other hand, is mainly ocean. Only a little territory (Chile and Argentina in South America, the far tip of Africa, New Zealand, and parts of Australia) have environments friendly to wine. Geography blessed the north with vast vineyard resources. The main land areas of the Southern Hemisphere—much of Brazil, most of Africa, the Indian subcontinent, and two-thirds of Australia—are too close to the equator to reliably produce winegrapes without some natural or technical offsetting factor. Even South Africa's vineyards would be too warm for fine wine grapes were it not for a cold current that flows up from Antarctica and keeps a lid on the heat.

The two wine belts are where wine was first born and where wine-drinking people migrated, the Greeks and Phoenicians first (to Italy and Spain), then the Romans (to France and Germany), followed later by conquerors and colonists from Portugal, Spain, and France to the rest of the world. Or, rather, to other parts of the wine belt, north and south. European settlers went outside the wine belt when necessary (drawn by oil or gold, for example), but they mainly moved within and between the wine belts where they found the climate friendly and could taste the food and wine of home.

As an economist, I find the wine belt fascinating. It is where most of the wine in the world comes from. It is, in fact, where most of *everything* in the world comes from! That 30–50 degree band holds much of the world's nonoil wealth and produces most of its GDP. It is possible for a nation to be poor in this wine belt (Moldova comes to mind), but it is hard for a country to be *rich* (except for natural resource wealth) outside of it. Geography isn't destiny, but it has some effect on the choices that Destiny gets to make.

That wine (and a high standard of living) should be made in New Zealand is therefore, at least in part, a happy accident, for if these islands had been placed a few degrees of latitude farther north or south, *vitis vinifera* grapes would have been an unlikely crop.

Winegrapes didn't get to New Zealand by accident, of course, and the wine didn't make itself. So as much as geography and Destiny played a part, the miracle of your wineglass is a people story.

FROM MISSIONARIES TO DALLY PLONK

Bibles and winegrapes came together to New Zealand in 1816, both planted by the British missionary Reverend Samuel Marsden at Kerikeri on the Bay of Islands on the North Island.[3] This fact serves as a reminder that many of the roots of today's complex global economy can be traced back to seeds planted by missionaries, who were often the most enthusiastic and determined globalizers of their day. French missionaries, Marist priests from Lyon, brought their own bibles and grapes in 1830, planting them first at Poverty Bay and later Hawke's Bay.

Commercial wine production started up in the 1830s when James Busby made wine to sell to British troops before leaving for Australia to operate a similar and more successful business there. It took a while for a real wine industry to develop, however, because British soldiers, settlers, and visiting sailors were all more interested in beer and spirits than wine. The colonial government didn't put much emphasis on wine or wine exports in part because of a strong temperance movement in New Zealand, but also because Australia had been chosen to serve as the "vineyard of the British Empire," thereby reducing British dependency on the hated French.

No one seems to have had any doubts that grapes would grow in New Zealand (thanks to that lucky accident of geography). Natural conditions were favorable, but market conditions were not. Many growers experimented with wine with greater or lesser degrees of success, but the industry didn't achieve a critical mass.

The wine industry in New Zealand didn't really take off until the next great wave of globalization in the years on either side of 1900. Immigrants from central and eastern Europe came to New Zealand, trading depression and war at home for jobs as farm workers and gumdiggers. They brought with them both a thirst for wine and the know-how to make it—supply *and* demand.

Thus many of the most famous names in New Zealand wine—their Gallos and Mondavis—are not British, as you might expect, or even French, as might be the case given French influence in the South Pacific, but Lebanese and Croatian. Assid Abraham Corban with his sons Wadier and Khaleel built Corban wines into the dominant New Zealand producer through the 1960s. Dalmatian gumdiggers Josip and Stipan Babic created the wine that bears their name today; Zuva and Nikola Nobilo did the same.

Ivan Yukich was the most successful of them all, however, building his Montana brand to be the country's largest today, absorbing Corban's before being absorbed itself by Seagram's of Canada and then ultimately by the French drinks conglomerate Pernod Ricard.

The inexpensive workingman's drink of a hundred years ago was called "Dally plonk" in New Zealand because the producers (and possibly also the consumers) were Dalmatian immigrants. The era of globalization that brought Dalmatian gumdiggers to New Zealand planted the roots of the cultural vines that grew the grapes that made the wine in your glass.

This period also produced New Zealand's first "flying winemaker," although "sailing winemaker" is more accurate historically. Flying winemakers are wine consultants who travel back and forth between the Northern and Southern Hemispheres giving advice and encouraging winemaking enterprises.

New Zealand's great winemaking consultant was named Romeo Bragato. Born in what is now Croatia and trained in Italy at the Regia Scuola di Viticoltura e Enologie at Conegliano, he sailed first to Australia in 1889, where the government employed him to advise winegrowers, before moving to New Zealand in 1902 where he held a similar post until 1909. Excerpts from Bragato's reports indicate that he recognized New Zealand's great wine potential, even singling out Central Otago as an ideal place to grow the Pinot Noir that it is celebrated for today. Interestingly, he promoted vineyard plantings just about everywhere in New Zealand except Marlborough on the South Island, which didn't impress him. Chances are good that the wine in your glass is from Marlborough, Bragato's undiscovered country.

THE THIRD WAVE

It would be nice to be able to say that New Zealand's comparative advantage in fine wine was quickly developed once Bragato and others identified it, but that wasn't the case. While some good wine was made, the bulk of production lacked distinction apart from sugar and alcohol. When Kiwis drank wine, they went for the same sweet, fortified productions that their Australian neighbors were gulping down.

It took one more wave of globalization to put this particular wine in your glass. Seagram's investment in Montana in the 1970s gave the firm the capital it needed to expand production. On the recommendation of another consultant—this one, I'm told, from California—Montana planted the first Sauvignon Blanc vineyards in Marlborough on the South Island at the Brancott Estate, virgin wine territory at the time. The wines were immediately recognized for their distinctive quality. It is tempting to say that the rest is history, but in fact just the opposite was the case.[4]

The birth of Marlborough wine had the bad luck to coincide with an era of spectacularly misguided economic policy in New Zealand. Like many less developed countries, New Zealand adopted the policies that political economists call Import-Substituting Industrialization. In an attempt to emulate Japan's postwar success, New Zealand raised import barriers, subsidized domestic production, picked "winning" sectors, and generally tried to grow a modern economy from the inside out. This is never an easy task and more so given New Zealand's limited population and resources.

The result in the wine industry was a vast increase in plantings of high-quantity, low-quality grapes as everyone aimed for the captive domestic bulk wine market—the market for Dally plonk. This led, predictably, to a glut of bad wine, which could not be sold at home or abroad, falling prices, and a general collapse of the industry. Having failed to develop by keeping imports out, New Zealand changed course and liberalized its economic policies, lowering trade barriers, eliminating agricultural subsidies, and embracing competition and global markets. The wine in your glass owes its existence—dare I say it?—to these neoliberal market reforms!

NEW ZEALAND WINE TRANSFORMED

A transformation of the New Zealand wine industry followed. Cheap bulk wines from Australia and then also Chile flooded in, capturing the bottom end of the market. Domestic Dally plonk was replaced with imported Aussie wine. The government paid winegrowers to rip out their old vines (a process called grubbing up) and replant with high-quality classic varieties like Pinot Noir and Sauvignon Blanc. Winegrowers began to focus on quality both because quantity no longer paid and because, with good imported wines now readily available, quality was the only way to compete. The crisis of the 1980s finally created the foundation for the wine industry that Romeo Bragato envisioned eight decades before.

That's how these great New Zealand wines came to be produced, but how did they get from way over there to way over here, in your glass? How did New Zealand supply connect with you and me, the demand side market? Globalization is the answer again.

In 1985 a Marlborough winemaker named Ernie Hunter entered his Sauvignon Blanc in the *Sunday Times* of London's annual wine festival competition, where it was unexpectedly voted the top wine. His Chardonnay scored big the next year, showing that Hunter's wines weren't flukes. This public success opened up the world's most important wine market, British supermarkets like Tesco and Sainsbury's, to Hunter's wines and soon to Marlborough wines and New Zealand wines generally.

At the same time Cloudy Bay, a Marlborough wine produced by the quality West Australian firm Cape Mentelle (now owned by the French luxury goods conglomerate LVMH—Moët Hennessy Louis Vuitton), also hit the British market through the parent company's distribution network and achieved spectacular success. A firm foundation for New Zealand wine exports was established.

Today the New Zealand wine industry is remarkably globalized, with more than two-thirds of its production earmarked for export. Britain remains the largest foreign market followed by Australia (where Kiwi white wines routinely outsell domestic products), the United States, and Canada. Foreign ownership dominates the wine sector. Pernod Ricard of France (Montana and Corban's, plus other brands) is the largest producer followed by the U.S. conglomerate Constellation Brands (Nobilo, Selaks, Monkey Bay, Kim Crawford, and several others). Other important brands including Cloudy Bay, Craggy Range, Clos Henri, and Whitehaven have international owners, too. New Zealand is both a destination and a home base for dozens of "flying winemakers."

British missionaries, Dalmatian gumdiggers, Canadian investors, California consultants, British supermarkets, French multinationals—and three waves of globalization—that's the unlikely story of how Marlborough Sauvignon Blanc came to be poured into your wineglass.

IT TAKES THREE WAVES

I would like to say that it always takes three transforming M-waves—missionaries, migrants, and market reforms—to bring a country's wine to the global market, but that's not always true. Missionaries did introduce wine to Chile and Argentina, two important New World producers. Jesuit missionaries brought wine to these countries in the sixteenth century, both for their own consumption and for use in religious observances. Missionaries were important in Mexico and California, too.

Merchants more than priests were responsible for the early wine industry in South Africa—the Dutch East India Company established the first vineyards there around 1652. The Cape of Good Hope was an obvious provisioning stop for ships sailing between Europe and Asia. Food, water, and especially wine were much in demand. Wine was especially valuable because its antibacterial qualities made it safer to drink than much of the water available at the time.

Mercantilism sometimes plays a role, too. The British developed a taste for wine hundreds of years ago when Bordeaux became English territory in 1152. For three hundred years Bordeaux was Britain's vineyard and the wines that the British call Claret were everywhere to be found. When Bordeaux returned to French hands, the British began what turned out to be a long search for a secure source of good wine. Winegrapes were introduced to Australia around 1800 in an attempt to create an alternative to France. Australia was envisioned as the vineyard of the British Empire, something that it became in the 1930s (and is again to a certain extent today), despite the long shipping distances involved, due in part to Imperial Preference trade policies.

Sometimes this first step is all it takes. South African wines had developed a global reputation by the seventeenth century, for example, and were a precious commodity in Europe. Constantia, a sweet South African white wine, was one of the three most famous wines in the world (along with Tokaji from Hungary and Contari from Moldova). It comforted Napoleon, who especially requested it, during his exile on St. Helena.

Early wine production in Chile was so successful that the Spanish government tried (unsuccessfully) to forbid new plantings (just as the Romans did centuries before in France) in order to limit competition for their own wines.

Missionaries are not always needed to create a vibrant wine industry, but migrants nearly always are. In California some of the pioneers were migrants who came with the Gold Rush and then discovered they would make more money selling wine to prospectors than panning for nuggets in the rivers and streams. Spanish and Italian migrants established a major wine industry in Argentina, for example, simultaneously importing supply-side know-how and demand-side wine-drinking habits. Migrants also played an important role in Australia. Swiss immigrants planted vines in the Yarra Valley, Dalmatians in Western Australia, and migrants from Silesia in the Barossa Valley and Riverland areas near Adelaide.

Migrants were even important in China. Changyu, China's oldest existing winemaker, was founded in 1892 to make wine for the large population of European expatriates in China at that time. Now its wine finds a market among China's growing urban capitalist class that expresses its worldliness in part through upscale consumer goods.

CRISIS AND CHANGE IN GLOBAL WINE

Missionaries and migrants were key components of the first two waves of globalization that swept wine to the far corners of the earth. They planted the grapes, but they didn't build the global markets. That was the role of the third global wave, which was powered by market reforms. And one thing that I have learned from studying wine economics is that market reforms seldom happen without a crisis to focus the minds of growers and policy makers.

We've already seen how crisis and reform were critical to the development of New Zealand's wine sector. Protectionist policies encouraged overproduction of low-quality wines. Too much wine to sell at home. Not good enough to sell abroad. Collapse, grubbing up, replanting, reform. New Zealand wine has done much better as a global competitor than it did as a protected industry.

Argentina, one of today's hottest wine regions, also endured a great wine crisis in the 1970s and 1980s. See if this story sounds familiar. Import protection and agricultural subsidies encouraged the production of huge quantities of cheap, strong, sweet wines. There was no incentive for quality production because quantity was all that mattered in the captive domestic market. (There was no export market—who would buy such poor quality plonk?) The crisis, when it came, was severe. Import restrictions were removed and a "grubbing up" program removed about a third of the existing vineyard area. The new market environment encouraged investment in quality production, both for the home market and for export. That's how Argentine wines came to live on your supermarket wine shelf.

The story is much the same for Chile, except that the reforms were more extreme. Half of Chile's vineyards were grubbed up in the 1990s and the focus was even more clearly on exports because of the collapse of the domestic market.

The story is different in South Africa and Australia, but the need for market reforms was much the same. South Africa actually had its great wine crisis in 1918, when overproduction and falling demand drove the industry to the edge of collapse. The crisis produced a unique solution, the creation of a strong winegrower cooperative, KWV. KWV allocated production quotas, set minimum prices, and made and marketed wine. With government help, it stabilized the protected Cape wine market and kept grower incomes high.

KWV was forced to abandon its cooperative structure in 1997 as part of South Africa's adjustment to postapartheid realities, which included access to previously closed export markets. Wine production was privatized and investment increased. KWV regulatory and administrative functions were transferred to the Wine Industry Trust, which aims, among other things, to use the wine industry as a tool to promote Black Economic Empowerment (BEE). The reappearance of South African wine on global markets can thus be seen as part of a response to a set of crises that reaches well beyond the vineyard.

Australia's surge into global wine markets in the 1990s was the result of intentional policy more than reaction to a crisis. The wine industry in Australia is highly concentrated, with most of the production under the control of a handful of very large firms. These businesses saw an opportunity for export growth and domestic market development. Industry-government discussions produced a 1996 report called *Strategy 2025* that set out a vision for Australia's wine future. The ambitious plan called for an organized push for increased wine volume (1996–2002), rising value (2002–2015) as Australian brands attained international stature, and then "preeminence" (2015–2025). Australians wines achieved their initial goals quickly, but the road to preeminence will be difficult. The Australian industry is in crisis as these words are written, with grubbing up, restructuring, and market reforms once again on the agenda. The future of wine in Australia is uncertain indeed.

TWO CHEERS FOR GLOBAL WINE

As you can see, the global market we take for granted today is really the result of a long, slow, complicated process punctuated by moments of terrifying crisis and fundamental reform. What should we think as we stand before the wine wall and survey the world of choice before us?

I'd like to give three cheers for global wine, but alas I fear it only deserves two. Globalization has certainly provided many benefits. As consumers, we benefit from more choices and greater competition, both of which work in our favor. Wine producers gain, too, in a number of ways. The global market for wine has helped create a global market for wine services ranging from technical production matters to financial services to those flying winemakers who help spread winemaking know-how.

Big wine companies also gain from the ability to source globally and sell globally. Increasingly it pays to read the fine print on wine labels. That Australian wine label may be affixed to a bottle containing South African wine when natural or market conditions make that the economic choice. I have seen "California" wine brands that contain Pinot Noir from Chile, Northern Italy, and France. The wine world is an increasingly small world and efficient global sourcing (via 24,000 liter disposable plastic bladders that fit neatly into ocean shipping containers) is doubtless here to stay.

So what's not to like about globalization? Good for wine drinkers. Good for producers, too. Well, economics is called the dismal science for a reason; economists get suspicious whenever they see a silver lining—they want to know where's the dark cloud that goes with it? So it should be no surprise that global gains must be weighed against costs.

Terroirists—a group we will meet later in the book—see globalization as a threat to the particular sense of place we associate with wine. Most globally produced goods could be made anywhere; they are defined by their *nowhereness*. Terroir is all about *somewhereness*.

Winegrapes are particularly sensitive to their growing conditions—they are able to express terroir better than most crops, a fact that Adam Smith noted in *The Wealth of Nations*. Wine drinkers seem to think that somewhereness is significant. Wine labels frequently give us much more information about the who, what, when, where, and how of the contents of a bottle of wine than is available for almost any other consumer product. (Ironically, the labels do *not* give the sort of nutritional data routinely found on generic cereal boxes!)

Terroirists recognize that sometimes global markets can save endangered local grape varieties and wine styles from extinction by creating a broader market for them, but they worry that pressure to grow "international" grape varieties like Merlot and Chardonnay and to produce wines that match an international market standard are too strong to resist. Soon, they fear, nowhere will replace somewhere . . . everywhere! This possibility makes it difficult to award the global market that third hearty cheer.

VICIOUS CYCLES

A darker cloud, from a strictly economic standpoint, is the tendency of wine markets to go through cycles of boom and bust and how globalization may affect this. Wine more than beer or spirits remains an agricultural product. The amount of 2009 Merlot available on today's market, for example, depends upon decisions made in 2009, when the grapes were harvested, and in years before that when the vines were planted. This lag between the time decisions are made and when market consequences are realized is a real problem.

Suppose, for example, that Pinot Noir is hot right now, so you plant more Pinot Noir vines in the hopes of cashing in on the trend. It will take at least three years for the new vines to bear grapes suitable for fine wine and another two years or more after crush (fermentation, oak aging, bottle aging) before your wine will be ready for the market. Will Pinot still be a hot commodity? Or a drag on the market? You can never really know.

Sometimes this fact produces a vicious wine cycle. High prices today discourage consumers but motivate growers and winemakers to expand production. Then all that new capacity comes online a few years later and it creates so much surplus that prices plummet. This of course motivates consumers, who love the new prices, but new plantings pretty much disappear. Result: shortage in a few years' time, when rising demand overtakes stagnant supply. Prices surge back up and the wine cycle begins once again.

Globalization can act as a shock absorber, stabilizing the cycle, especially if temporary surpluses here (Australia, for example) can be sold off there (the United States), filling in shortages there. But there's no guarantee that different wine economies will be coordinated in this countercyclical way. As wine markets become more integrated and international price effects are more important, it is entirely possible that global boom-bust cycles could appear, rocking the world of wine (and not in a good way).

The potential for a global wine bust (like the world financial crisis of 2008 but with different types of "liquid assets") is a sobering possibility. The creation of the global wine wall was a slow process, but not a steady one, punctuated by crises within countries as they adjusted to changing conditions. Global markets may make these crises less frequent but more serious. That's something to consider when you think about the future of wine.

Three waves of globalization—missionaries, migrants, and market reforms—helped create a world of wine, but they don't completely explain how that world came to rest on your upscale supermarket's wine wall. To get the full story, we will need to journey to an unlikely place. Grab your hat. We are going to London.

TASTING NOTES

A Rose by Any Other Name: Montana wines, which is owned by the French drinks multinational Pernod-Ricard, has been rebranded as Brancott Estate Wines, taking the name of the famous Marlborough vineyard where the first Sauvignon Blanc grapes were planted. The wines had previously been sold under the Montana brand almost everywhere except the key U.S. market, where the Brancott label was used, since Americans think of cowboys, not Chardonnay, when "Montana" is mentioned. Now Brancott Estate is the global brand.

Boom and Bust: The New Zealand wine industry continues to boom. New Zealand and Argentina are the fastest growing imported wines in the U.S. market today. Wine producers in both countries worry that boom may be followed by bust, but the actual wine "bust" is unexpectedly in California, where there are too few wine grapes, not too many. Years of low prices discouraged wine growers from planting new vineyards or renewing old ones. Now it appears that the supply of wine grapes will likely fall short of demand for several years—an indication that wine is ultimately an agricultural product and subject to agricultural cycles!

5

The Masters of Wine

Take a map (or better yet a globe) and mark an *X* at the center of the wine universe. This is not the simplest task in the world, but you should try anyhow.

The world of wine is usually defined geographically, as you know, by two climate bands that circle the globe, defining the temperate zone between latitudes 30 and 50 degrees north and south where wine grapes grow best. France, Italy, China, California are all in the north band. Australia, South Africa, Chile, and Argentina lie in the south. This is where most of the world's wine is made today, although the zone now extends closer to the equator (India, Thailand, Peru, Brazil) as winegrowers adapt varietals and techniques to hotter environments and nearer the polar regions, too, as global warming pushes vineyard limits. Researchers are seriously developing winegrape clones for the Estonian vineyards of the future.

THE CENTER OF THE UNIVERSE OF WINE

Where is the center of this expanding universe of wine? The answer to this question depends upon how you think about the world of wine. If you think about wine in historical terms, for example, then the center is near the Black Sea in what are now parts of Georgia and Armenia. That's where scientists have found evidence of extensive early *vitis vinifera* plantings.

The answer is different if we frame the question in quantitative terms. Going by number of bottles produced, the center of the wine world lies in

Languedoc, the huge Mediterranean arc of vines in the South of France. Languedoc-Roussillon, to give the region its proper name, is the world's largest vineyard where a half-million acres of vines are tended by over thirty thousand *vignerons*.

The average vineyard size is tiny, sometimes just a few acres, as a result of decades of division of family holdings. Such small plots are not very economical, of course, which helps explain why Languedoc is simultaneously the world's largest producer of wine and the world's greatest recipient of wine subsidies. In recent years the European Union (EU) has bought up millions of cases of surplus wine from Languedoc and other regions and distilled it into industrial alcohol. Although recent EU reforms promise to end these payments, pressure to continue them remains. As recently as 2009 the French government requested emergency permission to distill 600 million liters of surplus wine to support winegrower incomes.

Languedoc has the numbers when it comes to wine, but not the reputation (although many excellent wines are made there). To find the center of the wine world in terms of status, you have to travel from Languedoc up the 240 kilometers of the Canal du Midi to Bordeaux, the most famous wine region in France and the world. Although Burgundy may cry foul, and not without cause, Bordeaux reigns supreme in the minds of many wine enthusiasts, led by the famous *Premieur Crus* (first-rated growths) established by the Classification of 1855: Chateaux Lafite-Rothschild, Margaux, Latour, Haut-Brion, and Mouton-Rothschild (added to the list in 1973). Not all Bordeaux wines reach these heights (indeed most fall far short), but the region's reputation is established by these exceptional champions just as Languedoc's low status is due to its noteworthy failures.

Bordeaux with its classic chateaux and international reputation is what people imagine when they think about fine wines, but it is not the center of the market when those thoughts become action in the marketplace. No, the center of the world of wine *markets* is the least likely place of all—a place better known for drinking ale and spirits at about the same latitude as Calgary, Canada, in a climate long thought to be unfriendly to the vine.

The center of the wine world in economic terms is in the United Kingdom on Delamare Road in Cheshunt, Hertfordshire—north of London a few miles past the M25 ring road. What an unlikely place! Why is this center of the world and how did it get that way? Read on.

THE WORLD'S BEST WINE MARKET

Britain's consumers have relatively plentiful disposable incomes and are, as we will see, well informed by the wine press and well served by specialists and supermarkets; the wine culture is robust. The British drink about twenty liters of wine per capita each year, much less than France (about fifty liters per head) but a good deal more than the United States (less than ten) or the world average (less than four liters per capita).

There *is* a British winemaking industry that is growing in quantity and reputation (helped along by global climate change), but it remains small relative to domestic demand. Thus almost all wine in Britain is imported. This is one reason for the British market's central importance. Almost all the other countries with large wine demand also have large local supplies.

Great Britain is therefore the country with the largest wine imports in the world. Although the British consume only about 5 percent of the world's wine by volume (a bit more than Argentina and a bit less than Spain), this represents almost 17 percent of world wine imports—more than any other country. Germany is number two (about 16 percent) with the United States a distant third (about 10 percent). No other country comes close in terms of imported wine opportunities and, as we will soon see, the U.S. and German wine markets are distinctly different from the British.

One bottle in six of all the wine that trades from country to country ends up on a British shelf. This fact actually understates the importance of the British market in several ways, however. First, the one-in-six figure looks at the volume of wine imports only and inexpensive bulk wines (the wines that end up in boxes and jugs) dominate this figure. But British buyers are upmarket compared to the global average, so they punch above their weight in terms of wine spending. In fact British buyers account for nearly 20 percent of the money spent on wine in international exchanges (the United States accounts for about 18 percent, Germany about 12 percent).

Britain is also the center of the global auction market for fine wines, meaning that it is a key trading center that attracts buyers, sellers, investors, critics, and wine press. It is no accident that so many of the world's most influential wine writers carry British passports or write for British publications. This confluence seems to be shifting east to Hong Kong now as Asian buyers have come into the market and the Hong Kong authorities have ended their high tax on wine imports.

THE RISE AND FALL AND RISE OF THE BRITISH WINE MARKET[1]

Britain was not always the pint and pie culture popularized by Andy Capp cartoons. The Romans brought wine to Britain along with their empire's troops and religious practices, although the local wine, produced at monasteries as far north as York, could not have been very good. Britain had its own vast vineyards for three hundred years starting in 1152, when the future King Henry II married Eleanor of Aquitaine, which brought Gascony, including Bordeaux, under British control. Low import duties on Gascon wines helped cement cross-Channel relations for a period and encouraged wine drinking, especially among British elites. The eventual loss of those vineyards and then war with France caused Britain to turn away from French wines to those from Spain and Portugal and then, finally, from wine generally.

Faced with the need to generate war revenue in the nineteenth century, Britain imposed high tariffs on wine imports. Significantly, these were not excise tariffs (10 percent or 20 percent of value), but specific tariffs (*x* number of pence per bottle or gallon). Excise tariffs would have had an equal proportionate impact on wines of all prices, but specific tariffs introduced a bias against cheap wine.

To see this, suppose that the tariff is $10 per bottle, for example. The effect on a $100 bottle of imported wine is relatively small—the price rises by 10 percent and demand declines somewhat. Some people will like fine wine well enough to pay $110 for a $100 bottle, so demand slips but probably doesn't slide away. The impact on a $5 bottle of wine is enormous, however. Its relative price rises prohibitively to 300 percent of the pretariff amount. Who will pay $15 for a $5 bottle of wine? Its market evaporates.

The cost of shipping wine abroad, which is more or less the same regardless of the price of the wine, has something of this same effect. If it costs $50 to ship a case of wine from France, for example, the impact is proportionately greater for wine that sells for $5 per bottle than the $500 luxury product. This helps explain why that cheap but lovely bottle of local wine you enjoyed on holiday in Provence never shows up on your grocers' shelves here in the United States. By the time the transportation costs are paid—plus whatever import duties apply—it would no longer be cheap and you might not find it quite so lovely.

The British drinks market was thus split in two. Elites continued to drink and collect fine red Bordeaux wines that they called "Claret." The masses switched from wine to now relatively less expensive beer. And Britain acquired its reputation as a beer-drinking nation.

John V. C. Nye tells this story in his excellent book *War, Wine, and Taxes: The Political Economy of Anglo-French Trade, 1689–1900.*[2] He argues that British brewers were able to take advantage of technological innovations that allowed for large economies of scale in beer production. Once they had a near monopoly on the British drinks market, they could build huge factories to satisfy the captive demand at low production costs.

An interesting "invisible handshake" arrangement evolved, according to Nye, between the brewers and the revenue-hungry British state. The brewers permitted themselves to be taxed at fairly high rates in return for tariff protection from wine imports, which gave them a large captive market to exploit. The economies of scale in brewing were so significant as to make it profitable both for the brewers and for the taxman—so long as cheap wine was kept away.

Thus did war, taxes, politics, and economies of scale in beer manufacture conspire to convert Britain from wine to beer. The story of how it changed back is equally complex.

BRITISH WINE RESURGENCE[3]

Wine became cheaper in Britain as import duties were reduced on a wide range of products, including wine, as part of post–World War II trade liberalization. British tariffs on table wine fell in three steps, first in 1949 as part of postwar tariff reform, then again in 1973, upon Britain's entry into the European Community (EC), and once more in 1984 when the EC ruled that British wine tariffs must be "harmonized" or brought into line with those in other member countries. These duty and price reductions stimulated consumption in the price-sensitive British market.

Lower tariffs on wine didn't happen by themselves, however. Both domestic and international politics were involved. International politics appeared in the form of Britain's uncertain commitment to European unity and the single market initiative. Lower taxes on wine was one of the costs of greater influence in European affairs and freer access to European markets.

Brewers, the beneficiaries of high wine taxes, switched sides on this issue, changing the domestic political balance. British consumption of beer and ale fell dramatically in the postwar period, so brewers were looking for new profit centers to replace their declining pub sales. Wine and wine distributors and merchants were obvious targets and integrated drinks firms emerged, making, marketing, distributing, and selling all manner of local and global alcoholic beverages. Thus did the political opposition to lower wine taxes fall away.

Even more important, however, were several actions that increased competition among sellers and so both reduced price and increased convenience and selection. Britain's restrictive retail licensing laws were revised in 1962, giving supermarkets the ability to sell wine and liquor. This was a big change as previously wine was available mainly through specialized shops with limited hours and distribution. Sainsbury's, the big grocery chain, was the first to take up a wine license, followed quickly by competitors such as Tesco, Waitrose, and Co-Op. This put wine within reach of the everyday buyer who no longer needed to schlep to specialists such as Berry Bros. & Rudd or high street merchants like Threshers, Odd Bins, and Victoria Wines to make a purchase.

Wine was more available after 1962, but resale price maintenance agreements prevented true competition in the market for alcoholic beverages. Wine prices were set free in 1966, paving the way for the fiercely competitive market we see today. As the grocery chains expanded, their stores grew bigger and the wine walls became both larger and more diverse. The economic incentive to sell wine was very strong. The markup for many supermarket items is surprisingly low: just 5 to 10 percent for beer and spirits, for example, but wine prices can be 30 percent over cost and sometimes more.

Selling wine, however, isn't just selling wine (if that makes sense). It also sells complementary items (meat, fish, cheese, gourmet foods) as well as the store's overall image as home to the good life's consumable ingredients. High-end supermarkets scatter wine displays throughout the store as they market lifestyle choices, not just industrial packaged goods.

It worked. British wine consumption increased steadily, from about two liters per person in the early 1960s to about twenty liters today as consumers shifted from "on-premise" wine consumption (at pubs, restaurants, and wine bars) to "off-premise" drinking at home.[4] Supermarkets account for more than 70 percent of British wine sales today and their market share continues to grow.

MASTERS OF THE [WINE] UNIVERSE

The conditions were ripe for the rebirth of the Great British wine market, but one problem remained—sorting out the choices from among the thousands and thousands of wines that came knocking on Britain's door as its supermarket wine sector expanded. Building (or even rebuilding) a wine culture is not a snap in the era of global wine. Education is key and the British wine industry responded with the Masters of Wine program and *Decanter* magazine.

The Master of Wine (MW) is not a degree given by Oxford or Cambridge. It is a special designation created by the Institute of Masters of Wine, a fifty-year-old London-based, industry-supported nonprofit organization dedicated to wine education. The MW program was originally created for British wine traders, who obviously needed to be very knowledgeable to succeed in their profession, but it eventually expanded both in occupational and geographic terms. Today there are more than 275 Masters of Wine in the world scattered across twenty-two countries. Not surprisingly, Britain remains the center of MW membership and activities, reflecting its central position in the world wine market generally, with more than two-thirds of the world's wine masters.

The Masters of Wine program created an elite group of wine experts who have played an important role over the years in shaping the growth of British and now global wine markets. Some of the world's most famous wine critics and winemakers hold the MW designation. Jancis Robinson, Michael Broadbent, David Peppercorn, and Serena Sutcliffe are famous British MW wine critics, for example. Among the winemakers who have earned the MW title are Steve Smith in New Zealand and David Lake, Joel Butler, and Bob Betz in the United States.

It's hard to get a Masters of Wine. You need to work in the wine industry for at least five years and take special seminars that are often held at a major wine research center such as UC Davis, University of Bordeaux, Geisenheim University in Germany, or University of Adelaide. Then, once admitted to the MW program, you have to pass exams in four theory areas, stagger successfully through three 12-wine blind tastings, and write a ten thousand word dissertation on a topic relevant to the wine industry.

I don't think I am cut out to be a Master of Wine—I doubt that I could survive the blind tasting exam. But I think I would do well on the third exam, which is all about the business of wine. In fact, the published syllabi for the MW program suggest that about a third of the training focuses on wine economics, which makes sense when you think about it. Masters of Wine are all experts in sensory appreciation and evaluation, to be sure, and they know their regions and grapes and so on, but Britain wouldn't be the world's best wine market today if it had not purposefully applied specialized knowledge to the business of wine.

THE WORLD'S BEST WINE [MAGAZINE]

The Masters of Wine program created an elite corps of wine professionals to select and market wine to British buyers, but that still left the problem of educating the masses. People won't buy products they don't understand and the wine wall, as we have seen, can be a very confusing and intimidating place. This gap was filled in Britain in many ways. British newspapers introduced wine columnists and eventually wine fairs and competitions, selling wine and educating their readers in an attempt to grab and hold fickle readers. The *Financial Times*, probably the most influential newspaper in the world, publishes a column by Jancis Robinson MW, possibly the most influential wine critic in the world, in its weekend edition. The popularity of wine columns and the growing influence of wine critics culminated in 1975 with the founding of *Decanter*, the self-described "world's best wine magazine."

Based in London, *Decanter* is a monthly wine and wine-lifestyle magazine that is distributed in ninety countries, including, since 2005, China. It is arguably the most influential wine periodical in the world—a claim that American wine enthusiasts will find hard to swallow since most of them have never seen a copy. *Wine Spectator, Wine Enthusiast, Wine & Spirits,* and *Wine Advocate* are popular wine magazines in the United States (*Wine Spectator*'s readership is about 2.5 million, much larger than *Decanter*'s, reflecting the bigger American potential audience). *Decanter* is rarely seen in America, except by people like me who pay an arm and a leg to have it airmailed from Britain. If *Decanter* isn't popular in America, how can it be so important?

One answer to this question is that *Decanter*'s columnists and contributors include many of the most famous names in the business. Sometimes it seems like every article is written by someone with one of those "MW" designations after their name. The magazine is therefore very authoritative and its reviews and ratings get serious attention.

A second answer is that *Decanter* is important because it focuses on wines that are available in the British market. This market is the focus of worldwide attention and, unlike the United States, it is more or less a unified market. Wine in the United States is regulated as alcohol, which is treated in some regions as if it were a dangerous narcotic drug. The result is that there is no single U.S. wine market, except for a small number of brands that have invested in creating national distribution for their products; there are just the fifty-plus state and local wine markets, each with its own rules, requirements, and sales hurdles. This is one of the reasons *Decanter* is not as important in the United States as it is in the rest of the world. The domestic wines that make up most of the American wine wall are not widely distributed in the United Kingdom, while the vast global mix of wines found there are harder to purchase here.

The unified British market means that wines that are available *anywhere* in Britain are essentially available *everywhere. Decanter* has the luxury (from the U.S. point of view) of being able not only to recommend wines to its readers but also to tell them which retailers (stockists in *Decanter* jargon) can provide them. This means that in a practical sense the world of wine on offer to British wine drinkers is quite large—the envy of wine enthusiasts elsewhere.

Decanter is a full-service wine publication with something to offer almost any British (or global) wine enthusiast. There are interviews, topical essays, and regional travel surveys (drink this, stay here, try this place for dinner). *Decanter* obviously includes wine investors among its readers because it contains very detailed monthly reports on wine auction sales prices. Bordeaux reds are the main focus (vintages dating back to 1961), but white Bordeaux, Burgundy, and Port prices are also listed. It even publishes a wine auction index. This probably reflects Michael Broadbent's influence—he was for many years head of the wine auction practice at Christie's.

Decanter reports on this market and reviews the wines being sold, but its impact is much greater than this. It promotes wine (through tastings and awards, wine travel and events) and shapes the market, too, by drawing attention to new wine regions, makers, varieties, and styles. The magazine's global reach is thus intentional and has, along with other elements of the U.K. wine press, educated and encouraged consumers, building the foundation for the market of today.

Britain thus has everything to make it the leading global wine market: rich (by global standards) and educated consumers, expert professionals, a unified wine market, advantageous tax and trade policies, and sophisticated supermarkets to bring all the pieces together. What does the result look like? Well, Google that address I gave you earlier in the chapter (Delamare Road in Cheshunt, Hertfordshire) and you'll find out. That's the address of Tesco House, headquarters of the biggest wine retailer in the world, Tesco plc.

TESCO'S WORLD OF WINE

Tesco is (along with giants Walmart, Home Depot, and Carrefour) one of the largest retail chains in the world by sales; only Walmart makes more profits. From its home market in Great Britain, Tesco has expanded over the last thirty years into Ireland, Hungary, Poland, the Czech Republic, Slovakia, Turkey, Thailand, South Korea, Malaysia, Japan, China, and most recently the United States, where it rolled out its Fresh & Easy Neighborhood Market concept in the Southwest. There are cautious plans to expand into India next. Tesco operated more than 3,700 stores in fourteen countries in 2009 with 440,000 employees, 76 million square feet of sales space, generating more than £50 billion in sales from 50 million shoppers who pass through its checkout stands each week.

I don't know if all the stores in Tesco's global network sell wine, but I'll bet that most of them do. Drilling down into the corporate website I was able to download colorful weekly sale flyers for the Beijing and Shanghai stores that featured wines (from Chinese producers Great Wall and Changyu) prominently. I remember being impressed with the Tesco wine selection on my last visit to Prague.

Tesco was not the first British supermarket to sell wine (Sainsbury's has that distinction), but it has evolved into the largest wine retailer in the United Kingdom and, indeed, the world because it has aggressively and effectively harnessed the forces of global wine to serve the interests of local consumers. In the course of creating the world's most prodigious wine wall, Tesco (and the other British supermarkets) blazed the trail that brings wine to places and people who have never heard of Tesco.

Tesco sources wine from all over the world. The Tesco wine catalogue lists all the main global producers: Argentina, Australia, Austria, Bulgaria, Germany, Chile, France, Greece, Hungary, Israel, Italy, New Zealand, Portugal, South Africa, Spain, and the United States. The French listings are particularly detailed, as you might expect from Britain's wine history and proximity to French terroir. This embarrassment of riches (which you share indirectly of course, in the form of the wine wall in your local upscale supermarket) is a mixed blessing. More choices aren't always better choices if they are confusing or intimidating. How can you be sure that *this* Chilean Cabernet is any good or what *that* French white wine from an unknown appellation will be like? How can you be confident that your money won't be wasted on an inferior product?

The answer, which Tesco and Britain's other big wine retailers, including Sainsbury's, Waitrose, Asda (Walmart), and the others have discovered, is own-brand wines (or house brands as I like to call them). You might never feel confident in buying a mysterious bottle of red wine from Bulgaria, for example. Who knows what's beneath the cork and if it is drinkable. But you might be willing to purchase Tesco's Finest Bulgarian Cabernet Sauvignon. The Tesco name (or the name of an ersatz winery that a store invents for marketing purposes) provides some minimum guarantee of quality.

Tesco's catalogue and its wine wall are filled with house brand wines that sit alongside products from international producers. Thus the Beaujolais part of the wine wall map holds both the products of Georges Duboeuf and Louis Jadot (famous makers of these wines) and also Tesco Beaujolais Villages Reserve and Tesco Finest Fleurie. Over in the Bordeaux territory you may find Chateau Roc de Thau and Chateau Puy de Lignac alongside Tesco Claret, Tesco Claret Reserve, and Tesco Claret Vintage (at increasing price points, as you might expect from the names). Confident buyers may go for the Chateau, but many will choose the safety of the Tesco brand and the reliable reputation that comes with it. House brands account for more than 40 percent of supermarket wine sales in the United Kingdom compared with less than 2 percent in the United States.

Significantly, buying house brand wines is not necessarily a step to lower quality (although they generally sell at lower prices). *Decanter* tasting notes frequently recommend house brand wines from the major supermarkets and specialty shop chains. A £14.69 bottle of Sainsbury's "Taste the Difference" house brand Amarone della Valpolicella 2006, for example, received the International Trophy (highest award) for Italian red wines over £10 in *Decanter*'s 2009 World Wine Awards, beating out wines from hundreds of prestigious producers.

The house brand strategy gave Tesco and the others a way to build the market for wine. It also freed the supermarkets from dependence on smaller suppliers, no one of whom could possibly fill the huge pipeline that the supermarket sales system created. Rather, Tesco and Sainsbury's and the rest began to deal directly with suppliers around the world. On rare occasions they contracted with local cooperatives, which collected and blended grapes or wines from small-scale producers. The cooperatives could operate on the scale the supermarkets needed. Sometimes the supermarkets acted as *négociants*, buying and blending wine themselves. The most recent trend is for the supermarkets to actually become winemakers, purchasing grapes and sending teams of "flying winemaker" consultants around the world to make sure that the resulting products meet the needs of the British stores and their customers.

ONE SINGULAR [WINE] SENSATION

Tesco sells more than 320 million bottles of wine each year in Britain alone (one in four bottles in this important market). It is a wine-selling machine, using every available mechanism to market wine and build the brand. Tesco stores feature attractive wine walls, for example, tailored according to the demographics of individual stores. The selection is large, although not as obscenely diverse as at an American upscale grocery store. Big retailers like to work with a small number of suppliers and to focus on a limited number of SKUs (stock keeping units or products) that efficiently generate high returns. And, of course, there are the house brands to consider. Selling wine doesn't stop at the wine wall, however. Wine displays are strategically positioned near the fish, meat, and cheese counters as you will appreciate from your own experience. Wine tastings and wine-related events are organized by the no-fee Tesco Wine Club.

Wine, wine—everywhere. Tesco and its British competitors take the *everywhere* seriously, so their quest to sell wine doesn't stop when you leave the store. Internet wine sales are an important retail sector in Britain since nationwide shipping and delivery is not a problem as it is in the United States, where jurisdictional issues complicate every aspect of interstate wine sales. The Tesco Wine by the Case website provides consumers with a rather stunning array of wine choices that range from a discounted mixed case of "mellow reds" for £28 to a Vosne Romanee Domaine Hudelot Noellat 2006 Red Burgundy for about the same price, but for just one bottle. Tesco has captured about a quarter of all Internet wine sales in Britain.

Buyers earn ClubCard points both online and in the stores. The loyalty card system carefully tracks the purchases of each customer (and notes non-purchases, too, I suppose), providing data to guide store strategy and the opportunity to produce individualized checkout coupons to encourage wine drinkers to buy more or better wines or perhaps to try something different. Tesco was an early pioneer in loyalty cards and is thought to use this data very effectively.

Tesco goes to great lengths to reach British consumers whenever and wherever the urge to buy wine might hit them. Tesco and its U.K. competitors have established substantial wine stores in Calais, France, just minutes from Hovercraft ferry and Eurostar train stations. British consumers have long crossed the English Channel in search of duty-free bargains and British duties still make the trip an attractive excursion for some. Wine can cost about 25 percent less in Tesco's Calais store and online ordering makes stocking up quick and easy.

Tesco's latest (as of this writing) innovation is a smart phone app for wine lovers. Enjoying a nice bottle of Chianti at your favorite Italian restaurant? Want to know where to buy it? Well, launch the app and use your phone to take a photo of the label on the bottle in front of you. High-tech label recognition software will identify the wine, provide maker information and tasting notes, and even search through the Tesco online inventory so that you can order a case right now for immediate delivery. Tesco and wine are with you anytime, anywhere.

TESCO'S MARKET POWER

Tesco and the other British supermarkets have used wine to make money and to change the way at least some British shoppers think about grocery stores and even how they think about themselves. In the process, of course, these retailers have acquired a certain amount of power. Indeed, *Decanter*'s 2009 "Power List" of the most influential people in the world of wine ranks Tesco's wine director Dan Jago at number six—a few places behind Robert Sands, head of international giant Constellation Brands, and wine critic

Robert Parker, but ahead of French president Nicholas Sarkozy and E&J Gallo president Joseph Gallo. This power is put to a surprising number of uses.

That Tesco would use its market muscle to reduce wine costs is not unexpected. Volume purchasing has always been an excuse to press for lower prices. Tesco goes further, however. The New World wines in the Tesco lineup are shipped to Britain in bulk, in 20-foot shipping containers that contain giant plastic bladders holding thousands of liters of wine. The bulk wine is bottled once it reaches Britain, eliminating the cost of hauling fragile bottles halfway around the world. Tesco has even started moving the bulk wine to its bottling plant using Britain's historic system of canals, saving the expense of tanker truck shipment and lowering the wine's carbon footprint.

Tesco is very focused on innovation and uses its power to achieve it. Tesco has pressed its suppliers to switch from cork closures to screw caps, for example, in order to eliminate the 3 to 5 percent loss that is commonly experienced due to TCA cork taint (TCA refers to 2,4,6-trichloroanisole). Anyone who wants to get wines into the Tesco pipe had better not show up with a corkscrew (iconic brands excepted, of course).

Recently, Tesco has introduced the world's lightest wine bottle in an attempt to further reduce production and shipping costs and reduce environmental impacts. The new 300 gram bottles are 30 percent lighter than Tesco's previous lightweight bottle and much lighter, of course, than some of the heavyweight containers that one sometimes finds on the wine wall. Structural concerns require that the new bottle have a new shape—somewhere between the high shoulders of the classic Bordeaux and the soft silhouette of a Syrah or Burgundy. Tesco estimates that use of this special bottle will save 560 metric tons of glass for the ten million liters of wine that it imports in bulk each year, bottles in Britain, and sells under its own label.

Tesco's market power gives some customers access to good cheap wine but it also helps others get their hands on hard-to-find wines. The most sought after wines are often impossible to get, especially in single-bottle purchases. Sales are allocated and case purchases often required. Tesco's market power can cut through these constraints. As the United Kingdom's largest seller of Australia's Penfold's wine, for example, it is able to obtain qualities of cult wines like Penfold's Grange, which it makes available (at a high price, of course) to one and all.

ARRESTED DEVELOPMENT?

The picture I've painted of the British wine scene so far is really quite bright—it must seem really much too good to be true. So you should be a little suspicious. Economists hold that if something *is* too good to be true, it must be false (that's why economics is called the dismal science). The right way to think about Tesco, supermarkets, and the British wine market is that they are part of the incredible transformation of global wine today compared with the sorry state of the wine wall fifty years ago.

The supermarkets have created global supply chains that carry their house brand wines to Britain along with a great variety of products by winemakers large and small. Although each supermarket's selection is relatively small (compared with the fifteen hundred–plus wines I found at the Metropolitan Market, for example), the cumulative wine wall is perhaps the fullest in the world and the market for wines has expanded very significantly.

All silver linings so far; where's the dark cloud? Well, supermarkets are mass merchandisers, of course, and so they need to appeal to a mass market and, although they can shape that market somewhat, they must also reflect it. It's a fact of life.

One of the things I remember best from shopping in British supermarkets when I lived there in the 1990s was the focus on bargains. I was constantly being offered "25 percent Extra Free" or "Buy One Get One Free." You couldn't walk down a grocery aisle without being offered a bargain of this sort. BOGOF (Buy One Get One Free) was particularly common on the wine wall. This was the way the mass merchandisers tried to get the attention of mass consumers, and I expect that it trained them to expect bargains of this sort and to resist other kinds of incentives.

The problem, therefore, is the possibility of arrested development. Can the British wine market move beyond bargain-priced house brand wines and take advantage of the great potential that those house wines have helped create? Some wine critics are pretty pessimistic about this and predict that the future of British wine will be its increasing commodification. Wine will be like soap flakes, a quotidian purchase of unexceptional consequence. Critics are sad when they contemplate the prospect that wine could become so lifeless, so stripped of its finer qualities.

It is not clear that this dismal vision will come to pass, however. Certainly the British supermarkets are doing what they can to move their market upscale.

Tesco, for example, sells several ranges of house brand wines. Its Tesco wine products fit the cheap and cheerful bargain-hunter mold. The upmarket Tesco Finest series, introduced about ten years ago, was initially meant to give buyers the opportunity to move up a step, from say £3 to £6. Slowly, however, Tesco's Finest and one step higher Tesco Reserve have evolved into a small line of distinctive high-quality wines (with higher prices, of course) that have made even the critics wonder if this might not be a pathway out of the dead-end supermarket wine aisle that they so thoroughly fear.[5]

Tesco and its British supermarket competitors were instrumental in creating the global wine wall of today, so it makes sense that they will continue to be influential in the future. Their vertically integrated supply and marketing chains give us a vision of what tomorrow's mass market for wine could look like. But the future as seen through the Tesco lens is disjointed—like looking at a cracked mirror—because it seems to point in several directions at once: arrested development and mass-market BOGOF wines on one hand and the potential for more sophisticated evolution on the other.

How will the story end? It's too soon to draw any conclusions. We need to go back on the road and investigate how wine works in the other key markets. Fasten your safety belts—we are in for a bumpy ride.

TASTING NOTES

More Masters: There are now nearly 300 Masters of Wine spread across the globe (up from the 275 I mentioned on page 57), with many more studying to take the famously rigorous exam.

Follow the Money: British influence in the wine industry remains strong, as you might expect given Tesco, the Masters of Wine, *Decanter,* and so on. But the center of gravity of the wine auction market continues to shift to Asia and especially Hong Kong.

Death and Taxes: In its effort to reduce the fiscal deficit, the British government has imposed the highest wine taxes (import duty plus VAT) in Europe, threatening to kill the goose that laid the golden age. Or at least that's how many British wine consumers see the issue.

6

Curse of the Blue Nun

Germany presents many apparent contradictions to anyone interested in wine. You would expect German wine drinkers to prefer upscale wines, since their standard of living is high, to drink white wines because their Rieslings are so famous, and to be a net exporter of wine since German wines are so ubiquitous on store shelves around the world. All these stereotypes are false.

Germans make a lot of wine—about 3.5 percent of the world total, most of it white as you would expect since it is difficult to ripen red grapes so far north. But they drink a lot more wine than they produce—nearly 9 percent of total global demand—and increasingly prefer red wine to white. So while Germany is an important exporter of fine white wines, its biggest influence on the world wine river is as a red wine import market. Germany imports almost as much wine as Great Britain, so it has been a powerful force in shaping global markets. But Germany's wine rivers bear little resemblance to Britain's.

The most interesting thing about the Germans is not how much wine they drink, but what kind: much of it is the cheapest wine they can find, sourced from the lowest cost producers in Germany, Europe, and the world. Germany exports fine wine, but imports more of the bulk commodity. Retail prices start at €0.79 per liter in Tetra packaging (like a milk carton) and €1.19 per liter for bottled wine (French "vin de pays").[1] Prices are low and falling.

HOW GERMANY BECAME THE LAND OF ONE BUCK CHUCK

The story of how Germany became the land of rich people and cheap wine is an interesting one. German wine has been through repeated cycles of boom and bust. It hit bottom just a few years ago (that's where the Curse of the Blue Nun will come in) and is now on an upward path.

Vines have probably always grown on German hillsides, and although Emperor Probus (276–282 AD) is often given credit as the founder of organized viticulture in Germany, Charlemagne (742–814 AD) probably deserves more of the credit. Charlemagne ordered that vines be planted throughout his empire, today's Germany included. He sent forth both the vines (supply) and Christian churches (demand) with the result that German wines in the Middle Ages were predominantly red (to represent the blood of Christ) rather than the white wines that were better suited to the climate. Many of today's most celebrated vineyards were originally planted for monastic use.

Wine rose and fell in synch with German social conditions. A growing population meant the need for more food, including wine, which preserves the calories and nutrients of grapes (which would otherwise go to waste). War was as bad for wine as it was for people in general. The steep slopes of the best vineyards required very labor-intensive viticultural practices. Conflict took workers away from the vines repeatedly over the years, setting the industry back again and again. Sometimes it must have seemed like even Mother Nature conspired against the desire to produce good German wine. The peak of the wine industry's expansion in the fifteenth century had the bad luck to coincide with the "Little Ice Age," which pushed the margins of successful viticulture southward.

The battle between quality and quantity was fought repeatedly, with mixed results, foreshadowing contemporary wine debates in many ways. Quality wine producers attempted to organize geographic designations beginning in the 1830s, for example. They sought rules and regulations to govern planting, harvest, and winemaking practices. Quality producers were tired of having their regional brand undercut by the shady practices of others—a rising problem as transportation improvements extended market reach. Far-flung consumers, lacking local knowledge, were easier to fool and so reliable "brands" became more important. Many of the more mysterious aspects of German wine labels (quality designations such as Qualitätswein mit Prädikat and the wonderful but intimidating Trockenbeerenauslese) owe their existence to these early efforts to recognize and preserve quality.

The expansion of wine trade put a different sort of pressure on wine quality, too. Protectionist policies in Bavaria, Württemberg, and Prussia had the effect of sheltering bad local wine from competition with better products made elsewhere. When, in 1834, the three principalities entered into a Custom Union (the Zollverein, if you want the official name), tariff barriers dropped, good wine flooded into zones of low quality, and the game was up for those who would try to sell bad wine.[2] This is a pattern that I've seen repeated again and again in my study of wine market history. But this golden age (of trade and wine), like most of the others, did not last.

THE RACE TO THE BOTTOM

The dire economic conditions of the Great Depression of the 1930s forced German winemakers to look abroad for export markets to soak up excess production. The market segment they identified in Britain and elsewhere was more interested in cheap bulk wine (as you might expect given the stagnant economy) and unwilling or unable to master the complexities of German wine label code. Wine brands were invented to make the product easier to understand and shapeless, low-quality, sweetened, multiregion wine blends were produced to satisfy untutored consumer tastes.

Thus Liebfraumilch, a mild, sweetish white wine blend, and brands like Black Tower (sold in a cylindrical black glass bottle) were born.[3] They found a ready market abroad among young people recovering from an adolescent addiction to sweets and bargain hunters unconcerned with the loss of aroma, flavor, and nuance. Since both of these groups were quite large, this version of German wine was a hit.

German wine continued on this downhill path after World War II. Vineyard plantings expanded dramatically, crop yields spiked, and Liebfraumilch exports surged, accounting for two-thirds of German sales by the end of the 1970s. The quality German industry of your imagination—complex tangy white wines from steep, stony vineyards overlooking the Mosel and Nahe Rivers—well, these wines still existed, of course, but they were submerged under the tidal wave of cheaper, sweeter wines that shaped domestic demand and foreign perceptions.

The result, in terms of the global market, is the problem I call the "Curse of the Blue Nun." Now I admit that I haven't thought of Blue Nun wine in years. I remember it from the 1970s as an unsophisticated Liebfraumilch in a tall, thin blue bottle with a blue and white–clad nun on the label. She reminded me a bit of *The Flying Nun* television show (starring Sally Field) that ran from 1967 to 1970. The wine was about as serious as the TV show, but apparently it sold hundreds of thousands of cases to aspiring wine drinkers like me.

I didn't know that it was still around until I spotted it on a BBC television show featuring Oz Clarke, notable British wine critic, and James May, cohost of the popular automobile series *Top Gear*. Oz and James were touring California with wine guru Oz trying to teach neophyte James a bit about wine. James resisted, put off by wine's snobbish elitist ways.

Blue Nun appeared in a sequence where James bets Oz $100 that he can't identify an ordinary everyday wine in a blind tasting (from a plastic beer cup, as it turned out). Oz sniffs and swirls and makes a bad face. Terrible, he says. Disgusting. So bad that it couldn't be from America—market-savvy Americans would never make a wine this bad. This could only come from the Old World. "Blue Nun!" he shouts, winning the bet cleanly if perhaps unfairly (I suspect that azure-colored bottle gave him an unfair clue).

I'm not sure that Blue Nun is really as bad as that, but Oz Clarke's disgusted reaction makes my point. Blue Nun and brands like it established Germany's place on the lower tier of the World Wine Wall. The wines may not be cheap and nasty but they are not sophisticated, either. They are the comprehensible face of German wine abroad and that face, like the Blue Nun herself, is more or less a color cartoon.

THE BLUE NUN STORY

Blue Nun was by some accounts the first truly global mass-market wine brand, an unexpected distinction for a German wine. Its story therefore has some bearing on the globalization of wine. Blue Nun's roots go back to 1857 when one Hermann Sichel started a wine business in Mainz, Germany. I know little about the early days of Sichel's firm except that it managed to survive the political and economic chaos of the ensuing years, which in retrospect seems like a considerable achievement. The real story begins with the 1921 vintage, said to be one of the best. Sichel sought to export these wines abroad, especially to Great Britain, and the Blue Nun label was invented to facilitate foreign sales. One source holds that the nun on the label was originally clad in standard-issue brown robes, but a printer's mistake turned them blue and thus a brand was born.

The brand and the famous vintage it represented found a market in England, selling more than a thousand cases a year in the 1930s (quite a lot for a single brand of wine) according to the official company history. Volumes increased after World War II, rising to 3.5 million bottles in the United Kingdom in the 1970s before sales collapsed back to 800,000 in the 1980s. The quantity/quality trade-off finally came back to haunt Blue Nun, it seems, and the fashion for red wine started by the famous French Paradox discovery did not help either. Blue Nun itself was the original victim of the Curse of the Blue Nun: the simple, sweetish wines that make you will also break you. As tastes changed and wine drinkers sought to move upmarket, Blue Nun wine petered out (although 800,000 bottles is hardly a trickle). Passé to some, a joke (as with Oz and James) to others, that was and to some extent is Blue Nun today.

It is an overgeneralization to say that the whole of German wine suffered the Curse of the Blue Nun, but there is some truth in it. Great wines continued to be produced, of course, and snatched up by the educated wine elites (although not at the high prices they once earned), but Brand Germany was Blue Nun, Black Tower, and their Liebfraumilch shelf mates. German wine hit its lowest point.

This book reflects my optimism about how the global wine wars will turn out and this attitude extends to German wine, too. The bad news of the crisis of quality is matched by the good news that German wines have changed, even the big brands. Black Tower has moved upmarket into affordable quality wines, not just Liebfraumilch and not just white wines, either. It is the top German brand today. Sichel sold the Blue Nun brand to Langguth, another German maker, who also upgraded the wines. Blue Nun is once again a major brand, selling five million bottles in Britain alone in 2005. It is a German brand but, significantly, not just a German wine.

Popular wines from around the world are imported to Germany where they are bottled under the Blue Nun label. There is Languedoc Merlot and Cabernet Sauvignon, California Zinfandel, Australian Shiraz, Chardonnay from Chile, and a Rosé from Spain—all sold under the Blue Nun brand. There's even a Pinot Grigio from Germany, although its unlikely origin is not easy to learn from the front label.[4] Blue Nun Light is low alcohol (0.5 percent), low calorie (27 calories per 100 ml glass).

My personal favorite (perhaps because I've never had an opportunity to try it) is Blue Nun Sparkling Gold Edition. It's a light, fizzy wine infused with flakes of 22-carat gold leaf that glitter in the glass. Young women seem to be the target market according to both published sources and the look of the advertising copy. Women buy more wine than men, so this is not a crazy strategy, and young women are the market of the future, although the assumption that they are attracted to floaty, shiny things like gold bits is depressing if true. The idea that the friendly nonthreatening female image of the Blue Nun might appeal to women more than men never occurred to me . . . until now. German wine is back, but it has changed. Quality has improved—even the mass-market brands offer some more distinctive wines—but the reputation lingers, the legacy of the Curse of the Blue Nun.

GERMANY, WINE, AND THE ALDI EFFECT

Are you familiar with Aldi? You should be. Aldi is Germany's largest wine merchant. Aldi accounts for more than a third of all wine sold in Germany and 75 percent of imported wine sales.[5] Aldi defines mass-market wine in this critical market. If Blue Nun is the face of German wine abroad, Aldi is its inward-looking visage.

The business is named for Karl and Theo Albrecht, who founded Albrecht Discount, or Aldi for short, in Essen, Germany, in 1948. The brothers are said to be the richest men in Germany. They are, I suppose, the German equivalents of Bill Gates and Warren Buffett, top dogs on the U.S. wealth league table. The irony of this is hard to ignore.

Aldi is not a high-tech company like Gates's Microsoft or a high-flying investment business like Buffett's Berkshire Hathaway. It is a "hard discounter" supermarket chain. Its bare bones stores are stocked with a very limited selection of house-brand necessities. Hard discounters are a niche albeit a growing one in the United States. Walmart is a successful discounter, of course, but not a *hard* discounter because it still features many mainstream branded products, its prices are higher, and its stores a bit more posh. Aldi and other hard-discount stores drove Walmart out of Germany, but the U.S. market has been a tough nut for the hard discounters to crack until recently. American consumers are primed to buy brand-named products and they like lots of choice, marketing experts say, and so have been able to resist the house brands that hard discounters feature until the recent financial crisis, which has boosted Aldi's brand everywhere.

Germans are more willing to sacrifice brand names for low prices, apparently. Aldi and other hard discounters are dominant powers in German retailing. Ninety percent of German households shop at Aldi stores and 40 percent of all grocery purchases are made in hard-discount outlets. The fact that so much wine is sold in these stores should come as no surprise.

A typical Aldi store stocks fewer items in total—about fifteen hundred— than your typical upscale supermarket stocks on the wine wall alone. Altogether your local store in the United States provides ten times the variety of an Aldi. Most of the products carry one of the store's house brands—there are only a few "famous name" products. The goods are displayed, if that is the right word, in their original cardboard packing boxes. Customers snap up empty boxes to use to carry their treasures out the door, thus providing free and instant recycling. The stores have minimal staff to go with minimal selection, the checkout lines are long and, empty boxes aside, you better bring your own bag or be prepared to pay for one of theirs.

Aldi stores are more austere than Walmart stores, and they attract customers looking for basic value. At last count Aldi had eight thousand stores in eighteen countries (including the United States), divided into two groups: Aldi Nord (with a red, white, and blue logo) owned by Theo Albrecht, and Aldi Süd, owned by his brother Karl, with an orange and blue logo. The brothers had a falling out early on regarding whether they should sell tobacco products and, unable to resolve the issue, they divided operation of the business, one taking the north (nord) and the other southern Germany.[6] Later they divided the world market, too. Karl took Austria, Australia, Greece, Hungary, Ireland, Slovenia, and Great Britain and Theo got Belgium, France, Spain, Luxemburg, Poland, Denmark, and the Netherlands. They share the U.S. market in a unique way that will be revealed shortly.

Aldi found a market for very low cost house-brand wine and developed it. It is in part because of the Aldi effect that so much of German wine sales are in the market basement. About a quarter of all wine in Germany sells for less than $2 per standard bottle equivalent and about 40 percent between $2 and $5, much of it from low-cost producers in Italy, Spain, and Austria.

NAVIGATING THE ALDI WINE WALL

I went online to the Aldi Süd website to see if their wine wall had changed much since my last visit a few years ago. The selection was large by Aldi standards (more choices, for example, than on the canned soup aisle), but still much less than consumers in the United States or Great Britain would expect. Aldi stocks wines from Germany, Austria, France, Italy, Spain, South Africa, Australia, and the United States. I found just a few different choices from each country (just a single red and white from California, for example), mainly house brands and generics, with a few products made by well-known producers or from specific wine areas.

Looking at the Spanish wines (and concentrating on the reds as a German buyer would) I found a basic Rioja for €2.39 for a standard 750 ml bottle, a Rioja Reserva for €4.99, and special bottlings by Miguel Torres for €5.99 and €6.99. Among the French wines I discovered a Cru Beaujolais Fleurie for €4.99 and Champagne priced at €11.49. The most common price point was €2.49 per bottle, which works out to about $3.50 at exchange rates current when I made my search. There is a small selection of organic wines from Italy, too.

The most expensive table wine that Aldi sells seems to cost about $10, which is quite a lot less than the most expensive wine at your local upscale supermarket. But then Aldi's least expensive wine is a lot cheaper, too. Holding down the bottom of the wall and forming the foundation for the Aldi wine empire is a 1.5 liter Tetra Pak red wine that sells for €1.39. That translates into €0.93 per liter or about €0.70 per standard bottle (although it obviously doesn't come in a bottle). For mathematically challenged readers, this equates to a shade over $0.97 per bottle equivalent, or less than half the price of Two Buck Chuck.

I wonder what a 97-cent wine tastes like? I'm kicking myself for not buying a carton of the stuff when I was in Munich, but I was understandably diverted by the beer. The Aldi Süd website provides scant information. Origin: European Community (not even limited to a particular country much less a particular winemaking region). Grape Variety: different varieties—that's an exact quote. It sounds a bit like "dump bucket red," although I am sure it isn't like that at all. Flavor: lovely. Tasting note: "This mild red wine is subtly scented with cherry and raspberry and a little orange. It goes well with dessert, cheese, heavy soups, and roasts." (Thanks to Google Translate for compensating for my weak German skills.)

I trust that the flavor really is lovely, but my mind boggles just a bit trying to imagine a red wine that can be paired effectively with such a diverse range of foods. The Tetra Pak white, which sells for the same price, is also a pan-European mixed-grape product that has a "lovely" taste. It goes well with desserts, cheeses, salads, and poultry according to Aldi.

These are the wines that define the German wine market to the majority of its wine buyers. The bad news of course is that the Tetra Pak products seem to be so lacking in specific character, which is what makes wine interesting. The good news is that Aldi seems to be encouraging its customers to move up the ladder (even if it doesn't reach very high) and try products that promise to reveal a bit of terroir in their half-full glass.

HALF FULL? OR HALF EMPTY?

Aldi would seem to be a wine lovers nightmare and if the future of wine is more and more Aldi, I think many terroirists might consider suicide. But there is reason to doubt that the future (or the present) is quite so grim. When Britain's *Which* magazine (it advises subscribers which cars and which televisions to purchase) rated supermarkets in early 2010, it put Aldi and its hard-discount peer Lidl ahead of Tesco, Sainsbury's, and Asda. The rankings were the result of a poll of more than thirteen thousand British supermarket shoppers in 2009, a time of deep recession in Britain. (Waitrose and Marks & Spencer came in top of the table, if you are interested, with Aldi and Lidl tied for third place.)

British consumers seem to be satisfied with Aldi's value-driven model. They even seem to like the wine, although choices are limited—something like fifty regularly stocked wines with another thirty or so that rotate in and out during the year to provide a bit of variety. Wine critic Tim Atkin surprised himself by finding Aldi wine pretty decent. He was disappointed by the narrow selection, as you might expect, but he found a few wines to like including a Chianti Superiore with nice fruit and a bit of tannic grip selling for just £3.99.

The glass is half full here in the United States, too. The Aldi way of shopping has evolved quite a lot since the first American store, an Aldi Süd affiliate, opened in southeastern Iowa in 1976. The first stores took their hard-discount origins seriously, located in small spaces and stocking only about five hundred house-brand items. This is less choice than a typical convenience store with even fewer amenities. And they were closed on Sunday, which was until recently a standard German retail practice. The prices, of course, were very low, which seems to have been enough to attract a following.

Today, there are nearly a thousand Aldi stores in twenty-nine states, from Kansas to the East Coast. And today's Aldi store carries about fourteen hundred regularly stocked items, including fresh meat. Though the original Aldi concept has been modified somewhat, the core concept remains: "Incredible Value Every Day."

The good news here is that Aldi's U.S. push may also help drive wine deeper into the U.S. consumer mainstream. Inexpensive wine is part of the Aldi package in the United States, too (where local laws permit). It may not be very good wine (a matter of taste), but its market impact may not be entirely bad. Will Aldi's drive be successful? There is reason to think it will be. They seem committed to tailoring their hard-discount operations to local market conditions, which is important because markets have terroir as much as wine.

But there is a more important reason. *Both* German Aldi chains are present in the United States now, although you are probably not aware of them. Aldi Süd operates under the Aldi name, of course, with the same logo as in Germany. The owners of Aldi Nord invested years ago in a different chain, based in California and intentionally tailored for thrifty but upwardly mobile U.S. consumers. It's an upscale Aldi Nord chain and the stores have been very successful here.

Perhaps you've heard of them. They have limited selection, smaller stores, lots of house brands, and low prices. They even sell a lot of wine. The name?

Oh, yes. Trader Joe's!

Trader Joe's, the California-based U.S. grocery chain that caters to upscale customers who are looking for a bargain, is Aldi Nord in surfer shorts. The stores are small (compared to U.S. supermarkets), the selections narrow, and most of the products are house brands produced by outside suppliers, some of them in Europe. If you can't stop thinking that you are shopping at a European food shop when you visit Trader Joe's, well it is because you are.

And this explains the influence of the German market on the globalization of wine. Two Buck Chuck isn't really the revolutionary innovation that most of my friends seem to believe; it is simply Aldi's discount wine strategy transplanted to American soil, with low-cost wine from California's Central Valley rather than the low-cost producers in France and the Veneto that Aldi uses in Europe.[7] And it seems to be as popular in the United States as it is in Germany and everywhere else the Albrecht brothers (and the winemakers and retailers who have adopted their strategy) have set up shop.

Germany is recovering from the Curse of the Blue Nun and the limitations of the Aldi model of wines. For a long time German wine was defined by a particular idea of low-cost generic products and low-quality branded goods. Its quality Rieslings aside, it doesn't seem like wine enthusiasts have much reason to give Germany their thanks. But don't rush to judgment—we have one more wine market to visit.

The United States will soon overtake Britain and Germany to become the world's most important wine market. America is the famous melting pot and this is true for wine as well. It's the place where Tesco, Aldi, and Blue Nun come together to create a third image of the future of wine.

7

America's Hangover

The United States recently assumed the title of "World's Largest Wine Market" (measured by dollars spent)—a tribute to America's large population and great wealth more than to its love of wine alone. While the American totals are huge—supersized, if you will—we still lag far behind many other countries in terms of per capita consumption.

Average wine consumption in the United States has risen to a bit more than a case of wine per person per year (or about two cases plus per wine drinker, since fewer than half of all Americans drink any wine at all).[1] This is a lot more than we drank fifty years ago, but Old World wine consumers in France, Italy, and Spain drink nearly five times as much per person; the British drink about twice as much. Even Canadians drink more wine on average.

America thus presents a puzzle—a major wine producer, the largest market in the world, but suffering from a bad case of arrested development in terms of its national wine culture. The source of this syndrome is easy to perceive and how it is treated in coming years will do much to shape the future of wine.

The problem is simple. American wine is suffering from a hangover. But it isn't a hangover created by some barrel-draining bottle-gulping Bacchanalian binge. America is still recovering from the Prohibition era (1920–1933), when production and sale of wine and other alcoholic beverages was all but banned. Prohibition's impact on wine in America and the peculiar pattern the market took once wine was legal again continue to shape the world of wine today.

THE PROHIBITION PARADOX

Wine, the "temperance beverage" according to its advocates, was banned along with all other alcoholic beverages during the "Great Experiment" of Prohibition. Or at least that's what most people think. Banning wine—letting the vineyards go to ruin, allowing America's wine culture to shrivel—that would have been bad. But what actually happened to wine in America during Prohibition was even worse.[2]

Wine consumption actually increased during Prohibition. How is this possible, since wine was illegal? Well, the truth is that the Volstead Act provided three loopholes that wine producers and consumers exploited for all they were worth. It was legal for commercial wineries to make and sell wine for religious and medical purposes. Sacramental wine and prescription wine kept a few American wineries in business, albeit at low production levels (I suppose it is possible that some of this legal wine might have made its way onto the black market).

The biggest loophole, however, was the provision that allowed for limited home production of wine. It was against the law for an Italian American family in Brooklyn to buy wine, but they could legally make two hundred gallons of it at home for nonintoxicating family use. Two hundred gallons! That's about a thousand bottles a year, a lot more wine than most Americans were drinking before Prohibition.[3] Plenty of wine for the family and maybe a bit left over for friends and even under-the-table sales. Okay, a lot left over for other purposes.

The wine loopholes, combined with attempts to more tightly regulate other forms of alcohol, encouraged wine production and consumption during the long Prohibition years, but in a way that corrupted the idea of wine and crippled the development of a sustainable wine culture.

Wine is many things to many people, which is why it is so interesting, but during Prohibition it was really just one thing: a widely available semilegal buzz. Wine was reduced to its alcoholic content in the minds of many producers, consumers, and (especially) regulators. The idea that it was a valuable cultural component or temperate, healthful food product—well, those notions basically disappeared. We still suffer from the hangover effect of this transformation, with wine that is heavily taxed and regulated and subject to tight distributional controls.

America's taste for wine changed, too. Wine that is consumed with meals is different from wine that you drink to get numb. Sweet, high-proof wines were the beverage of choice and it took decades after 1933 for drier table wines to reestablish themselves in American life in an important way.

Most important, however, is the fact that the wine itself changed. Because of the two hundred–gallon loophole, much of the wine that American's drank during Prohibition was utterly revolting. It was made by fumbling amateurs, not trained professionals. It was made at home, with rudimentary equipment, not in clean and well-supplied cellars. And it was made with grapes that traveled hundreds and sometimes thousands of miles by truck and rail to get to the cities and towns where home-winemakers lived.

I can only imagine what the grapes must have looked like when the amateur winemakers got them home. My friends who make wine pick their grapes in the early morning hours and then rush them to the cellar, to process them at the peak of freshness and before bacteria have a chance to do their smelly work. I'll bet the grapes that were loaded onto railcars in California were in sorry shape when they reached their final destinations in Chicago and Philadelphia!

So wine consumption rose during Prohibition, but the culture of wine went into a steep spiral of decline. Wine drinkers changed (into alcohol drinkers), the wines changed (they got much worse), and even the grapes themselves changed. Given the realities of the Prohibition wine market, winegrowers focused on thick-skinned grapes that would survive shipping in place of more delicate varietals that would make better wine. It made sense in the short run, of course, but it added one more barrier to the revival of wine once the Prohibition era came to a close.

GALLO AND THE REBIRTH OF AMERICAN WINE

A lot of my wine snob friends turn up their noses at Gallo wines and others like them, but I think you have to appreciate the role they have played in the rebirth of wine in America. Ernest and Julio Gallo founded their eponymous California winery in 1933 just at the moment when production and sale of wine became legal once again. The American wine industry, as you can probably appreciate, was in a sorry state indeed.

In addition to all the problems I've just listed, add one more. The death of Prohibition did not mean the end of wine market controls. The federal government turned over wine distribution regulation to state governments while retaining certain controls in the Treasury Department's Bureau of Alcohol, Tobacco and Firearms.[4] This act did even more to fragment the wine market by subjecting it to both several layers of regulation (federal, state, local) and multiple systems of distributional controls. Interstate wine trade was subject to a maze of rules and regulations and each state's internal wine market was different. In theory the end of Prohibition created a huge potential market for wine in America, but in practice the new regime replaced one huge barrier to wine with hundreds of smaller ones.

Gallo and the other wine pioneers of the era evolved around the bottlenecks they confronted. The most obvious key to their success was that their professionally made wine was of much higher quality than the rotgut homemade stuff that buyers had grown accustomed to. But you shouldn't imagine that their aim was to make fine wines to rival the best of Burgundy and Bordeaux. The fragmentation of the American market and the corruption of the American palate meant that American wine needed to be targeted at the mass-market middle, where a broad enough consumer base could be found to make the big investment in multistate distribution worthwhile, not the fine wine heights.

The early strategy for Gallo and other post-Prohibition pioneers was to make large quantities of wine and ship them in bulk (in railroad tanker cars for the most part) to clients across the country who would bottle the wine and sell it under their own label. It was an economical system, since the extra weight of the bottle was added close to the final buyer's market, and one that put most of the burden on meeting local liquor regulations on the local bottlers and distributors who were best situated to deal with them.

Wineries like Gallo grew quite large, with storage capacity denominated in the millions of gallons, but they were not household names and didn't promote national brands. They supplied commodity wines to local firms that bottled and sold wine but rarely made it. Growing grapes (under contract to a winery) and making wine and selling it were surprisingly discrete links in the mass-market wine commodity chain.

World War II changed all that. More than half of the fleet of wine tanker railcars that were key to the prewar wine system were conscripted—used to transport industrial alcohol used to make armaments. The best way to get wine to market during World War II was to bottle (and brand) it at the winery and use readily available boxcars to ship cases of wine across the country. In a matter of months, the tank car shortage turned companies like Gallo from anonymous bulk wine producers into nationally distributed bottled wine brands.

This pattern persisted in the early postwar years and is responsible for the way the wine wall looked back in the 1960s. A pretty thin selection, except in big city specialty stores, because the fragmented market structure made national distribution prohibitively costly for most winemakers. Top-shelf wines came from the Old World. American wines were aimed at the mass-market middle and below, wine drinkers whose palates were still recovering from the Prohibition hangover.

Excellent wines were being made in America, but in tiny quantities with limited distribution. The industry was defined by wines like Gallo's successful Thunderbird, a lemon-flavored, fortified White Port. This looked to be the dark future of American wine. And then came Robert Mondavi.[5]

THE JULIA CHILD OF WINE

I like to say that Robert Mondavi tried to do for American wine what Julia Child (public television's "French chef") tried to do for American cuisine: revolutionize it by convincing Americans that they could not just imitate the French but maybe better them at their own game.

Julia Child succeeded, although not by herself of course. American cuisine was transformed by her books and *The French Chef*, which aired from 1963 to 1973. She changed the idea of food in America. American ingredients, French techniques. Bring them together and cooks could be chefs.

Robert Mondavi did the same thing for wine. He was convinced that American grapes and Old World techniques could produce world-class wines. And he was right. When the Robert Mondavi Winery opened in Oakville in 1966, it was the first major new investment in Napa Valley in decades and it changed everything (not by itself, of course) and paved the way for a distinctly American vision of fine wine that coexists today along with a Gallo-tinted image of mass-market wines.

Although there are hundreds of tiny boutique wineries, I think it is fair to say that the American way of fine wine, as Mondavi defined it, thinks big. Mondavi didn't so much make wine and create a winery as he built a brand that could be successfully marketed. The brand defined Mondavi and it also defined Napa Valley (and helped make it famous) and in a way it defined the New World of wine, too.

The Mondavi winery wasn't just a vineyard and production facility, it was a destination. Mondavi knew that wine and a story sold better than wine by itself, so he set out to create a facility that would glow with a particularly California aura. It stood alone in the 1960s as an outpost of fine wine and it stands alone today, even though it's surrounded by other wineries it inspired.

Robert Mondavi Winery became known around the world for the quality of its signature Napa Valley Cabernet Sauvignon wines, but that's not really the wine that built the Mondavi brand in my opinion. I think it was the Fumé Blanc, an oaked Sauvignon Blanc with a trademarked French-inspired name. Sauvignon Blanc is a money wine—I call it Chateau Cash Flow—because you make them fresh and release them young. Return on investment is recouped much quicker than with red wines that need years in the barrel.

The Fumé Blanc, using grapes from Mondavi's famous To Kalon Vineyard and other sources, was exactly what was needed to jumpstart upscale wines in America. It was, first of all, a distinctive wine that deserved its premium (but still affordable) price. French sounding but not really authentically French in substance or style, it was the ideal first step up for aspiring Julia Child *French Chef* viewers. It was profitable, too, I'll wager, and provided funds for other projects. And it was a brand (Robert Mondavi Fumé Blanc) that could be marketed vigorously and used to build the bigger brands and projects that were always on big-thinker Robert Mondavi's mind.

THE AMERICAN WAY OF WINE

Gallo and Mondavi showed that it was possible to overcome the Prohibition hangover in the United States. Gallo did it with reliable quality, trustworthy brands, a consumer-driven strategy, and sufficient scale to make national distribution economically feasible. Eventually, having built this foundation, Gallo moved upmarket to more sophisticated wines. Especially in the early years, however, Gallo didn't try to shape America's wine culture so much as to find ways to reach out to it.

Gallo today is the largest wine company in the world. It makes or distributes nearly fifty wine brands that range from bottom-shelf value wines like Peter Vella, Carlo Rossi, and André sparkling wine to single vineyard Gallo Family Vineyard wines and the historic Louis M. Martini brand. The Gallo brand portfolio includes wines from Australia (Black Swan, Clarendon Hills,

McWilliams), Argentina (Don Miguel Gascon, Catena Alamos), Spain (Las Rocas, Martin Côdax), South Africa (Sebeka), New Zealand (Starborough, Whitehaven), Italy (DaVinci, Bella Sera, Ecco Domani, Maso Canali), Germany (Pölka Dot), and France (Red Bicyclette).

Why so many wines brands? Well, globalization is one answer, of course, although it's only part of the story. As we will see in the next section, the New World wine wall is complex and highly stratified since it is organized around what consumers might want to buy rather than what winemakers might want to sell. Powered by its huge investment in a national (and increasingly international) distribution system, Gallo has the resources to put its products in most of the important market spaces.

Reputation was the key factor in Mondavi's success and he built powerful brands (brand Fumé Blanc, brand Napa Valley, brand Robert Mondavi himself) that could be marketed successfully to a wine audience that included wine neophytes, wine enthusiasts, and Julia Child's audience of aspiring French chefs.

Robert Mondavi thought big, as his Opus One partnership with Bordeaux's famous Rothschild family makes clear. But thinking big isn't always enough. The Mondavis went "public" in an attempt to achieve Gallo-like scale, trading their family-business traditions for a corporate wine structure to get capital for expansion on both national and global scales. The plan backfired and in 2004 the Mondavi empire was acquired by New York–based Constellation Brands for one billion dollars.

Scale and reputation don't guarantee success in American wine, obviously, but it is hard to overcome the Prohibition hangover without them. There is reason to believe that together they define the future of wine in the world's largest wine market. Or at least that's what I discovered when I started buying wine at Costco.

COSTCO AND THE FUTURE OF WINE

Costco is the largest wine retailer in the United States and arguably the top fine-wine merchant in the world. Costco sold more than a hundred thousand cases of $100 Dom Pérignon Champagne in 2006, according to one source, an indication of its market power even at the higher reaches of the wine market. Costco's notable success reflects its ability to leverage the methods of Tesco and Aldi to break through the bottlenecks that the U.S. wine market presents.

Costco is a members-only "big box" discounter with more than five hundred warehouse stores in the United States, Canada, Mexico, Puerto

Rico, Great Britain, Japan, Korea, Australia, and Taiwan. Its fifty-six million household and business members pay $50 to $100 per year (depending upon membership category) to get access to Costco's low prices, good service, and private label products. The stores are large and relatively austere. They look more like factory floors than retail sales areas. In fact they *are* factories in a way, where the customers do much of the work (in the same happy spirit as Aldi shoppers) and are happy with the bargain, especially if they score a tasty snack sample along the way.

The merchandise is stacked in ground-level boxes and crates and inventory is stored on industrial shelves that reach toward the roof. Shoppers push over-size trolleys and flat-bed carts through the aisles, loading up on economy-size packages of irresistible material goods. Although Costco is in many ways a temple of consumer excess, its low prices, Spartan shelves, and humble stacks make you feel almost virtuous when you walk out with a fully loaded cart.

You won't find everything in a Costco—there are far fewer product lines (or SKUs) than in a typical Walmart store, for example, or a big French Car-refour *hypermarché*, and usually only one or two product choices. Some of the products are packed in humongous sizes intended for business or restaurant use, but the prices are famously low and the reputation for quality is unques-tioned. Consumers seem to have adjusted to Costco by turning their homes and apartments into soft good storage units.

Costco sold more than $2 billion worth of televisions in fiscal 2007, ac-cording to the company's website, and 110,432 carats of diamonds (including a single ring that sold for nearly $200,000). Costco members filled more than 28 million prescriptions, bought more than 2.5 million pairs of eyeglasses, took home more than 35 million rotisserie chickens, and scarfed down over 75 million hot dogs. It is no surprise, therefore, that Costco sells a lot of wine. Members bought almost $500 million worth of fine wine in fiscal 2007 and spent over $1 billion overall on the 75 million bottles of wine they lugged out of warehouse stores.

The wine aisle at Costco doesn't look much like the wine aisle in your local upscale supermarket. Most supermarkets provide a surprisingly large selec-tion of wines—hundreds or even thousands of different wines are constantly on offer. A typical Costco store on the other hand has a rolling inventory of only about 100–120 wines at any given time. This is only about a tenth of the number of brands that your supermarket stocks, although it is perhaps ten times the number of choices of any other product category in a typical Costco warehouse, with the possible exception of books.

Selection is obviously much narrower at Costco, so value and quantity sales are the key. If you've shopped for wine at Costco, you already know that you can spend as little as about $5 or less for a bottle of simple table wine and as much as . . . well, as much as you want, really. I have seen Dom Pérignon on the Costco rack as well as a Heitz Cellars Martha's Vineyard Cabernet Sauvignon a few years ago.

One way that Costco reflects wine globalization is obvious: they bring global wines to the American market by offering products from France, Italy, Spain, Chile, South Africa, Germany, Portugal, Australia, South Africa, and New Zealand. But Costco's global connections run deeper than just the origins of the wine.

COSTCO AND THE GERMAN MODEL

You would think that Costco's wine strategy would be based upon the Germany discount model, since Costco is a high-volume low-price warehouse operation and that's the way most wine is sold in Germany. The maximum markup on wine is just 14 percent above wholesale price.[6] This is much less than the standard rule of thumb of about 30–50 percent for retail wine and 150 percent or more for restaurant sales.

But the resemblance between Costco, an American discounter, and Aldi, the German budget king, is superficial at best. The average "bottle" of German wine is sold in a discount store, often with a house-brand name, and costs a little more than a euro per liter. I put "bottle" in quotes because sometimes it comes in a 1 liter juice-box-type container. Decent quality for less is what the German market seeks and the discount chain's reputation for value seals the deal.

Costco's wine aisle looks a bit like Aldi, with volume wines stacked in their cardboard cases. But Costco's cheapest wines are much more expensive than the Aldi standard. Top-selling brands include Kendall-Jackson Vintner's Reserve and Robert Mondavi Woodbridge. These wines are meant to be good-value famous-brand wines for upscale shoppers, not rock-bottom private-label bargains. Value wines are positioned just down the aisle from carefully arranged wooden cases that display carefully selected fine wines with prices that start at about $10 and go steadily upward from there.

I guess that you could say that Costco appeals to the German wine drinker in all of us, but doesn't go as far as Aldi would, either in the United States or in Germany, to reach that market. The U.S. retailer that best represents the German wine model isn't Costco; it is Trader Joe's, the upscale surfer dude gourmet store, with its discount wines and big displays of Two Buck Chuck. And that's not an accident, as we learned in the last chapter, since TJ's is owned by Theo Albrecht, one of the Aldi founders.

So although you might think of Costco as the home of German-style inexpensive wine because of it discount warehouse store image, that's not really accurate. Costco is something a bit different.

COSTCO AND THE AMERICAN SYSTEM

Although Costco is an American company and most of its stores are in the United States, it doesn't really present the classic American wine market system, either. The U.S. model is built around brands owned by wine companies with strong distribution systems, not discount stores with private labels like in Germany. Winemakers big and small seek to establish a brand or reputation that will help them sell their wines to consumers who need a trustworthy indicator of value and/or quality. Americans typically look to brands for quality/value information when shopping in general and so it is natural that wine brands are important here, too.

Because there are lots of market segments for wine and many competing brands within each segment, the American system demands lots of variety and choice. This is how your supermarket wine aisle became so extravagant. If you have three or four competing brands for each type of wine at each significant price point, well the numbers of choices quickly adds up.

The Costco system rejects this whole idea, offering only a hundred or so different choices. Obviously not all brands and all varieties of wine and all price points are covered. And yet, interestingly, many of my wine loving friends tell me that Costco's wine selection is great.

Some of the big sellers in the $10.99-plus "fine wine category" are brands you might recognize—La Crema Chardonnay, Kendall-Jackson Grand Reserve Chardonnay, Santa Margherita Pinot Grigio, and Beaulieu Vineyards Napa Valley Cabernet, among them. These are large volume producers who can reliably fill Costco's huge pipeline—wine marketing the American way. These may not be the wines that customers would select in a grocery store setting, with more choices at more price points, but they buy them up at Costco and feel that they are getting good value for the money.

Interestingly, however, Costco also stocks wine from many much smaller producers—wines that are likely to sell out and not be replaced as limited inventories are used up. A team of regional wine buyers customizes the selection for each local area. This idea runs exactly opposite of the American model, which supposes that buyers seek consistent, reliable supply and that retailers want to deal with a small number of producers with many brands each. Costco aims to create what it calls a "treasure hunt" atmosphere in the fine wine aisle, where buyers will not always know exactly what to expect and learn to snap up new items that delight them and come back often to see what's new.

So why does Costco sell so much wine? It isn't because it gives American wine buyers what they expect or even what they would probably say they want. The reason, I think, is that it gives them something that is different. Costco, more than anything else, is Tesco on steroids.

TESCO ON STEROIDS?

A typical Costco store bears little physical resemblance to the Tesco supermarket I used to shop at in England, but the Costco wine strategy, well, that's a different story. The British system works by lending the reputation of the store to its wine wall, encouraging customers by giving them more confidence. If Tesco/Costco sells it, then it must be a good value.

The use of private-label wine has been the signature tactic of British supermarkets and it is probably not an accident that Costco has followed suit. A good example is the Kirkland Signature Central Otago (New Zealand) Pinot Noir that I found on one Costco expedition. Pinot Noir is hot these days (the *Sideways* fad) and Central Otago Pinots have developed something of a cult following. So it is very interesting to find this wine in a warehouse store.

The Kirkland Signature label first appeared in 2003. The wines are relatively small lots (around two thousand cases each—large for many wineries but small for Costco) and specially created by selected winemakers who are sometimes identified on the label and sometimes, for various reasons, kept secret. The wines are scattered out among the warehouse stores and when they are gone they're gone. New wine releases are staggered throughout the year so that serious (or curious) buyers have reason to check back frequently to see what's new.

Now we can begin to appreciate why Costco is so successful as a wine retailer. Their list of wines is not large compared to other retailers, but they provide a rolling selection of pretty interesting and sometimes unexpected wines (at good prices, but that goes without saying). Costco buyers suspect that it must be a good value to get on the Costco shelves and know that any particular wine might not still be there next week or next month. Better run back and buy more now if you want it. So people keep coming back.

The fact that the Costco system bears a striking resemblance to the British wine model is not an accident. The Costco wine program was created by David Andrew, a Scot who began his career selling wine in London. After working as a fashion model in Europe and literary agent in Los Angeles, Andrew returned to London and to wine, studying at the Institute of Masters of Wine. He approached Costco with the idea of building a wine trade at the warehouse store in 1998. The British model, transplanted to the American warehouse, was a quick success.

So, is Costco the future of wine? My answer is yes . . . and no. Costco shows us that the globalization of wine is not just about populating the wine wall with hundreds of bottles from dozens of countries or stooping to a global least common denominator standard. Costco is successful because it sells American consumers wines from all around the world in supersized Aldi-style stores using a marketing model like the Tesco marketing model that made Britain the center of the wine universe. Costco blends in a bit of German thrift and lots of American brand names with British wine-selling savvy.

The fact that the Costco system works in the United States is not surprising—it is an American company, after all. But it is significant because as globalization brings more and more countries and their consumers into the wine market, the ability to overcome the sort of obstacles and bottlenecks that define American wine will be increasingly important.

The future of wine? Aldi, Tesco, and Costco are part of the story, but wine is too complex to be reduced to retail market strategy. Wine buyers are as complicated as wine is itself. The battle for the future of wine pits Martians versus Wagnerians, as we see in the next chapter, and depends critically on a miracle—the Miracle of Two Buck Chuck, which is the subject of the next flight of chapters. There is much still to be done in our investigation of the future of wine.

But first it's time for a tasting!

Globalization Tasting

Each of the three main sections of *Wine Wars* (I call them "flights" after the term for a selection of wines to be tasted together) concludes with a suggested wine tasting intended to allow you to consider these ideas in a different way, one that draws upon all of your senses. Wine is the perfect choice, don't you think?

For the Globalization Tasting I would like you to taste through a flight of Sauvignon Blanc wines. I choose Sauvignon Blanc because it is truly a global variety—it shows up in many corners of the wine world from France to New Zealand, Chile to California, India to Israel. Maybe it's because the grape variety is so adaptable. Or maybe, as we've just learned, because it's a Chateau Cash Flow wine that doesn't take forever to turn a profit.

Buy three or four bottles of Sauvignon Blanc, call up some friends, taste the different wines, and talk about how the world of wine has expanded since you started drinking wine. What wines should you pick? Here are my suggestions, inspired by the chapters you've just read.

- Start with France. Sauvignon Blanc is grown in several French regions, but it is generally not labeled as such because of the DaVino Code—the French think of wine as geography (places) not horticulture (types of grapes). When in doubt, choose Sancerre, the Sauvignon Blanc wines made in the eastern part of the Loire Valley in France.

- Now follow the missionaries, migrants, and market reformers to New Zealand and sample a Marlborough Sauvignon Blanc. Choose the most recent vintage you can find because freshness is a good thing with these wines. If you can afford it, try Cloudy Bay, since it was one of the first Kiwi wines to hit world markets, or a Brancott Estate, since that's where the first Marlborough Sauvignon Blanc vineyard was planted. But don't worry if you cannot find a particular wine—any one will do to start.
- I think you should look to California for the third wine. Get the Mondavi Fumé Blanc if you can or something else if you can't (Geyser Peak is a reliable and affordable choice). If you are ambitious and have any money left add a fourth wine—choose a Sauvignon Blanc from an unlikely or unexpected place. South Africa would be appropriate, since we've talked about its wine history. Chilean wines are good values—some are made by French "flying winemakers." Israeli wines are interesting, too, and Washington State produces good examples of this variety. Really, you can't go wrong—just pull the cork (or twist the cap).

Whichever wines you select, I think you will find them interestingly different from one another despite being made from the same type of grape. As you enjoy the colors and aromas, tastes and textures, consider the miracle of globalization that has brought all these wines to your table. And ponder a bit the puzzle that cornucopia of choice presents.

Cheers!

Flight Two
THE MIRACLE OF
TWO BUCK CHUCK

Martians versus Wagnerians

Thomas Pinney devotes the last few pages of *A History of Wine in America: From Prohibition to the Present* to what he sees is a fundamental battle for the *idea* of wine in America. It is a conflict between Martians and Wagnerians, he says.

Martians and Wagnerians? Little green men versus opera-singing Rhine maidens (or maybe *wine* maidens)? No, it's even stranger than that.

The Wagnerians are inspired by the ideas of Philip Wagner (not the opera-writing Richard), a Baltimore journalist, viticulturist, and winemaker especially active in the years that bracket World War II when America's Prohibition hangover was especially severe. Wagner believed that wine should be an affordable part of ordinary life and a constant companion at mealtime. Pinney writes that

> Wagnerians are always delighted to have a bottle of superlative wine, but their happiness does not depend on it, nor are they so foolish as to think that only the superlative is fit to drink. Their happiness *does* depend upon wine each day . . . good sound wine will not only suffice. It is a necessary part of the daily regimen.[1]

Wagnerians sing an appealing but fundamentally radical song in the American context, where wine is just one of many beverages and not always the cheapest or most convenient to purchase. Regulations that treat wine as a controlled substance are very anti-Wagnerian.

Wagner founded Boordy Vineyards in Maryland and was well regarded by wine people from coast to coast. He is an important figure in the history of American wine, according to Pinney, and one whose idea of wine lives on in many forms. I guess you could say that Two Buck Chuck is a Wagnerian wine, for example, although I think there's a lot more to Wagner's idea of wine than just low price.

Wagner promulgated his populist vision by promoting the so-called French hybrid grape varieties on the East Coast and elsewhere. I think he wanted America to be Vineland (the name chosen by the Viking explorers), a country covered with grapevines and abundant with honest wine. This is easier said than done, however, as Pinney's history makes clear.

Martians are inspired by Martin Ray's idea of wine. Whereas Wagner was disappointed that America lacked a mainstream wine culture, Martin Ray was upset that the standard was so low in the years following the repeal of Prohibition. He persuaded Paul Masson to sell him his once great winery in 1935 and proceeded to try to restore its quality with a personal drive that Pinney terms fanatical.

He did it, too, making wines of true distinction—wines that earned the highest prices in California at the time. His achievement was short-lived, however. A winery fire slowed Ray's momentum and he finally sold out to Seagram's, which used a loophole in wartime price control regulations to make a fortune from the Paul Masson brand and its premium price points, starting a trend of destructive corporate exploitation that forms a central theme in Pinney's book.

The Martian view, according to Pinney, is that "anything less than superlative was unworthy, that no price could be too high, and that the enjoyment of wine required rigorous preparation."[2]

Ray's history is therefore especially tragic since his attempt to take California wine to the heights through Paul Masson ended so badly. Paul Masson today is an undistinguished mass-market wine brand—as un-Martian as you can get.

When wine enthusiasts of my generation think of Paul Masson (now part of the Constellation Brands portfolio), it is often because of Orson Welles's classic television ads, where he straight-facedly compared cheap California fizz to fine French Champagne and proclaimed, "Paul Masson will sell no wine before its time." What time is it? my wine-drinking friends used to joke. Oh . . . it's time!

Martians and Wagnerians have two very different ideas of wine and it is a shame that one needs to choose between them. It seems to me that wine could and should be *both* a daily pleasure and an opportunity for exceptional expression. The good isn't *always* the enemy of the great. But many people see it that way, including Pinney, who reveals himself to be a Wagnerian and expresses concern that the Martians have won the battle for wine in America. "The tendency of all this folderol is to exclude wine from a place in everyday life and to isolate it in a special sphere open only to a privileged elite, or, worse, to tourists on a spree."[3]

> The people who write about wine in the popular press largely appear to be Martians who take for granted that anything under $20 a bottle is a "bargain" wine and who routinely review for their middle-class readership wines costing $30, $40, $50 and up. Even in affluent America such wines can hardly be part of a daily supper. They enforce the idea that wine must be something special—a matter of display, or of costly indulgence. That idea is strongly reinforced by the price of wine in restaurants, where a not particularly distinguished bottle routinely costs two or three times the price of the most expensive entrée on the menu.[4]

"No wonder," Pinney concludes, "that the ordinary American, unable to understand how a natural fruit product (as wine undoubtedly is) can be sold for $50 or more a bottle, sensibly decides to have nothing to do with the mystery."

I guess I am a Wagnerian, too, if I have to choose, but I'm not as pessimistic as Pinney. Can wine be both common and great? Why not? Wine isn't one thing; it is many things to many people. No purpose is served, in my view, by monolithic thinking.

What are wine drinkers *really* looking for? Are they Martians or Wagnerians or something else? That's the bottom-line question that I want to probe in this part of the book. And I want to see where Two Buck Chuck fits into the answer.

WHAT ARE WINE DRINKERS LOOKING FOR?

Americans (or at least many of them) have unexpectedly come to love wine, something that seemed impossible just a few years ago. The wine wall has been transformed, from a rack of Thunderbird to a selection of global proportions. But have we embraced wine in our peculiar American way and, by loving it, destroyed it? And is Two Buck Chuck the shaft of our deadly Cupid arrow? Only one way to find out. Away we go!

Here we are again, back at the wine wall of your neighborhood upscale supermarket, but this time I want you to look at the people, not the wine, because we are interested in the mainstream market for wine. Hang around a while and see if you can draw any conclusions about the "typical" wine buyer. Young or old? Male or female? Rich or poor? Expert or novice? Do they reach up to the more expensive bottles on the top shelf or stoop down for the economy-size boxes and bottles at the bottom?

It is actually pretty interesting to be an amateur wine wall anthropologist, so I hope you give it a try. The first thing that most people notice is also the most important: there doesn't seem to be a single, "typical" wine customer, although there are several types of ritualized behaviors. Some people launch surgical strikes, efficiently plucking bottles from the wine wall and disappearing into Meat or Fish or Produce. Others linger in particular areas, reading the tags that are affixed to the racks, which are called "shelf talkers," and sometimes picking up bottles to read the label more closely. Other buyers seem to be lost: they wander around like a driver looking for a house number on an unfamiliar street until finally grabbing a bottle or just walking away empty-handed.

Does your supermarket have a wine steward or someone who lingers in the neighborhood of the wine wall to offer assistance? This is an increasingly common feature of upscale grocery stores. If so, you might note how many customers ask for advice, how many accept help when it is offered, and how many prefer to confront the wall one-on-one.

The anthropology of the native wine wall culture is an interesting study, but it has its limits, too. To get a better understanding of what is driving wine buyers and their behavior you would need to do more detailed research, to know more about the people and their motivations and to take into account all the market factors, like income and ethnicity, that affect demand for any consumer good.

SEQUENCING WINE DRINKER DNA

Fortunately we don't have to go to the trouble of designing a research methodology to sequence wine buyer DNA in the United States because multinational wine giant Constellation Brands has already done it. They call their study Project Genome and the results that have been released to the public go a long way toward helping us understand both the people who come to the wine wall and how the wall has adapted in response.[5]

The first phase of Project Genome was released in 2005. A bank of one hundred questions was administered to a panel of thirty-five hundred U.S. wine consumers in the largest organized study of wine buyers at the time. A further study, released in 2008, tracked the behavior of ten thousand wine consumers using Nielsen Homescan® data. The Nielsen company (the same people who release television ratings) has created a "mini-USA" consumer panel, according to their website, where participants fill out surveys and scan the barcodes of their purchases. Nielsen measures consumer attitudes and purchase behavior within multiple purchase channels, including warehouse clubs, supermarkets, mass merchandisers, drug stores, liquor stores, and wine shops. The scan data were supplemented with online interviews. Constellation Brands is using the wine data to shape strategies for their constantly evolving portfolio of product lines.

So what are wine buyers really looking for? Well, according to Project Genome, your amateur anthropology was on the money: there really isn't a single, "typical" kind of wine buyer. Wine drinkers come in all sizes, shapes, and colors. It is, however, possible to identify six wine market segments, which Constellation has named Enthusiasts, Image Seekers, Savvy Shoppers, Traditionalists, Satisfied Sippers, and Overwhelmed.

By far the largest group of wine buyers are "overwhelmed." They represent about 23 percent of the people you see at the wine wall, but they buy only 13 percent of the wine and produce only 11 percent of wine market profits. If you see someone walk up and down the wall and then walk away empty-handed, well it's probably an Overwhelmed consumer.

It is easy to see how someone could be overwhelmed by the wine wall, with its hundreds of labels in dozens of categories at many price points. What you might see as a world (literally) of interesting options, an Overwhelmed consumer sees as a crazy-quilt montage. Overwhelmed consumers are interested in wine, otherwise they wouldn't be standing at the wall, but they want and need help.

The first phase of Project Genome seems to have concluded that Overwhelmed consumers have pretty unsophisticated tastes. When asked what kind of wine they bought, many said "blush wine"—White Zinfandel. But the

Nielsen scanners revealed that in fact their purchases were much more varied that this. The reason they said White Zin was because they couldn't remember what they bought, a fact that shows just how confusing they find the wine wall (or a restaurant wine list) to be. I suspect that this market segment accounts for the popularity of so-called critter wines—wines with pictures of cute little animals on the label such as penguins and kangaroos, dogs and cats, birds and fish.

What do Overwhelmed wine buyers want? They want wine to be simpler, friendlier, easier to understand. Yes, isn't that what we all want out of life?

WINE AS A LIFESTYLE CHOICE

Overwhelmed buyers are the largest group, but they obviously don't buy the most wine. The Wine Enthusiast market segment accounts for just 12 percent of all wine buyers, but they purchase 25 percent of all wine in the study and produced nearly 30 percent of wine profits. Enthusiasts are at the opposite end of the spectrum from their Overwhelmed friends. They are looking for more than wine—they want a "wine experience," which I take to mean wine . . . and a story about the wine. So they are looking for sophisticated information about wine of the sort that causes Overwhelmed consumers to bolt for the exit.

Wine is a lifestyle choice for Enthusiasts, who are likely to read wine publications, make wine an important part of socializing, and take wine-related trips and vacations. They are more likely to live in affluent or cosmopolitan areas, according to the study, but I have found Enthusiasts pretty much everywhere.

Image Seekers are the third wine market group that Project Genome identifies and, as you might guess, these are affluent individuals who use wine, along with other material goods, to construct an identity. They seek status and validation through wine and wine-related activities such as tastings and tours. Image Seekers represent 20 percent of all buyers but make 24 percent of purchases and produce 25 percent of wine profits.

Image Seekers are not necessarily as well informed as Enthusiasts because they are often new to wine and still learning and experimenting. They might grow up to be Enthusiasts (Image Seekers tend to be younger), but not necessarily. There are a lot of products that an Image Seeker could use to construct an identity—clothes, cars, watches, smart phones, you name it. They will try anything once and spend a lot of time on the Internet searching for wine information. When in doubt, they are likely to buy wines with higher ratings or higher price tags.

MIDDLE MARKET WINE

Three very different (but roughly equal-sized) groups make up the solid middle of the wine market in the Project Genome study: Traditionalists, Savvy Shoppers, and Satisfied Sippers (I imagine these names were coined because they look good on a PowerPoint slide—I feel a little bit silly typing them here). Together they make up 45 percent of the wine buying public.

Traditionalists seek the familiar and tend to buy well-established brands, which they see as reinforcing their traditional values. Project Genome doesn't provide a lot of information about Traditionalists and I wonder what their "traditional values" really are? I'm guessing that this is code for a certain comfort zone and resistance to change. So I cannot imagine a Traditionalist buying a screw cap wine except by accident—the traditional rituals of the cork are too important. France, Italy, California—that's probably where the wine comes from in this household, with familiar names on the labels. New Zealand or Oregon? Probably not.

Satisfied Sippers actually represent the smallest market segment. This predominantly female group knows what to buy and buys it, often in 1.5 liter bottles. Wine is a consumer product and they know exactly which brands they like. Although they are 14 percent of all wine buyers, Satisfied Sippers buy just 8 percent of all wine and generate only 7 percent of profits. Given all the options available, it is kind of sad that someone could become so completely uncurious about all the wines on the wall. On the other hand, it is even sadder that so few people are so happy with wine that they see no reason to change.

I think that Satisfied Sippers are the past of wine, not its future. They are remnants of times past when there were very few choices and only a few national brands. Wine drinking fifty years ago for many Americans was probably about finding your brand (of wine, beer, cola) and sticking with it.

The final group are the Savvy Shoppers and I guess they are the extreme center of the U.S. wine market. They make up 15 percent of the market, buy 15 percent of the wine, and account for 15 percent of wine profits. They are value driven—they want to buy an $8 wine that tastes like a $12 or $15 dollar wine—irrespective of the fact that wines don't taste like price points. Savvy Shoppers seek satisfaction from a good wine value; because I have friends in this category I know that they are sometimes even happier with the bargain price than they are with the wine itself. They are treasure hunters looking for a deal.

WHAT KIND OF WINE BUYER ARE YOU?

So what kind of wine buyer are you? And where do your friends and family fit into the Project Genome taxonomy? I suspect that many readers will say that they don't really identify with any one of these wine buyer profiles, which is understandable, since we tend to be complicated individuals and these are broad and intentionally simplifying aggregates. Chances are that you are a mixed breed, perhaps part Enthusiast with a bit of Traditional value seeker tossed in.

I have developed several tests to help me identify and classify wine buyers according to Project Genome profiles. The first one is the Costco test. Costco is the single biggest wine merchant in the United States and so I'm guessing that they have figured out how to present themselves to the wine market in a user-friendly way. I haven't been to every Costco with a wine department, but all the ones I have visited are laid out the same way. A certain part of the store is set aside for the wine wall and two areas are created. One end features less expensive wine, usually well-known brands, often in 1.5 liter packages, stacked in the original cardboard boxes and offered for middle market prices, say $5.99 to $10.99. (Ironically, as I will explain in the next chapter, these less expensive wines are actually sold at "premium" price points in wine industry lingo.)

Close by this warehouse-style wine display is a much more upscale presentation, a long wooden case where wines are displayed on their sides, not upright, with informative labels giving wine critic scores for recent years. The displays remind me of big cradles that invite buyers to pick up bottles and cuddle them a while before dropping them into the big shopping carts. There are just a dozen or so bottles of each wine here versus cases and cases of each product at the other end of the wall, a subtle suggestion that you'd better buy now, before supplies run out.

Which end of the wine wall you gravitate toward will tell you what kind of wine buyer you are. If you spend most of your time in the value wine section, then you may be a Satisfied Sipper or a Savvy Shopper. You know what you like, you want to buy in quantity, you don't need anyone to tell you about it. Indeed, according to Project Genome, Satisfied Sippers buy about 16 percent of their wine at warehouse stores like Costco.

Wine Enthusiasts and Image Seekers won't spend much time among the stacked cases of ordinary wine. They will find themselves drawn instead to the other end, where a rotating selection of fine wines (prices at $10.99 and up) is presented in a more sophisticated way with at least some more detailed information that will appeal to wine geeks. The fine wine section gives Image Seekers good opportunities to experiment with wine while Wine Enthusiasts can gain satisfaction by applying their esoteric knowledge of wine to the complex set of choices presented. You don't have to read wine magazines or columns to get the most out of Costco's upscale wine wall, but it helps, so people who see wine as an integral part of their lifestyle are most comfortable there.

There is a special Trader Joe's version of this test that you can perform, if there is a TJ's store near you. Trader Joe's also segments its wine displays in the stores I have visited. There is a traditional supermarket-type wine wall in one part of the store with several hundred wines from all around the world on display at discount prices. Then, scattered around the store, often on "endcap" end-of-aisle displays, are piles of cases of particular deeply discounted wines. I call these displays "haystacks" because they often take that form as the cases are stacked four or five high and also because at least some of these wines are often very unfamiliar and so TJ's is sort of encouraging its customers to find the needle (good value wine) in a haystack. The biggest haystacks usually contain Charles Shaw (a.k.a. Two Buck Chuck) wine, Trader Joe's signature product.

I suspect that Wine Enthusiasts shop at Trader Joe's for its gourmet foods, but I don't know how much wine they buy there. My intuition is that TJ's wine wall appeals more to Image Seekers, who are attracted by the experimental opportunity that TJ's eclectic wine selection provides. It's cool to shop at Trader Joe's and double-cool to try a Chilean Carmenere—that's an irresistible opportunity for identity-driven consumers.

Trader Joe's also attracts Savvy Shoppers and Satisfied Sippers. You can probably find the Savvy Shopper group all over the store because while Trader Joe's products in general are not always cheap, they do have a reputation for consistently good value, and that's what the Shoppers are seeking out. Satisfied Sippers are most likely found near the Two Buck Chuck haystacks. Once they've decided that the Charles Shaw wines that sell for as little as $1.99 a bottle fit their needs, they have little reason to look elsewhere.

TALK TO ME

My theory is that you learn a bit about what sort of wine buyers your friends are by following them around as they shop at Costco and Trader Joe's because

I think these stores have rather purposefully arranged the wine wall to attract certain types of customers. Here's one final test that you can try in almost any wine-selling establishment: the shelf talker test.

Shelf talkers are those little signs that you find attached to the shelf or bins on the wine wall. I have been to stores where only a few wines have "talkers" and to others where nearly every wine is annotated with a tag. Shelf talkers take many forms.

The simplest and in some stores the most common is the discount tag. The shelf talker's message is clear: $14.99 / $5 off / $9.99. This wine is on sale. This is a lure meant to attract Savvy Shoppers and it works, even when nearly every wine on the wall is always "on sale," thus making the whole notion of regular retail price something of a joke.

The second most common kind of shelf talker in my experience is what I call the Number Tag. It gives a thumbnail wine rating from Robert Parker's *Wine Advocate, Wine Spectator,* or some other wine critic or publication. These tags are extremely effective and are also useful because they sell both wine and wine publications (at one point Costco had an exclusive agreement with *Wine Enthusiast* magazine to use their wine ratings in Costco stores). A number tag gives an otherwise anonymous wine instant credibility. You may not know what it will taste like, and you may not like it when you get home, but you made the purchase based upon recognized expert opinion, and that's better (or seems better at least) than throwing darts at the wine wall to make a choice.

Wine critics don't always agree in scoring wines and the whole notion of numerical ratings of wine is problematic, too, but the number tags work nonetheless. Image Seekers look for them so that they can take satisfaction in buying a 91-plus wine while Savvy Shoppers use them to make complex points per dollar wine value calculations. Satisfied Sippers don't need talkers, because they know what they want, although a little positive reinforcement doesn't hurt. Barefoot Wines, a Gallo value brand, makes sure that each of its wines earns a medal in a wine competition and this information always appears on the label and sometimes on a shelf talker.

Traditionalists don't really need shelf talkers either because they are just looking for the Mondavi Woodbridge or Antinori wines they always buy. Too many tags make it difficult for them to find their standby brands.

Wine Enthusiasts, on the other hand, live for shelf talkers. They look for the hand-lettered ones that provide brief but memorable narratives about the wine, the winemaking family, the region or vintage or varietal. Enthusiasts especially appreciate the story behind the wine and these miniature wine chronicles suit them to a T. Especially the hand-written ones, even if the story told is actually downloaded from the winery or distributor website. Type "wine shelf talkers" into your Internet search engine, hit enter, and see what I mean.

Wine buyers are complicated people. If you want to know what kind of wine buyer you are, just pay attention to where you buy wine and how and to what sort of consumer cues you respond—discount price, buying convenience, critic ratings, or detailed narrative. Each of these factors guides a strategy designed to appeal to certain types of wine buyers.

MARTIANS, WAGNERIANS, AND THE FUTURE OF WINE

Martians, Wagnerians, Savvy Sippers, Image Seekers—American wine buyers seem like a pretty confused lot. They buy different wines for different reasons at different prices at different types of stores. They seem to come from different planets, if you know what I mean. It's hard to see what they have in common.

But that's precisely the point. Although Martians moan when they hear me say it, the world of wine (and even the fine wine submarket) is enormously varied. And while you might like to think that you can ignore everyone but Martian Enthusiasts, the fact is that everyone will influence how wine develops in the future, even (or perhaps especially) the most confused and least informed.

And while you might like to believe that Overwhelmed wine shoppers and the rest are only an American phenomenon, the fact is that as globalization expands the wine world, bringing more wines to more wine drinkers, it makes wine both more diverse and more confusing.

It's easy to explain why America doesn't have a "traditional wine culture" that uniquely defines its idea of wine—Prohibition explains that. But the world has become more like America in this regard than we might like to admit. The idea that recovering teetotaler America is an exception is probably a myth.

One of my students wrote a paper on "The Postwar Decline of the Old World Consumer" that probed the question of why per capita wine consumption in Old World countries has fallen so rapidly over the last fifty years. This falling demand is a key factor in the continuing global wine glut and especially the EU's notorious wine lake. David, the author, turned the question around: why, he wondered, was consumption so high in the first place?

The most intensive wine consumption in France, Spain, and Italy in the early postwar years was among laborers and rural workers who expended great energy in their jobs and required high caloric intake. Rough local wine (of the sort that is in excess supply today) was a cheap source of this energy. As European economies modernized and living standards rose, the demographics of wine consumption changed. Fewer people engaged in grueling, hard physical labor. Life was easier, living standards higher, and better nutritional options presented themselves.

Not surprisingly, as the need for wine's cheap calories declined so did its consumption. Other factors were at work, too, but rising living standards explain an unexpectedly large proportion of the wine consumption decline.

Romantically, we Americans associate wine with the good life and wonder why Europeans would turn away from it. But for some Europeans, at least, wine was part of the hard life and they may be happy to have moved away from it. The wine world will just have to adjust. Old World consumers today are as diverse and sometimes befuddled as Americans and tend to respond to the same motivations. Any theory of the future of wine will have to take their many faces into account.

WINE IN ASIA: AWAKEN BACCHUS!

And that brings us to Asia. If Europe was wine's past (in terms of a defining influence) and the huge American market its probable present, it stands to reason that Asia is the future, or at least will be an important part of it. Many of the world's new wine consumers in the next fifty years will be located in countries that lack a well-defined idea of wine. They will be in China, India, and Japan. Their influence has already been strongly felt in the wine auction world (which is shifting from New York and London to Hong Kong) and in wine's most important futures market (Bordeaux *en primeur* sales).

I've spent the last two weeks watching a nine-part Japanese television miniseries that is based upon a twenty-plus-volume Japanese manga (graphic novel) called *Kami no Shizuku* (Drops of God). Have you heard of it? No? Then read on, because *Kami no Shizuku* seems to be changing how millions of people outside the traditional wine enthusiast core are thinking about wine.[6] Maybe, just maybe, it is a clue to the future of wine.

Wine geeks like to think of wine as a very serious subject, all vintages and terroir and malolactic fermentation and so on. It is hard for us to accept that something as sacred as wine could be influenced by popular culture. But we know that it happens. The 2004 film *Sideways*, for example, is said to have set off the Pinot Noir boom in the United States and brought to an end a previous Merlot bubble. It also romanticized wine in a way that cannot have hurt wine sales overall. No wonder wine tourists come to the Santa Barbara area to drink the same wines, eat the same foods, and visit the same wineries as the film characters Miles and Jack (played by actors Paul Giamatti and Thomas Haden Church).

Sideways had a big effect on the wine world. The *Kami no Shizuku* effect seems to be several orders of magnitude larger. The reason you may not have heard about it is that this wine-quake is centered in Tokyo, not New York, Los Angeles, or London. The ongoing comic book series, written by Shin and Yuko Kibayashi, first appeared in 2004 and has sold more than half a million copies in Japan alone. The Nippon television series that I've been watching on DVD premiered in January 2009 and reached millions more.

The Kibayashis were ranked number fifty in *Decanter* magazine's July 2009 "Power List" of the wine industry's individuals of influence. *Kami no Shizuku* is arguably the most influential wine publication for the past twenty years, according to *Decanter*.

Kami no Shizuku set off a wine boom in Asia, where, much as with *Sideways*, Enthusiasts rush to taste the fine wines (mainly from France, mostly Burgundies and Bordeaux) that are featured in each storyline. The rising sales of these iconic wines has been good for these particular producers, but I think the larger effect has been to draw millions of Asian consumers into the market and help them to develop a personal sense of wine.

I've been trying to decide how to explain *Kami no Shizuku* and why I think it has had such a profound effect on wine in Asia and soon, perhaps, around the world. One reason is that it is a good story and that is always important. The Nippon TV series is pretty much a soap opera and you know how addictive those are!

But I think the real factor is that *Kami no Shizuku* presents a different idea of wine. Wine is presented as a sort of mysterious but not impenetrable secret society (think *Da Vinci Code*), with its own history, geography, rituals, language, and traditions. It is a mystery waiting to be solved. The reward for mastering its intricacies is a kind of divine communication (hence "Drops of God"). Wine can communicate a time and place, an emotion or experience. Tasting wine even allows the living to talk with the dead, in a way that the story makes clear but I won't reveal here.

The story's handsome young protagonist is upset with his wine-obsessed father for never leaving flowers on his mother's grave. He always leaves wine—Domaine de la Romanée Conti Richebourg 1990, if you are interested. Later, as he begins to learn the language of wine and unlock its secrets, he discovers that this Burgundy is the truest expression of the love that flowers are meant to represent—not a dozen flowers, but a field of them.

"Awaken, Bacchus," he says, when he wants to move beyond the physical senses to taste the memories and emotions that lie hidden in the wine glass. Who wouldn't want to have such a transformative experience? Who wouldn't want to see what mysteries wine can reveal?

Kami no Shizuku seems to have unleashed two forces in Japan and perhaps eventually around the world. One is the competition for status and self-esteem through the conspicuous consumption of the trophy wines featured in the comics and television series. This materialistic competition is even part of the plot! It is nothing new; although I'll bet French wine producers were thankful for it during the economic crisis. It is a sort of Martian vision of wine: fanatical, but not exactly what Martin Ray had in mind.

The other force is a more Wagnerian sort of quest—this one for meaning and fulfillment—with unruly Bacchus an unlikely guide. The competition here is more subtle and inward-looking, but the rewards are much greater (another lesson of the story).

Both quests are important from an economic standpoint, but it is only the second one that has the potential to awaken a new kind of audience for the pleasures of wine by waking up the Bacchus inside us all.

Two Buck Chuck, the famous $1.99 wine sold in Trader Joe's stores, has awakened Bacchus for millions of U.S. consumers. What's the secret of Two Buck Chuck? Everyone thinks it's finding a way to make very low cost wine. Maybe, but I think there's a bigger secret.

They Always Buy
the Ten Cent Wine

When Tyler Colman (a.k.a. the Internet's Dr. Vino) organized a competition for Wine Person of the Decade, I nominated Fred Franzia. No one (with the possible exception of Jesus Christ, who turned water in wine—a miracle!) has done more to bring inexpensive wine to the masses.

Two Buck Chuck (a.k.a. Charles Shaw wine) is the brand of very inexpensive wines that Fred Franzia's Bronco Wine Company makes for exclusive distribution through the Trader Joe's chain. The wines sell for $1.99 in California ($2.99 in some other states), which accounts for the "two buck" nickname. Total sales over the first five years of the brand (2002–2007): 300 million bottles (twenty-five million cases) and counting.

Two Buck Chuck (TBC) was made possible by a worldwide glut of wine grapes in the early years of the twenty-first century. There was a lot more wine made than people would buy (Franzia himself was part of the glut, with perhaps thirty thousand acres of vines in California's Central Valley, where yields are high and production costs low). Bulk prices fell, creating a profitable opportunity for someone like Franzia, a nephew of Ernest Gallo who understands how to make wine in industrial quantities. Franzia's wineries have storage capacity for 100 million gallons of wine, according to *Wine Business Monthly*.[1] He partnered with the Trader Joe's people, who know how to distribute and market it efficiently, and Two Buck Chuck was born.[2] TBC aimed to find a big demand for a big supply, and it did.

People think that the miracle of Two Buck Chuck is that they can make and sell a wine so cheaply, but that's really not so hard. Remember that wine in Germany often sells for a euro per liter—that's *one buck*, Chuck! The trick isn't making an inexpensive wine—that's very doable—it's getting people to overcome their beliefs about price and quality and buy it. Once you have made a decent wine that you can sell for less, you need to get buyers to look down from their accustomed layer of the wine wall and try it—and to serve it to their friends without fear of humiliation.

THE PRICE OF EVERYTHING

Oscar Wilde observed that modern people know the price of everything but the value of nothing, and I suppose this problem applies to wine. Wine's value is particularly uncertain because of the impossibility of knowing what's really in a bottle until it is opened combined with rather great differences in taste (and ability *to* taste) from person to person. Price is relatively easy to discover in wine, its value . . . well that's another matter.

The problem of reconciling price and value—and what to do about it—has brought us back to the wine wall to see what role price plays in the wine buying decision. Students learn the law of demand in Econ 101—lower price, higher sales. But this assumes that quality is both certain and uniform, which isn't the case with wine, as an examination of the wine wall's vertical layers will demonstrate.

When we think about the geography of the wine wall, we usually focus on its horizontal layout rather than its vertical arrangement. Horizontally, the wine wall moves from international wines through domestic wines to sweet and fortified wines in a number of more or less standard patterns. The Old World wines are arranged by region (Chianti, Burgundy, Rioja) and New World wines by varietal name (Chardonnay, Merlot), and so on. A walk down the wall's horizontal axis in a good store is a quick tour of the wine world's best-known landmarks, the famous names and places that attract our attention. But it is the vertical arrangement that pays the bills.

Have you ever noticed how the wine wall seems to be arranged according to price? Where do you find the most expensive wines on the wall? I think you know—they are usually on the top shelf (a term that signifies high quality) so that you reach up to get them. The most expensive wines stand prominently on top of the wall; buying them may be a reach, something you do for special occasions only, but it is an uplifting experience nonetheless.

Where do you find the least expensive wines? Although it isn't a hard and fast rule, the cheapest wines tend to congregate at the bottom of the wall, where you have to bend or stoop to find them, thus uniting the physical act with its psychological result, unless you think of yourself as a treasure hunter, in which case you'd be looking to find overlooked gems lying on the ground.

The rest of the wines on the wall are layered almost like the geological strata that you sometimes see on riverbanks or road cuts. Only the layers don't run oldest to newest as in nature, on the wine wall it is cheap to expensive.

If you stand at the wine wall and stare straight ahead you will discover your wine merchant's target audience. All along the wall, from New World back to Old, the price range at eye level will be about the same. If this is where you normally look for wine, then congratulations, you've found your place on the wall.

FINDING THE WINE PRICE COMFORT ZONE

Wine buyers are complicated people with complex tastes, but in one respect we are simple folks: we tend to buy most of our wines of whatever vintage or variety within a fairly narrow "comfort zone" of price, which corresponds to one or two vertical shelf "strata" on the wine wall. Rabobank, the Dutch bank that provides financing to many global wine businesses, divides the wine wall into six layers.[3] The price points that divide the layers vary from country to country (you can imagine that Germany is different form Britain, for example) and depend on the type of store and its clientele, but here's the basic pattern, running from bottom to top.

- Basic wines, often packaged in 1.5 liter bottles or bag-in-box "casks" sell for less than $5 per bottle equivalent (the Rabobank study puts that price at less than €3 in Europe). I found several wines in the value section of Costco including a Chilean Cab-Merlot blend at $6.99 for the 1.5 liter bottle ($3.50 per bottle equivalent). All of the Two Buck Chuck wines fall into this category. Or maybe they have a category of their own: extreme value wines (X-wines—I like that!). About 50 percent of all the wine purchased in the United States comes from this part of the wine wall.

- Popular Premium wines costs about $5 to $7 (€3–€5 in Europe) and account for about a third of total wine volume. Some wine marketing experts give the name "fighting varietals" to this layer of the wine wall because the wines tend to have fairly generic designations (California Merlot, South Australian Shiraz) with a particular emphasis on brand name and grape variety. This is a wine identity that is easy to communicate and lends itself to catchy brand names and colorful labels. Australia's Yellow Tail wines, which often sell for about $5.99 per bottle, fit neatly into this part of the wall.

- Premium wines sell for $7 to $10 (€5–€7). These tend to be branded wines, too, but promoted in a different way and often with a more specific regional designation. Gallo, for example, has a number of wine brands positioned at different layers on the wall. Its casual Barefoot Cellars brand sits at the top of the Popular Premium stratus, with a $6.99 typical price. Redwood Creek wines, another Gallo line, are positioned for the Premium market and sell for about $7.99. The Redwood Creek label is more formal and traditional than Barefoot's irreverent "footprint" logo and there is a suggestion of an association with a particular vineyard. I guess the label looks more French (and therefore more expensive) than a Barefoot or Yellow Tail bottle.

- Super Premium wines sell for €7–€14 in Europe, which would be about $10–$20 in the United States, but I think our Super Premium stratum is a bit thinner than this—I think $10–$15 is our range, with another layer, call it SP-plus from $15 to $20. I note that Kendall-Jackson tends to position its Vintner's Reserve range of wines below $15 and place the Grand Reserve wines above $15, which tells me that the economic geology of the market must change at this point. They price their vineyard-designated wines in the next layer up, which is . . .

- Ultra Premium. These wines sell for €14–€150 in Europe or perhaps $20–$200, which is a huge range that invites further segmentation. Wines in this price range are insignificant in terms of quantity, but tremendously important from a profit standpoint. The difference in production cost between a $5 wine and a $50 bottle is much less than the ten-times difference in price, so wine profitability generally rises with price (so long as buyers will pay that price, of course). In addition, high priced, highly rated wines can sometimes lend status and prestige to lesser parts of the family. Beringer Private Reserve Napa Valley Cabernet Sauvignon ($100-plus, Robert Parker rating of 95) lends credibility to the $20 Beringer Knights Valley wine and its $11 cousin, the Beringer Third Century North Coast Cab. (Farther down the wall you'll even find an $8 Stone Cellars by Beringer wine, which the maker bills as a sort of "starter" Cabernet Sauvignon for consumers just getting into fine wines).

- The very top of the wine wall holds the Icon wines, which cost more than €150 in Europe, or say, $200 in the United States. These "Martian" wines make up a tiny fraction of all wine sales, but they get disproportionate attention in the wine press and among wine enthusiasts. Do not expect to find these wines in your upscale grocery store. I have sometimes seen them in good wine shops—always sitting on the topmost shelf of course—there less to sell than to show that the shop owner has style, taste, and good connections in the industry. Some Icon wines are famous for being impossible to buy—you have to get on the winery's exclusive list. This makes them even more desirable, of course. Having the wine—and the wine club membership that goes with it—is a powerful status symbol for certain iconic wines.

The wine wall's vertical stratification, Basic to Popular Premium, and on up the wall, is convenient, since it makes it easy for you to know where to look for wines in a certain price range. But there is more than convenience at work here. Many wine buyers, no matter what they say about their tastes and preferences, fundamentally choose wines based on their price. Even wine buyers who are comfortable experimenting with new varietals from new locations seem to return again and again to a price comfort zone.

Suppose, for example, you are an $8 wine buyer. This means that you are pretty comfortable paying about $8 for a bottle of wine. You may think that $12 wine is better (and buy it for the weekend) and that $5.99 wine isn't quite as good (you buy it for parties, to save a little money), so you stick pretty close to your comfort zone as a rule.

The wine wall's organization is therefore intended to be convenient, to make you comfortable, and to provide a little psychological feedback—you really should reach up to that more expensive brand rather than stooping for the cheaper stuff. This isn't the only way to organize a wine wall, of course, so it is interesting that it is so nearly ubiquitous.

THE ERNEST GALLO EFFECT

The built-in assumption of the wine wall is that more expensive wines are better wines and worth reaching up for. People are always looking for a $10 wine that tastes like $20 and wine critics and marketers rather boldly reinforce this idea. People often say that they like Two Buck Chuck because it doesn't taste like it costs $1.99. It may not be distinctive, but it tastes better than you'd expect for the price.

It's pretty easy to tell that price isn't a very good indicator of quality in wine. Since you seem to be spending so much time hanging around the wine wall, pick up one of the wine magazines that are often displayed there and turn to the back for the wine ratings to see if the most expensive wines get the highest scores. I picked a magazine randomly and found this information in a review of red wines from Australia. The highest score (92 points) went to an expensive wine ($70), but the next two wines varied in price a good deal—$152 and $20—and both received 91 points. Over in the California ratings, a Beringer Napa Valley Cabernet for $35 outscored an iconic single-vineyard wine selling for $215.

The problem of judging a wine by its price reminds me of an old story about the early days of the Gallo winery. Ernest and Julio Gallo built their business in the years after the repeal of Prohibition according to a strict division of labor: Julio made the wines and Ernest sold them. The story is told of a sales call that Ernest Gallo made to a New York customer in the dark days of the Depression. He offered sample glasses of two red wines—one costing five cents per bottle and the other ten cents. The buyer tasted both and pronounced, "I'll take the ten-cent one." The wine in the two glasses was exactly the same. Clearly, the customer wanted to buy an identity—the image of someone who wouldn't drink that five-cent rotgut—even if he couldn't actually taste the difference.

They always buy the ten-cent wine, Ernest Gallo said. I wonder how much things have changed since the days when Ernest Gallo made his calls? Two recent studies provoke this question.

The first, which has been widely reported, is a study that was published in the Proceedings of the National Academy of Sciences that showed that test subjects displayed the Ernest Gallo effect.[4] Their ratings of wines changed when they were given price information—even bogus price information. Identical wines received different ratings depending upon price information provided. "Expensive" wines, naturally, were rated higher than their inexpensive twins. This shows how strong the psychological effect of price can be. Consumers want to believe that higher priced wines taste better, even if they can't themselves appreciate the difference. Pulling the cork transforms desire into belief.

A second study, released by the American Association of Wine Economists, answers the question: Do more expensive wines actually taste better than cheaper ones? The answer, based on a large sample of blind tastings, is that there is no correlation between price and wine evaluation (or maybe a modestly negative one due to the fact that more expensive wines are often tannic in their youth and unpleasant to the untrained palate). This will be no surprise to readers of wine publications like *Wine Spectator*, as noted earlier. Sure, the top wines are usually expensive, but there are also a lot of costly wines that get low ratings:[5]

These findings will bring great satisfaction to my friend and part-time research assistant Michael Morrell, who prides himself on drinking cheap wines, trusting his own tastes not ratings or price "signals" of quality. Michael would buy the five-cent bottle every time.

This brings us back to the miracle of Two Buck Chuck. If you put an equally cheap Two Buck Chuck clone in your typical upscale supermarket, it's entirely possible that no one would buy it because they would assume low quality based upon the low price. That's where Trader Joe's comes in. Trader Joe's has a reputation for selling upscale products for a bit less—for providing *relative* value.

Cheap wine at Safeway? How can it be any good? The same cheap wine at Trader Joe's? How *bad* can it be? That tiny difference (like Ernest Gallo's ten-cent price) makes all the difference.

Only Nixon could go to China, as the old Vulcan proverb goes, and only Trader Joe's could sell Two Buck Chuck—for two bucks. Reputation is key here on the wine wall. Let's see how it is made.

THE CONFIDENCE GAME

The reason that wine buyers are willing to try a product as improbable as Two Buck Chuck is that they have confidence in it—borrowed confidence in this case (based upon their trust in Trader Joe's) but confidence nonetheless. They may not know exactly where the wine is from (California is a big place) or exactly what it will taste like (there are a lot of variations on your basic Chardonnay) or even if it will taste like the last bottle of TBC they purchased (TBC is blended from so many different wine sources that it is impossible, I'm told, to assure consistent taste, even with Fred Franzia's huge stainless steel blending tanks).[6] And of course they pay a ridiculously low price.

And yet upmarket customers confidently load cases of the stuff into their shopping carts in a retail setting defined by its surfer-dude theme and owned by a German discount store magnate. The key to Two Buck Chuck isn't the wine or the price, it is the confidence that buyers have in the store and their purchases. Take away that confidence and Two Buck Chuck would disappear as well.

The wine wall is huge, as we have seen, and price is not a very reliable guide to quality. Wines taste different from each other, obviously; they taste different from year to year because of Nature's unpredictability, they taste different over time as they develop and eventually decline in the bottle, and they taste different to different people based upon both sensory skills and differences in preferences. You might say that wine's defining attribute is uncertainty. Some people love to take risks—they buy lottery tickets and recklessly purchase wines based on label art. The chance of winning is almost the same. Other people are so intimidated that they walk away from the wine wall with empty hands and hearts. The rest of us? Well, we try to cut the odds as best we can.

As the wine wall has become more crowded, with more domestic wines and more international choices, wine brands—like Two Buck Chuck—have grown in importance. Brands are one successful strategy in the Confidence Game. The idea of a brand is to inspire confidence through consistency. People go to McDonald's because they know what they will get in terms of choice, quality, and value. There is little chance that they will have an unexpectedly excellent, transformative culinary experience, but there's not much chance that they will be badly disappointed, either. They get what they expect to get. That's what makes McDonald's such a powerful brand—its consistent reliability.

Wine branding is not a new phenomenon. Although people tend to associate the branding trend with New World wine, especially U.S. and Australian, in fact the Europeans invented the system and in some respects are still masters of it.

The French traditionally define their wines by place not grape—the *appellation* identifies the wine first, and private producer brands are often secondary. Their AOC (Appellation d'Origine Contrôlée) system began as a simple geographic designation like America's AVAs (American Viticultural Areas) but developed into something more complicated and, well, more French. Originally AOCs were all about fraud prevention—protecting the reputation of honest Champagne winegrowers, for example, by making it illegal to put the Champagne label on a wine made mainly from grapes grown in other regions. This assurance, it was believed, would give the Champagne regional "brand" greater value.

And it did, but this led to a different kind of fraud. Some producers cut corners and overcropped, making cheaper, poorer wine that could legally wear the geographic designation because of the grapes' origins. The only way to protect the region's reputation (and the value of its brand) was to regulate both *where* the grapes were grown and *how* the wines were made. And so the contemporary AOC system was born.

It seems to me that the French, who famously reject the idea of branded products in their popular antiglobalization rhetoric, are in fact the world's most successful practitioners of the branding art. If you think of Champagne and Beaujolais as brands, which they are, and not just regions or styles of wine, this becomes instantly clear. Beaujolais Nouveau, the ultimate Coca-Cola wine, was purposefully developed as a global brand. And of course, such French firms as Möet-Hennessy Louis Vuitton are the most successful purveyors of branded luxury products, including wine, in the world. (Möet-Chandon Champagne, Cloudy Bay Marlborough Sauvignon Blanc, and Terrazas de los Andes Argentinean Malbec are all LVMH brands.)

Globalization has been part of the shift in brand strategy. As the global market expands and brings in new consumers, the company-based branding system is simply more successful than the old geography-based grower-driven branding system because it is easier to understand and promote. It gives wine to consumers who are accustomed to purchasing branded products in a format that they can easily understand.

THE MARKET FOR LEMONS (AND WINE)

Brands are nothing new and they are more than just a marketing tool. Brands can serve a very useful economic purpose because of wine's inherent uncertain nature. The Nobel Prize–winning economist George Akerlof wrote about the difficulty of making a purchase with certainty in a famous paper on "the market for lemons."[7] Buying a used car, for example, is difficult because it is hard to tell if a particular vehicle is a "lemon." Some cars, even those made by reliable manufacturers, are simply plagued by problems. Lemons happen. It is not in the seller's interest to disclose this fact, so when you buy a used car, you have to accept the risk that you might be buying a lemon. This uncertainty drives down the price of *all* used cars, according to Ackerloff, even the good ones. There are a variety of solutions to this problem, many of which are techniques for the seller of a nonlemon to communicate this fact to buyers, thus differentiating good cars from bad and gaining a higher price.

Do you see where this is going? Although I have never tasted wine made from lemons, I have drunk a lot of lemon wine in my time. The fact is that some wines or some vintages are lemons and you cannot be sure if you have a lemon until you open the bottle. Solution? Well, the whole wine rating industry exists because of the lemon wine problem, doesn't it? Robert Parker and *Wine Spectator* play the same role for wine that *Consumer Reports* does for cars and washing machines.

Brands are another solution to the lemon problem. If brands represent a reliable indicator of quality or consistency (these are not always the same thing), then they communicate valuable information to buyers, who are seeking that knowledge. Result (if successful): more confidence among wine drinkers and a higher overall demand for wine. With the market demand for wine growing and becoming more complex in the New World, the value of brands has increased correspondingly.

One final reason for the rising importance of wine brands is distribution. I have noticed that every industry tends to organize itself around solutions to its biggest bottleneck—the factor that represents the biggest impediment to efficiency. Distribution is the biggest problem in the United States and some winemakers solve this problem by becoming distribution machines (that's part of the Gallo story) and some distributors have been turned into winemakers, either directly or through strategic alliances (that's part of the Yellow Tail story).

Here, very briefly, is the distribution story. Retailers prefer to deal with a small number of distributors in each product category, so size matters in distribution. On the wine aisle, these distributors need to provide product at several different price points (because retail wine buyers purchase by price more than any other factor) in a large number of different categories (think of all the different varieties and regions to cover)—and do it in a way that will reduce consumer uncertainty not increase it, reducing the lemon fear and increasing sales.

Brands like Two Buck Chuck address the lemon issue, and portfolios of brands are necessary to provide wines in different categories at each critical price point and to create the breadth and scale that retailers seek. The wine-makers who can do this the best will become the leading wine companies of the future.

The key to success in the wine business is understanding what to do with lem-ons? Who knew? What else can economists teach us about wine?

Well, the economist's motto is *de gustibus non est disputandum*, which is variously translated from Latin as "you can't argue about taste" or, sometimes in jest, "it is disgusting not to dispute." Both translations apply to wine. Ev-eryone's taste is different. And everyone is a critic!

TASTING NOTES

Big Box Wine: The Two Buck Chuck effect continues to spread across the United States. More major national retail chains have introduced their own private label wine brands, including Target's popular Wine Cube, 7-Eleven's Yosemite Road, Sonoma Crest and VitAlma, and the Oak Leaf Vineyards wine that is sold exclusively at Walmart. Walmart?!

Bargains Galore: The Grocery Outlet chain of "hard discount" stores has carved out a distinctive niche in the United States selling closeout and over-stock wines at bargain prices. Now, it seems, there are consumers who always buy the five-cent wine!

10

Everyone's a Critic

Wine critics are the bond-rating agencies of the wine market. Their scores and written reviews give many wine buyers the confidence they need to make what really is a risky purchase. At their best, wine critics serve a useful function of reducing uncertainty about what's in that bottle and whether it is worth the price.

But wine critics are often accused of playing a less-than-useful role. Jancis Robinson, one of the most influential critics in the world, accused her profession of displaying "parasitical" behavior.[1] Robert Parker, the American wine expert who publishes *The Wine Advocate*, is often accused of exercising undue influence over the wine industry. If you want to get ahead in the global wine market, it is said, you need to make big wines to suit his particular taste. High "Parker numbers" are a guarantee of market success, they say.

Everyone has opinions about wine—everyone's a critic—but some opinions matter more than others. The future of wine will depend in part on who wields palate power and how. That's cause enough to provoke an investigation of wine critics and their discontents.

THE MARTHA STEWART OF WINE?

Jancis Robinson is a good example of how wine critics operate at the top of the league. Robinson is the Martha Stewart of wine—and I don't mean that as an insult. Martha Stewart (and her company, the tellingly named Martha

Stewart Living Omnimedia) pushes out a consistently attractive lifestyle message through all known communication forms. Stewart's work has sold lots of books, magazines, and advertising space while it has given her fans the confidence to try all sorts of lifestyle products and projects.

Jancis Robinson is almost equally omni, if that makes any sense. As a wine economist, I know her best from her informative weekly wine column in the *Financial Times*, but that's only the tip of the iceberg. Subscribers pay £69 or $99 per year to get access to the complete contents of her "very personal, obsessively updated and completely independent" website, JancisRobinson. com, which includes wine ratings, wine tourism information and news, and opinions produced as she and her small staff travel the world to participate in wine tastings and events.

Jancis Robinson is the author or editor of a slew of wine books, including *The World Atlas of Wine, The Oxford Companion to Wine, Jancis Robinson's Wine Course, Jancis Robinson's Wine Tasting Workbook: How to Taste, Jancis Robinson's Guide to Wine Grapes,* and *Tasting Pleasure: Confessions of a Wine Lover.* Two sets of DVDs are available, too, based upon her BBC wine series: *Vintners' Tales* and *Jancis Robinson's Wine Course.* Her work is witty, opinionated, and informative: it is no wonder she is so sought after. I understand that her tasting of global wines is one of the hottest tickets at the World Economic Forum meetings in Davos, Switzerland. She receives a constant stream of invitations to attend wine dinners, judge wine competitions, and speak at wine events. It's a tough life, I guess, but someone has to do it.

Wine critics like Jancis Robinson are important because their rock star reputations and acknowledged expertise can lend credibility to those with whom they associate. Other wine critics, with national, regional, or local audiences do the same work, just not on a global scale. Robinson is a skilled taster, of course, but more than that she is a "flying critic" who can judge wines, wine producers, wine regions, and wine organizations in a global context. Her evaluations of individual wines may be objective, as her website indicates, but like all the top wine critics she has strong views on the big questions in the world of wine and the mix of fact and opinion can be controversial, especially as with wine in matters of taste.

THE EMPEROR OF WINE

The wine critic industry is complex and multilayered, but attention inevitably focuses on the top of the pyramid: the King, the Czar, the Top Dog. The title of the world's most influential wine critic is perennially in dispute, as you might guess. For a long time the battle seemed to be between traditional British critics, like the prolific Jancis Robinson or the esteemed Michael Broadbent, versus the upstart American Robert Parker, publisher of *The Wine Advocate*. Now, however, a new challenger has appeared who might represent the future of wine criticism.

I met the guy everyone thinks might be the New Emperor of Wine at a big event called Taste Washington, where I was pouring wine for my friends Mike and Karen Wade, owners of the award-winning Fielding Hills Winery. He's a thirtyish fellow from Belarus via New Jersey. He was walking around in a white and green New York Jets jersey, something Michael Broadbent would never do, and people treated him like a god or, if that's too extreme, like the ultimate wine VIP.

The Old Emperor of Wine is Robert Parker; that's the title Elin McCoy gave him on the cover of her book, *The Emperor of Wine: The Rise of Robert Parker and the Reign of American Taste.*[2] Parker is often cited as the most influential wine critic in the world. His writing on Bordeaux wines helped make these products objects of global interest and fueled American and now Asian interest in these wines. I suspect that every successful Bordeaux producer or investor owes a debt of thanks to Robert Parker. Jacques Chirac awarded him the Legion of Honor for his service to France and her wine industry, a fact that irritates everyone who disagrees with him, especially French winemakers who do not benefit from his ratings.

Parker is controversial because of the perceived power of his palate. Parker has particular tastes, it is argued, and winemakers who cater to those tastes receive big Parker numbers and are rewarded handsomely in the marketplace. And yet the French hate him. Parker is one of several villains we meet in the film *Mondovino*, where the heroes are the winemakers and enthusiasts who reject Parkerization, which is the production of big, intense, highly extracted wines at the expense, his critics say, of style, finesse, and tradition. They disagree with his idea of wine, or perhaps they just resent that an American could be so influential. Power and taste—those are the issues in *l'affaire* Robert Parker.

Robert Parker is more than a wine critic, he is a business model. Parker scrupulously avoids conflicts of interest, accepting no payment from anyone with a financial stake in wine, so he must sell his knowledge and opinions to pay the bills. He does this successfully in a variety of ways including subscriptions to his magazine *The Wine Advocate* ($75 per year in the United States);

his frequently updated Internet wine site, eRobertParker.com ($99 per year); and sales of his many books and buyers guides ($30 to $75). People will clearly pay a lot to learn Parker's opinions. They will pay even more to meet him in person. Dinner with Robert Parker appears occasionally on charity wine auction lists. I don't think I have ever seen it go for less than $10,000 although I admit I don't follow these things closely.

Parker's reign is coming to an end, however, according to an article by Michael Steinberger in a magazine called *The World of Fine Wine* ($300 per year in the United States—wow!). Parker is getting older and slowing down, Steinberger writes, overwhelmed by the global expansion of the wine industry. He's slowly turning over the chores to a stable of hired tasters with regional specialization and in the process losing his hegemony over global wine.

THE X EMPEROR

The New Emperor, the one I met in Seattle, represents a different business model and a different idea of wine. His name is Gary Vaynerchuk and he is director of operations at the Wine Library, a wine store in Springfield, New Jersey, that is owned by his family, immigrants from Belarus. You can see Vaynerchuk in action on his website, tv.winelibrary.com. His daily ten- to twenty-minute wine tasting webcasts ("The Thunder Show") draw a growing audience—I have seen estimates that range from sixty thousand to ninety thousand viewers a day. They come for a completely different experience of wine.

Go to your computer and watch one of Vaynerchuk's wine reviews right now. Yes, do it now. His real-time reviews may change the way you think about wine, but even if they don't, they will transform how you think about wine critics. The narrative is zany and over the top. The "tasting notes" are instant, personal, confident, and detailed. I admit they make me wish that I could taste as much in a glass of wine as he does. But it's his business and he does it with gusto. The surround sound experience (complete with the *splurt* as he spits into a NY Jets bucket) will either delight or appall you, but it probably will not leave you unmoved.

Gary Vaynerchuk is to traditional wine criticism as the X Games are to the Olympics. It's the same game, more or less, but intentionally taken to a new level, X for extreme. Like the X Games, I'm not sure his style is to my taste, but it fascinates me. Like the X Games, I suspect it is an experience that will appeal instantly to young people who are drawn by the combination of extreme bungee-jumping pure adrenalin rush and geeky technical detail. Like the X Games, I think it is probably here to stay.

The New Emperor embodies a new business model, too. Parker studiously avoids conflict of interest. Vaynerchuk accepts such conflicts as inevitable and moves on. Wine Library TV is given away free on the Internet, not sold on a subscription basis (another appealing factor for young people, who often resent being asked to pay for web content). The webcasts generate business for the store, however, and for other enterprises, including a book, *101 Wines Guaranteed to Bring Thunder to Your World.*

I asked Vaynerchuk about his audience demographic and he said it was everyone—young (as I would guess) and the not-so-young, too. Some of the viewers clearly have means. When Rob Newsom's "ultra-premium" Boudreaux Cellars Cabernet Sauvignon appeared on "The Thunder Show" and received a rave review, orders started to pour in and he was sold out in just a few days. Interestingly, Rob didn't know that Vaynerchuk had reviewed the wine. But a call came in from London asking for a case, then Brussels, then Paris. Then he started to piece together the story. He had been "Thundered," to coin a term, by the economic impact of Gary Vaynerchuk's Wine Empire 2.0.

Each webcast is annotated with sometimes hundreds of viewer comments and suggestions. "You—with a little bit of me—are changing the world of wine." That's how Vaynerchuk closes each show and, although you could argue with the proportions given, there is not much doubt about the conclusion.

One particularly interesting part of the New Emperor's empire is Cork'd (www.corkd.com), a wine social-networking website (Facebook for wine geeks, I guess). Cork'd aims, like the widely admired website CellarTracker, to turn the tables on wine critics by collecting reviews from wine drinkers themselves, many of whom are very knowledgeable, so that the ratings are free, interactive, and reflect the tastes of an (hopefully) informed consensus.

Although Vaynerchuck announced in January 2011 that he was winding down the Cork'd website to make room for other wine-related enterprises, I think the trend is well established. Blogs, Facebook, Twitter, and other social media have made potential critics of us all.

Globalization and technological change are so intertwined that they sometimes seem to be the same thing, but they are not. Globalization is the stretching and intensifying of transnational processes. Technological change facilitates and sometimes transforms this process. You can have globalization without technological change and vice versa, but they are most powerful (and transforming) when combined.

This distinction is important in wine. Globalization has stretched the world of wine and created the vast, confusing, and uncertain expanse of the contemporary wine wall. It has increased the influence and therefore power of wine critics and the wine media. They are middlemen, bond-raters, promoters, and lifestyle advisors.

Technology simultaneously magnifies these effects, by making information available at lower cost, and undermines them by weakening the control of existing hierarchies. The globalization and technological effects of which Gary Vaynerchuk is a convenient symbol may have an unexpected outcome. Rather than "democratizing" wine and dumbing it down, it seems to me that they are creating a world of well-informed enthusiasts—a world where critics are more important, but paradoxically everyone's a critic.

WHICH WINE MAGAZINE?

Wine enthusiasts spend a lot of time and money on magazines and guidebooks, and I guess they are never sure if they're getting the best advice. One of my blog's most common referring links is the Google search query "world's best wine magazine?" Want to know the answer? Read on.

If you were going to read just one wine magazine, which one would it be? I decided to use my university students to try to find out. They are plenty smart and know a lot about wine, but they don't (yet) spend much of their time reading these publications. Perfect subjects for a little media analysis experiment.

I passed out copies of what are perhaps the three most influential wine magazines on the planet and asked my students to analyze them in terms of point of view, intended audience, and, of course, which one they would want to read. The three magazines were *Wine Spectator*, *Decanter*, and *The Wine Advocate*.[3] *Wine Spectator* has the highest circulation of any wine magazine in the United States and probably the world. *Decanter*, a British publication, sells fewer copies, especially here in the United States, but has global reach. Robert Parker's *Wine Advocate* is a subscription-only publication. Most people don't actually read the *Wine Advocate*; they just see the rating numbers and blurbs on wine wall shelf talkers promoting particular bottles. It's very influential despite its limited distribution.

The magazines are different in almost every way. They certainly represent three different ideas of wine. Which is best? Well, that depends.

My students quickly labeled *Wine Spectator* a "lifestyle" magazine and this isn't just because it has nonwine or tangentially-related-to-wine "lifestyle" articles about food, travel, celebrities, and so forth. The advertisements were the giveaway to them. While many wine companies advertise in *WS*, so do the producers of many luxury and designer products.[4] Most wine magazines are lifestyle publications; they just have differing ratios and proportions of wine, wine-related, and pure lifestyle editorial content. Taken together, the editorial content and the advertising (plus the "coffee table" large format) gave my students a strong sense of a plush lifestyle publication. Wine is part of that world, they said, but not the only part of it. Some were attracted to this lifestyle image and others repulsed. They all found it fascinating.

Decanter is a lifestyle magazine, too, but that's not what struck my students. Compared with *Wine Spectator* they noted a more specific wine focus and talked about finding deeper analysis of wine regions and issues. I'm not sure if this is really true or if it reflects *Wine Spectator*'s high advertisement page count, which might make it seem like there is less wine content. But for whatever reason *Decanter* seemed more seriously interested in wine as opposed to lifestyle, according to my students. *Decanter* has a different approach to wine ratings, too. Whereas *Wine Spectator* has many wine reviews in the back covering new releases from the United States and many international regions, *Decanter* typically features in-depth review articles on just two regions. You get more breadth of coverage with *Wine Spectator* and more depth with *Decanter*.

Wine Spectator made good browsing, one student said, and sometimes that's just what you want, but *Decanter* would be better to read.

My students were shocked by *Wine Advocate*. Nothing in their experience had prepared them for a "just the facts, ma'am" wine publication. Black type on tan paper. No photos. No ads. Page after page of winery and wine reviews, focusing on three or four regions in each issue. Not for browsing. Not for reading. You have to study *Wine Advocate* to get anything out of it, they said.

Who reads *Wine Advocate*? No one would read it for pleasure, according to the students. (I disagree—geeky baseball fans read columns of statistics on their favorite sport. I think there is a similar wine reader.) You would read it for business—because you are a wine retailer, distributor, investor, or maybe own a restaurant. This, they said, was a magazine for readers with a serious professional purpose.

So which one is the best? I know my answer. If I could read only one it would be *Decanter* because I think it is more focused on the supply and demand issues I write about. It's a wine magazine written by and maybe for "Masters of Wine" who care a lot about commercial concerns. Unfortunately, *Decanter*'s specific consumer wine advice is mainly irrelevant to me since the British market it covers is so different from my wine wall here in the United States. Very few U.S. wines (apart from the big multinationals) successfully break into the British market, for example, and so we get little space in *Decanter* compared to wines from Europe and Australia. The market here is just the reverse.

My students weren't willing to choose a "world's best wine magazine." They could see strengths and weaknesses in all three. One student said it boiled down to a trade-off between accessibility (*Wine Spectator*) and authenticity (the more detailed analysis of terroir you find in publications like *Wine Advocate*) and there's no perfect balance between them. In wine, as in many other areas of life, we want both accessibility and authenticity, and I guess my students have already become both surprisingly self-aware of their position in this struggle and skilled at negotiating the complex space it creates. Interesting.

World's best wine magazine? No such thing. It depends on who you are, what you are looking for, and your particular idea of wine.

SHAPING THE INDUSTRY

The wine critic industry is built on the core service of evaluating wines and providing consumer and investment advice to wine buyers—sorting out the lemons from the rest, I guess you could say. But, as we've seen, the business model aims to leverage this position to sell a variety of wine-related goods and services, including wine books, wine magazines, and website subscriptions and advertising in them, wine events, wine tourism, and wine lifestyle products. Wine critics may not have an economic interest in the success or failure of any *particular* winery, but they do have a strong reason to want the wine industry to grow and succeed, since they are a part of it, and their opinions and publications can shape the bigger industry.

Wine consumers love rankings. Top 10 lists, top 100 lists, 50 best buys—these are a way wine critics influence the industry's development. But the rankings are seldom exactly what they seem. A wine magazine's Top 100 ranking, for example, is almost never a listing of the year's highest scoring wines. Most of the 95-point-plus wines are effectively unobtainable and why publish a list if no one can use it—it doesn't help the consumer and doesn't help build the market that ultimately feeds the critic industry. So these lists are typically qualified in several ways—high ranking, wide distribution, good value. The qualifications give the critics enormous scope to include or exclude individual wines and even whole wine regions, and I suspect that they have used this freedom to create your Great Wall of Wine.

This is most obvious in the geographical diversity of the top wine lists. The original Top 100–type lists were populated mainly by iconic wines from France, Italy, and California. A typical list today is much more global, including Australia, New Zealand, Chile, Argentina, South Africa, Spain, Portugal, and of course the Washington and Oregon regions of the United States. Some of this increase in global diversity reflects the way the wine market has stretched to include New World producers. But I suspect that wine critics have actually encouraged this by drawing attention to new wine regions with good value wines by including them in the top lists.

Wine critics reflect the industry they review, in other words, and also shape it. Promoting these wines is good for the wine business and therefore good business for the wine critics. Bottom line: I think we can thank the critics for many of the changes we've seen on the wine wall. And blame them, too.

THE NUMBERS RACKET

People turn to wine critics to tell them what's really inside that expensive bottle (or that cheap one) and how various wines compare. Some critics are famous for their detailed wine tasting notes (Michael Broadbent comes to mind here) that provide comprehensive qualitative evaluation of wines, but with so many choices in today's global market it is almost inevitable that quantitative rating scales would evolve. They simplify wine evaluation, which is what many consumers are looking for, but they have complicated matters, too, because there are many critics who often disagree and no standard system to provide the rankings.

The first problem is that different wine critic publications use different techniques to evaluate wine and different rating scales to compare them. Robert Parker's *Wine Advocate*, the *Wine Spectator*, and *Wine Enthusiast* all use a 100-point rating scale, although the qualitative meanings associated with the numbers are not exactly the same. It is perhaps not an accident that these are all American publications and that American wine readers are familiar with 100-point ratings from their high school and college classes.

In theory a 100-point system allows wine critics to be very precise in their relative ratings (an 85-point Syrah is a wee bit better than an 84-point Syrah), although in practice many consumers may not be able to appreciate the distinction. Significantly, it is not really a 100-point scale since 50 points is functionally the lowest grade and it is rare to see wines rated with scores lower than 70, so the scale is not really as precise as it might seem. I have seen publications that don't bother to rate wines that score below 80 and I think the bottom of the score sheet is creeping up toward 85.

Any professor or teacher will tell you that there has been both grade inflation and grade compression in recent years and this applies to wine critics too, I believe. A grade of B (85 points) is the new C.

The 100-point scale is far from universal. Many European wine critics rate wines out of 20, not 100. The 20-point scale actually corresponds to how students are graded in French high schools and universities, which says something about its origins. The enologists at the University of California at Davis use a 20-point rating scale, too, as does British wine critic Jancis Robinson and *Decanter*, Britain's self-proclaimed "world's best wine magazine."

The Davis 20-point scale gives up to 4 points for appearance, 6 points for smell, 8 points for taste, and 2 for overall harmony, according to my copy of *The Taste of Wine* by Emile Peynaud. The Office International du Vin's 20-point scale has different relative weights for wine qualities; it awards 4 points for appearance, 4 for smell, and 12 for taste. Oz Clarke's 20-point system assigns 2, 6, and 12 points for look, smell, and taste. It's easy to understand how the same wine can receive different scores when different critics used different criteria and different weights.

Decanter uses both a 20-point scale as well as a simple guide of zero to five stars to rate wines, where one star is "acceptable," two is quite good, three is recommended, four is highly recommended, and five is, well I suppose an American would say awesome, but the British are more reserved. Dorothy J.

Gaiter and John Brecher (who used to write an influential wine column for the *Wall Street Journal*) also use a five-grade system; they rated wines from OK to Good, Very Good, Delicious, and Delicious(!).

The five-grade system allows for less precision but is still very useful—it is the system commonly used to rate hotels and resorts. *ViniD'Italia*, the Italian wine guide published by Gambero Rosso, uses a three-wineglasses (*tre bicchiere*) scale that will be familiar to European consumers who use the *Michelin Guide*'s three-star scale to rate restaurants.

WINE AND FIGURE SKATING?

It is natural to think that the best system is the one that provides the most information, so a 100-point scale wins, but I'm not sure that's true. Emile Peynaud makes the point that how you go about tasting and evaluating wine is different depending upon your purpose. Critical wine evaluation to uncover the flaws in wine (to advise a winemaker, for example) is different in his book from commercial tasting (as the basis for ordering wine for a restaurant or wine distributor or perhaps buying wine as an investment), which is different from consumer tasting to see what you like.

Many will disagree, but it seems to me that the simple three or five stars/glasses/points systems are probably adequate for consumer tasting use while the 20- and 100-point scales are better suited for commercial purposes. I'm not sure that numbers or stars are useful at all for serious, critical wine evaluation—for that you need Broadbent's detailed qualitative notes. Wine critic publications often try to serve all three of these markets, which may explain why they use the most detailed systems or use a dual system like *Decanter*. Wine is a multidimensional experience—one that engages all the physical senses and a few senses beyond that. Reducing this rich pallet of sensory cues to a single number is kind of ridiculous. There is no way to avoid losing a lot of valuable information.

In economics we learn that numerical measures are either *cardinal* or *ordinal*. Cardinal measures have constant units of measurement that can be compared and manipulated mathematically with ease. Weight (measured by a scale) and length (measured in feet or meters) are cardinal measures. Every kilogram or kilometer is the same.

Ordinal measures are different—they provide only a rank ordering. If I asked you to rate three wines from your most preferred to your least favorite, for example, that would be an ordinal ranking. You and I might agree about the order (rating wines A over C over B, for example), but we might disagree about *how much better* A was compared to C. I might think it was a little better, but for you the difference could be profound. Ordinal measurements are less definite than cardinal ones in this regard, but they are appropriate and necessary when all we can do is know how several things compare relative to each other rather than relative to an absolute standard.

To use a familiar example from sports, they give the Olympic gold medal in the long jump based upon a cardinal measure of performance (length of jump) and they give the gold medal in figure skating based upon judges' ordinal scores, which are relative not absolute measures of performance (in the United States they actually call the judges' scores "ordinals"). Figure skating ratings are controversial for the same reason wine critics' scores are—because they rely so much upon relative judgment instead of absolute measurement.

So what kind of judgment do we make when we taste wine—do we evaluate against an absolute standard like in the long jump or a relative one like the figure skating judges? The answer is both, but in different proportions. An expert taster will have an exact idea of what a wine should be and can rate accordingly, but you and I might only be able to rank order different wines, since our abilities to make absolute judgments aren't well developed.

This is one reason why multiwine social blind tasting parties almost always produce unexpected winners or favorites. The wines we like *better* (relative) are not always the ones that are *best* (absolute) when evaluated on their own. Ordinal and cardinal are just different, like apples and oranges (or Pinot Gris and Chardonnay). Imagine what the long jump would look like if ordinal "style points" were awarded? Imagine what figure skating would look like if the jumps and throws were rated by cardinal measures such as distance and hang time? No, you're right—it wouldn't be a pretty sight.

Economists are taught that it is a mistake to treat ordinal rankings as if they are cardinal rankings, but that's what I think we wine folks do sometimes. I've read that the famous British wine critic Jancis Robinson, who studied mathematics at Oxford, isn't entirely comfortable with numeric wine ratings. Perhaps it is because she appreciates this methodological difficulty.

LESSONS OF THE JUDGMENT OF PARIS
Or maybe she's just smart. Smart enough to know that *your* 18-point wine may be *my* 14-pointer. It's clear that people approach wine with different

tastes, tasting skills, expectations, and even different taste buds, so relative rankings by one person need not be shared by others. This is true of even professional tasters, as the Judgment of Paris made clear.

The Judgment of Paris (the topic of a great book by George M. Taber) was a 1976 blind tasting of French versus American wines organized (in Paris, of course) by Steven Spurrier.[5] It became famous because a panel of French wine experts found to their surprise that American wines were as good as or even better than prestigious wines from France.

An article by Dennis Lindley in the *Journal of Wine Economics* casts doubt on this conclusion, however.[6] It turns out that these experts disagreed as much as they agreed about the quality of the wines they tasted. The 1971 Mayacamas Cabernet, for example, received scores as low as 3 and 5 on a 20-point scale along with ratings as high as 12, 13, and 14. It was simultaneously undrinkable (according to a famous sommelier) and pretty darn good (according to the owner of a famous wine property). If the experts don't agree with each other, what is the chance that you will agree with them?

Does this mean that wine critics and their rating systems are useless and should disappear? Not likely. Wine ratings are useful to consumers, who face an enormous range of choices and desperately need information, even if it is practically problematic and theoretically suspect. Wine ratings are useful commercially, too. Winemakers need to find ways to reduce consumer uncertainty and therefore increase sales; wine ratings serve that purpose.

And then, of course, there is the wine critic industry itself, which knows that ratings sell magazines and drive advertising.

As globalization brings more unfamiliar wines to the market, the wine wall choice will become increasingly complex and uncertain. The Confidence Game will grow in importance. This will accelerate the shift in power to those seen as reliable guides through the lemon-studded wine thicket. Wine critics and their ratings seem poised to gain even more power than they already have. But will they?

Power is shifting in the wine business and we need to know where it is going to be able to predict the future of wine. That means we must return to the wine wall and consider the situation of the Wine Whales—the big multinational wine businesses—and what I call the McWine Conspiracy.

TASTING NOTES

Distant Thunder: Gary Vaynerchuck has moved on and is no longer in the running for the title of New Emperor of Wine. His Wine Library TV "Thunder Show" morphed in 2011 into a short-lived video reviewing site called "Daily Grape," which is now closed. Vaynerchuck's most recent book is *The Thank You Economy*, about communication and marketing in the age of social media.

The Spiderman Principle: In the future no one should have as much power as Robert Parker has had—this according to Robert Parker himself, who is reducing his reviewing activities at his famous journal, *The Wine Advocate*. I wonder if Parker knows the Spiderman Principle: with great power comes great responsibility!

Everyone Really Is a Critic: Meanwhile, Millennial generation wine drinkers are being closely studied by wine marketers who see them as the consumers of the future. So-called Millennials don't seem to pay as much attention as prior generations did to authorities like Parker or even Vaynerchuck. Instead, research suggests, they take their cues from each other—the recommendations of friends both virtual (think Facebook) and real. So I guess now everyone really *is* a critic.

11

The McWine Conspiracy

There is a certain specter that invades the minds of wine enthusiasts when they sleep, turning their dreams of the future of wine into nightmares. I call the apparition McWine and right away you know what I am talking about and why it is so disturbing.

No one wants to live in a McMansion, get treatment at a McHospital or attend a McUniversity. Who would want to drink McWine? Putting a "Mc" (for McDonald's, obviously) in front of a noun diminishes it, removing all individuality, reducing it to a cookie-cutter, least common denominator, mass-market McProduct. McWine is to wine as a Chicken McNugget is to chicken, which is to say that the resemblance is pretty faint.

The defining elements of McWine are these. It is the product of a huge and impersonal multinational corporation. It is a U.S. business, of course, reflecting U.S. values (profit first!) and exporting unsophisticated U.S. tastes. Mc-WineCorp produces vast quantities of highly processed inexpensive brand-name wines that are distinguished, if that's the right word, by their lack of distinguishing characteristics apart from simplicity and industrial character. There is little reason to drink these wines from an aesthetic standpoint, yet their low cost and convenience make them almost irresistible. Soon they are everywhere and real wine, wine with character, wine that reflects its terroir, is an endangered species.

It isn't difficult to see evidence of a McWine conspiracy, if you are so inclined. Two Buck Chuck, for example, is the classic McWine. Bronco Wine cranks out millions of cases of the stuff each year and happy Trader Joe's customers haul it away for as little as $1.99 per bottle. While some people see Two Buck Chuck as a value—a $5 wine for $2 that has forced $5 wines to up-grade quality—others see it as a giant step in the race to the bottom. Only an upscale store like Trader Joe's could tempt American wine buyers to behave like Germans apparently and trade quality and taste for lower price.

But the McWine effect goes well beyond Two Buck Chuck. If you look at the best-selling wine brands in the world, for example, you see McWines everywhere. The number one global wine brand in 2004, for example, was Franzia, a California bag-in-box wine made by The Wine Group (they purchased the brand from Fred Franzia years ago). Carlo Rossi (Gallo) was second followed by Tavernello (the number one wine in Italy), Twin Valley (Gallo), and Almaden. Beringer made the list due in part to the success of its White Zinfandel. Two Buck Chuck appeared at number fifteen on the league table, trailing brands like Livingstone Cellars (Gallo), Sutter Home (more White Zin), Jacob's Creek, Chenet (from France), and Yellow Tail. Freixenet, the Spanish maker of mass-market Cava sparkling wine, seemed a bit out of place at number fourteen on the list.

I don't have a more current list of the best-selling brands (Gallo, the Wine Group, and some of the other large producers are privately held and do not release sales or financial data), but I'm confident that although the particular brands would be different, the basic McWine profile would stay the same.

McWine paranoia is heightened when you look closely at the wine wall. At first you'll be comforted by the huge number of choices. Obvious McWines like Franzia and Carlo Rossi take up only a relatively small space on the shelves—a good sign, yes? On closer examination, however, you'll notice that the McWineCorps have insinuated themselves into every nook and cranny of the wine wall.

McWine corporations don't sell just one wine; they manage large *portfolios* of wine brands that fill the wine wall to the brim. Each of the largest Mc-WineCorps aims to have a brand on each shelf of the wine wall corresponding to each important price point. Thus, for example, Gallo has its Carlo Rossi and Peter Vella wines holding down the bottom of the wall. As we move up we find other Gallo brands, including Turning Leaf, Barefoot Cellars, Redwood Creek, Dancing Bull, Rancho Zabaco, MacMurray Ranch, Gallo of Sonoma, Louis M. Martini, and Mirassou. Over in the sparkling wine section you'll see Gallo's André and Ballatore along with flavored-wine drinks like Bartles & Jaymes and Boone's Farm. Gallo is even found in the imported wine sections, with brands including Red Bicyclette and Pont d'Avignon (France), Bella Sera, Da Vinci, Ecco Domani, and Maso Canali (Italy), Black Swan and McWilliams (Australia), and Whitehaven (New Zealand).

Now you can see why the wine wall is so spectacularly vast. For every price point on the wall there will be a brand or two from Gallo and each of its Mc-WineCorp competitors. Each brand will have several products (Chardonnay, Pinot Grigio, Shiraz, and the rest). So many brands, so many price points, so many products, it doesn't take long for the wall to fill up, squeezing out (this is part of the conspiracy theory) smaller wineries that don't benefit from Mc-WineCorp's efficient distribution machine.

The wine wall *looks* like a world of choices, but pretty soon you get the feeling that they are all coming from just a few big factories. It's so depressing; it could drive you to drink beer! No, wait, stay with me. The McBeer problem is even worse!

MORE BAD NEWS

The picture does not improve very much if we move from retail wine sales (off-premises in the lingo of the trade) to restaurant and lounge sales (wine for on-premises consumption). Upscale restaurants of the sort that receive *Wine Spectator* awards get the most attention in the press, but so-called casual dining restaurants are where the volume of wine sales is greatest. The top ten individual wines (by volume not value of sales) in 2008 were (cue drum roll) . . .

1. Kendall-Jackson Vintner's Reserve Chardonnay
2. Cavit Pinot Grigio
3. Beringer White Zinfandel
4. Sutter Home White Zin
5. Inglenook Chablis
6. Ecco Domani Pinot Grigio
7. Mezzacorona Pinot Grigio
8. Copper Ridge Chardonnay
9. Yellow Tail Chardonnay
10. Franzia White Zin[1]

None of these is an expensive wine and the #1 K-J is probably the costliest of the lot. The best-selling restaurant (on-premises) wines are high-volume, widely distributed, inexpensive wines—just the sort that recession-ravaged consumers who want to trade down (in terms of price) and switch over (to a more relaxed view of wine) might find appealing.

Using the rule of thumb that a glass of restaurant wine sells for about the wholesale price of the bottle, these wines would sell from about $5 (for the Sutter Home) to maybe $8 (for the K-J Chard) per glass—and I suspect that a lot of this wine is sold by the glass. An affordable luxury, as they say.

The list changes only a little if we look at the data for wine brands (as opposed to specific wines):

1. Kendall-Jackson
2. Sutter Home
3. Beringer Vineyards
4. Franzia WineTaps
5. Inglenook
6. Yellow Tail
7. Copper Ridge
8. Cavit
9. Woodbridge
10. Salmon Creek (Bronco)

The complete list of the top twenty brands is dominated by America's three largest wine companies with three brands each: Constellation Brands (Woodbridge, Taylor California Cellars, and La Terre), Gallo (Copper Ridge, Barefoot Cellars, and Ecco Domani), and the Wine Group (Franzia, Inglenook, and Almaden). These three giants have large brand portfolios and strong distribution machines. They get their wines into every nook and cranny, both retail and on-premises sales. You can see the results virtually everywhere.

Only four of top twenty are international brands (Yellow Tail, Cavit, Ecco Domani, and Mezzacorona). I think the fact that three of these four are Italian wine brands says something about the importance of Italian-restaurant chains, including especially Olive Garden, in the American wine market.

If you are someone who dines mainly at three-star restaurants where the wine list is really a leather-bound book that is handled with biblical reverence (and White Zinfandel must be a typographical error), the facts I've just stated about what America drinks when it dines out are probably pretty discouraging. The McWine conspiracy to kill the soul of fine wine seems very real indeed. Who is to blame?

YELLOW TAIL AND BLUE [NUN] OCEAN WINE

It is easy to paint Gallo as the ultimate McWineCorp and its various wine wall products as quintessential McWines. But it is also unfair. If you really want to locate the McWine conspiracy, you have to look more closely at the global wine market. Carlo Rossi, the world's best-selling wine brand, is only really noteworthy because so much of it is produced by a single company, Gallo. It is a dirty little secret that basic wines like Carlo Rossi are the volume leaders in every wine market (or at least every one that I am familiar with). It's true in the United States, in Germany (obviously), and even in France. The difference is that cheap French wines come from hundreds of local producers, not one large company. There is nothing particularly different or sinister about Gallo based on its production of commodity-type wines. These wines are part of the long tradition of wines.

If you are looking for a real McWine, you need to look for a wine that has been custom designed to be a McWine—the result of the same sort of intentional product creation and development that gave us the Big Mac and the Egg McMuffin. You don't have to look very far to find such a product. It is made in Australia and called Yellow Tail.

Yellow Tail has in recent years been the best-selling imported wine in the United States. Yellow Tail accounted for 11 percent of all U.S. imports in 2005. This one wine brand represented about 8 percent of all Australian wine production. In 2009, when depressed market conditions caused Australian wine exports to plummet, Yellow Tail sales stayed strong; Yellow Tail accounted for one bottle in five of all Australian international sales.[2] Yellow Tail sells more wine in the United States than all French producers combined.[3]

The winery is located in a small village (population about a thousand) called Yenda in the Riverina region of southeast Australia. It's a big operation. The warehouse can store 900,000 cases of wine at a time and the bottling line next door is the fastest and loudest in the world, filling thirty thousand bottles per hour (two more lines are planned to increase capacity). It isn't the biggest winery in the world, but it's in the top ten. Total production is about 11 million cases, of which about 8.5 million are exported to the United States.

It is a sophisticated factory, with blending facilities that assure that each bottle tastes just like the one before. Yellow Tail is expanding in every imaginable way: more varietals (an Australian Pinot Grigio), a Reserve line of wines sourced from cooler-climate vineyards, and now sparkling wines, too. The Yellow Tail's distinctive yellow-footed rock wallaby "critter" is everywhere.

Why has Yellow Tail been so successful? Some business analysts argue that it's because the Casella family that owns Yellow Tail have created something that is new. They don't call it McWine; they tell the Yellow Tail story in terms of Blue Ocean versus Red Ocean.

The oceans in question are markets. Blue Oceans are markets for new products. Red Oceans are markets for existing products. Why are they red? I don't really know but based upon what I saw last summer on the Discovery Channel's "Shark Week," I'm willing to guess that existing markets are a tough environment to enter. You've got to compete with well-adapted predators who will cut you up badly if you aren't really strong (Red Ocean = bloody ocean—get it?). A Blue Ocean, on the other hand, is uncontested open water. You've got a much better chance of profit if you can stake out the market for a new product before the competition gets there.

So how is Yellow Tale a Blue Ocean product?[4] According to one article it is because Yellow Tail isn't wine as we know it—it's a whole new thing. People don't really like wine, the article suggests. Even the Casellas don't like it (is this possible—they are an Italian winemaking family that emigrated to Australia in the 1950s, planting their own vineyards in the 1990s?). It's very tannic and acidic and people aren't used to those qualities except in tea. Who wants to pay $6 a bottle for something that is bitter and sour? The key to Yellow Tail was the realization that wine without tannin and acid could be very appealing, especially to the majority of Americans who really don't like wine or at least don't drink it very often. (It was designed to appeal to the 85 percent of nonwine drinkers, according to the article, while not offending the 15 percent who already like wine. That's 100 percent, if my math is correct. No wonder it is so popular.) Yellow Tail isn't as strong a brand in Great Britain—maybe it's because the British actually like wine, acid, tannin, and all.

The Red Ocean, then, is the market for wine and the Blue Ocean is the market for wine that doesn't taste like wine. (You might call it the Blue Nun

Ocean in honor of a popular semiwine wine of the 1970s.) If this analysis is correct, then you can see why Yellow Tail is such a success. But you can also see why its success might be short-lived (and why, therefore, Casella may be moving into other markets). The Blue Ocean of semiwine was quickly populated by competing predator species. Two Buck Chuck is an obvious example, but there are really dozens and dozens of copycat critter wines out there. Fred Franzia even created a $2.99 Australian wine called Down Under to compete directly with Yellow Tail.

The trick for Yellow Tail is thus how to succeed now that their Blue Ocean is turning Pink. If you are looking for McWine, then look to the Casella family in Australia, who created it, and the William J. Deutsch Company of the United States, who have marketed it so effectively.

MCWINECORP REVEALED

Yellow Tail's Blue Ocean story aside, it is easy to finger Gallo as the ultimate McWineCorp. But it's not. Its Carlo Rossi isn't McWine—it is just the leading brand in a large but crowded commodity market segment that is of declining importance almost everywhere. And Gallo isn't really McWineCorp either. This is true in part because Gallo isn't a corporation. For all its size and market influence, it remains a family-owned firm, with the sort of long-term commitments that family firms are known for. Private ownership (often by family members) is actually one of the most interesting features of the wine business. Most of the small and boutique wineries are family owned, of course, but some very large wine companies are private not public creatures.

If you want to find America's McWineCorp, don't go to Modesto, California—Gallo's hometown. Head toward Canandaigua, New York, the headquarters of Constellation Wines, the winemaking division of Constellation Brands, once the largest wine company, now #2 behind Gallo.

Have you ever had a bottle of Constellation Wine? I'm not sure there is such a thing. But you certainly have tasted wine made by Constellation Brands. How Constellation came to be the number one wine company is an unlikely saga.

The story began in 1945 when Marvin Sands founded Canandaigua Industries Company for the purpose of selling bulk wine to East Coast bottlers. It took only a few years for the company to become interested in making and selling their own wines. A winery was built in Petersburg, Virginia, to make

Richard's Wild Irish Rose, a sweet, fortified (18 percent alcohol) concoction that was immediately popular and soon bottled at five different locations across the country. You would have seen it on the wine wall in the 1960s— alongside Gallo's Thunderbird and similar products.

The company acquired a number of eastern wineries and brands and continued to grow until 1972 when it changed its name to Canandaigua Wine Company and became a public corporation the next year. Over the next quarter century the company built a brand portfolio, acquiring J. Roget, the best-selling (read cheapest) sparkling wine brand, Sun Country wine coolers; Marcus James wines (imported from Brazil at one time, I understand); and other brands including Italian Swiss Colony, Cribari, Cook's, Paul Masson, Taylor, Almaden, and Inglenook. Canandaigua went beyond wine, becoming a classic "drinks" company through its acquisition of spirit and beer brands.

The company changed its name to Constellation Brands in 2000 and continued expansion, acquiring Vincor, a large Canada-based wine multinational, and then Robert Mondavi, the Napa Valley legend, along with the Australian wine giant BRL Hardy, 40 percent of the Italian producer Ruffino, and an incredible list of U.S. brands.

Constellation's 2006 annual report was titled "Strength in Numbers" and the numbers were huge: more than 200 brands (wine, beer, spirits) sold in almost 150 countries, $4.6 billion in net sales, and 10,000 employees. Richard Sands, of the founding family, was CEO, and Rob Sands was president. At its peak, Constellation produced perhaps 50 percent more wine than Gallo (Gallo is a private company and doesn't release financial data, so estimates of its wine volumes are necessarily uncertain). That's more than 120 million cases in 2005 compared to about 75 million, if you want numbers.

More impressive to me are Constellation's constellation of brands, which range from Richard's Wild Irish Rose to quality wines like Robert Mondavi, Simi Winery, Ravenswood, Kim Crawford, Franciscan, and Monkey Bay. More stars than there are in the heavens—isn't that how they used to describe the MGM movie studio? Well, there is a constellation of wine stars headquartered in upstate New York.

THE BRIDGET JONES EFFECT

At this point it would be really easy to conclude that the McWine effect that started this chapter is real. Big corporations getting bigger, churning out vast quantities of McWine, covering the wine wall with a Blue Ocean of un-complicated semiwine plonk. The future of wine, in this scenario (which is reminiscent of the Berry Bros. & Rudd forecast reported earlier in this book) is dismal indeed.

I am suspicious of the race to the bottom scenario. I don't think this is the future of wine. More like the past than the future, I believe. It starts with Two Buck Chuck itself, which I think has actually raised the overall quality of inex-pensive wine by setting a higher lower limit. If you can get Two Buck Chuck for $2 or a little more, then a $5 wine needs to be a lot better or customers will turn away. Raising the quality bar in this way cascades up the wine wall to the consumer's benefit.

Then we have the problem of the real McWine, those one-dimensional Australian wines and their global clones. The boom in McWines has faded be-cause consumers find it easy to get bored with simple products and move on. The wine writer Oz Clarke described one aspect of this as the "Bridget Jones effect."[5] Apparently Bridget Jones, the movie character, drowns her love life sorrows in huge glasses of inexpensive Australian Chardonnay. She's a loser, she thinks, so it must be loser wine. British Chardonnay sales took a steep dive as a result. It's hard to take a wine phenomenon seriously if all it takes is a few tearful entries in Bridget Jones's diary to pull the plug.

The most important indicator that the future of McWine may not be what you'd expect comes from the ultimate McWineCorp itself, Constellation, which seems intent on reinventing itself. Informed by the results of Project Genome, Constellation is moving upmarket.

It has been interesting to trace Constellation's continuing transformation through its annual reports. Yes, I know, wine writers don't really worry about annual reports and SEC filings, but wine economists do. The 2006 annual re-port, as I mentioned earlier, was titled "Strength in Numbers" and focused on the number of brands and products on the Constellation portfolio. By 2007 the annual report's theme had changed to "The Right Mix." It's important to have the *right* brands (and people and programs) it said. Quality matters at least as much as quantity, maybe more. "Cultivate"—a horticultural metaphor—was the theme in 2008. Growth, but not random growth. The acquisition of Clos du Bois, the leading super-premium brand, accompanied by sales of a number of product lines, including especially bottom-shelf Inglenook and Almaden, signaled a transformation, but to what?

The 2009 annual report announced a new company motto: "To elevate with every glass raised. To enhance life experiences and occasions; to continually raise the bar with respect to the quality of our people, our products and our performance; and to make a positive difference in the communities in which we live and work." Maybe it's just PR, but this doesn't sound like the McWineCorp stereotype. Maybe it's a smokescreen, but I think that it reflects the fact that while cheap wine sells (always has, always will) the focus of even huge businesses like Constellation Brands is no longer on McWine.

A BOTTLE OF WHITE? A BOTTLE OF RED?

I began to suspect that the McWine conspiracy was a bit overblown when some friends invited me out to dinner. If you want to see the state of the art in American restaurant wine programs, follow your nose in the direction of the local shopping mall and get in line for a table at Olive Garden. Olive Garden's seven hundred–plus restaurants sell more wine than any other restaurant chain in the United States and its sales and education programs are a positive part of the transformation of American wine culture. Olive Garden is the optimistic future of American restaurant wine.

How does Olive Garden, a chain best known for its bottomless salad bowl and endless supply of tasty bread sticks, sell so much wine (half a million cases in 2006, according to one source, probably much more than that today)? The short answer is education. Americans like wine and enjoy having it with food, but they are intimidated by everything about wine and need education before they are comfortable embracing wine. You've gotta learn 'em before you can turn 'em (into mainstream wine consumers).

The educational process at Olive Garden starts with staff, the people who are best placed to influence customer choice. Early on, Olive Garden established a relationship with the family that owns Rocca delle Macìe winery in Tuscany. Specially selected staff travel to Italy each year to live, shop, eat, drink, cook, and in general soak up knowledge and experience that can be used and shared back home—a nice employee incentive that pays off in higher wine sales.

Back home, in partnership with several California wineries, Olive Garden has established a similar institute in Napa Valley. Many restaurants expect that their waitstaff will pick up wine knowledge—Olive Garden really works at it by providing literally hundreds of thousands of hours of training. Of course, it has the chain-wide scale to make this investment pay off.

So Olive Garden staff are likely to know their wine list (thirty-seven wines from Italy, California, Washington, and Australia, thirty-five of which are available by the glass) and which wines match well with different dishes. But how do you get patrons to try them—and especially to move out of their comfort zone and try something new?

The answer is . . . wait for it . . . to give away free samples! Patrons at many Olive Garden restaurants (this is America—local regulations vary) are offered small samples of different wines along with advice on menu pairing. The Italian house wines are the Principato brand made by Cavit that sells for $5.35 a glass and $32 for a 1.5 liter bottle meant to be shared family style. Bottle prices of other wines range from $21 for the Sutter Home White Zin on up to $110 for Bertani Amarone. Most choices are in the $24–$34 range.

Olive Garden takes the free sample idea seriously, giving away thirty thousand cases of wine in 2006 and presumably more today. That's more than five million tastes, according to my back-of-the-envelope calculation. And it's worth it, both in terms of wine sales and customer satisfaction. Customers like the wine, once they've had a chance to try it, Olive Garden says, and it helps them enjoy the whole family dining experience more. No argument here—I can see how having one of those 1.5 liter bottles on the table would help a family relax and enjoy their meals.

The Olive Garden website continues the education process for customers who develop an interest, with basic "Wine 101" information along with an interactive guide to pairing specific wines with particular menu items.

The Olive Garden system sells wine, obviously, and it sells the idea of wine in a very healthy way. Olive Garden customers are more likely to try new wines and have fun with wine, I think, because they trust the Olive Garden brand. Olive Garden has obviously invested a lot in its wine program and in research about what will appeal to its customers. There is less perceived risk in trying something new at Olive Garden. This is perhaps especially important in selling some of the Italian wines, where both the producer (Mandra Rossa, for example, or Arancio) and wine name (Fiano or Nero d'Avola) would be unfamiliar to most diners.

In a way, Olive Garden has the same advantage when it comes to selling wine as Trader Joe's and Costco. The seller's trusted brand gives buyers confidence in making an otherwise uncertain purchase. Olive Garden is big enough and smart enough to make the investment required to pursue this wine strategy. It's a good thing in terms of the development of a healthy American wine culture, but it does contribute to the consolidation of the industry, noted at the beginning of this chapter. Olive Garden needs large, reliable supplies of each wine to make its system work (minimum quantity seventy-five hundred cases, I think), which rules out smaller producers.

But Olive Garden doesn't have to be everything to everyone and there is plenty of room in the marketplace for other types of restaurants and wine programs. If Olive Garden helps introduce middle America to a healthy idea of wine, it will have done a great service. And I think that's exactly what's happening.

DESPERATELY SEEKING SOMEWHERE

Olive Garden's success does not define the future of restaurant wine or of wine more generally—every element of wine is too complicated to be reduced to a single case. But it does show, to me at least, that a healthy balance can sometimes be struck, one that reflects the impact of globalization and takes advantage of the Two Buck Chuck brand wine dynamic.

Terry Theise, an *über terroirist* wine importer, frames the issue this way.[6] The wine debate comes down to *pragmatists* versus *romantics.* Romantics, he says, fret that market forces (globalization and Two Buck Chuck in my framework) are lowering the ceiling of fine wine (a very Martian attitude). In their search for broader markets they risk sacrificing truly distinct wines. If individual taste is replaced by some least common denominator market standard, much of wine's special appeal is lost.

I can see the romantics' point. It seems to me that the world is increasingly stretched and fragmented, processed and globalized. Many elements of our everyday lives are efficient, impersonal, and shallow. The things we buy and use could come from anywhere and end up anywhere. Anywhereness is the same as nowhereness in my book, the lack of real personality or a distinctive sense of time and place.

Given the prevalence of nowhere, it is not a surprise that we desperately seek somewhere to fill the empty places in our lives. This is what makes wine especially appealing to so many people today. Wine has the ability to express somewhereness, the intangible quality we often call *terroir.* More than most products, we know (or can find out) who made a particular wine and how, in what place at what time. Wine somehow manages to hold all these messages together and to show us through its variations the influence of personality, the impact of nature, time, and place.

Wine is more likely than most products to be a shared experience, too, consumed in a social setting, the subject of conversation and perhaps some collective introspection. Music once filled these gaps (and still does to some extent) because we typically listened to it in the company of others. Now the iPod has made music an efficient but more solitary experience. Thank God there is no equivalent iWine (at least not yet).

Desperately seeking somewhere—that's who and what we are. But this romantic viewpoint doesn't tell the whole story. Pragmatists argue that the average quality of wine has never been better, according to Theise. They don't notice that the quality ceiling has come down, if it has, because their concern is the floor, which is rising. Access to global markets and increasing competition make it difficult to sell bad wine or to justify buying it. Life is too short to drink bad wine, as they say, and it is easy to find something better.

Theise fears the risk of the falling ceiling and acknowledges the fact of the rising floor. I don't know what you think of Two Buck Chuck—some of my friends love it, some hate it (or at least hate the idea of it), and others, well, they love to hate it. But whatever you think, it must be said that bottom-shelf wine used to be much worse than Two Buck Chuck is today.

"The pragmatists need to realize there are risks inherent in their aesthetic. And we romantics need to realize certain things too," Theise says.

> We have misapplied the concept of *terroir* to excuse flawed wines. This concept is precious. We need to respect it, and use it with care. We have been guilty of a form of puritanism; if it tastes unpleasant it must be virtuous. The pragmatists ought in turn to acknowledge theirs isn't the only form of pleasure. There are worlds alongside the sensual, and wine can be intellectually and spiritually nourishing, and people can desire these experiences, and the true hedonist isn't threatened by them.[7]

"I wonder," Theise concludes, "if we cannot all unite behind the value of diversity. I would like to think so. . . . I want to live in a world of thousands of different wines, whose differences are deeper than zip-code, each one of which shows me the unending variety and fascination of this lovely bit of green on which we walk." I'm not sure whether Terry Theise is a Martian or a Wagnerian at heart, but I agree with his vision of the future of wine. There are a lot of McWine forces that threaten to standardize wine, but there are also counterforces that want to protect wine's diversity. Olive Garden has a little of both—a focus on large volumes but also educating consumers and introducing them to new ideas of wine. And it seems to me that other parts of the McWine conspiracy might, when studied closely, provide a similar hopeful balance between ceiling and floor.

What role will the Martians and romantics play in the future of wine? An important one, I think. But before we examine the "revenge of the *terroirists*" we have one more trip to the wine wall to make, to find three bottles that tell us something about the future of wine.

12

The Future of Wine
in Three Bottles

I've got three bottles sitting here on my desk. They are the future of wine, or at least what a lot of people think will be the future. We need to find out what's in them, so it's time to pull some corks.

(Pulling corks—hmmm—that's actually more of a metaphor than a real activity today. Only one of my three bottles is sealed with a natural cork closure. But that's part of the future of wine, too.)

The first bottle isn't really a bottle at all. The wine is packaged in a type of container that is sometimes called a cask, which sounds good, and sometimes a box or "bag-in-box," a less appealing name, because of the airtight plastic bladder that holds the wine in the box. The cork is really a spigot that lets you draw out wine without letting in air. This is the future of wine at the bottom of the wine wall.

The second bottle comes from the top shelf (if it is on the wine wall at all). You are more likely to find it in a specialist shop or on a restaurant wine list (although you may stumble upon it at Costco, too). It comes in a heavy glass bottle and is sealed with a cork. It represents a different future of wine.

The third bottle is a bit more lightweight (it might even be plastic) and is closed with a Stelvin closure—a screw-cap device developed by Alcan Packaging company that is sweeping across the wine wall, replacing natural corks. What is most distinctive about this wine is not the bottle, however, or what's on the bottle top. It's the label that draws your attention here and the strong brand association it represents.

These bottles symbolize three different types of wine and the business models that go with them. They are not the past, present, and future of wine (like the ghosts in *A Christmas Carol*) or three different *potential* futures of wine. They illustrate three *simultaneous* trajectories that will likely shape the industry in the years ahead as globalization and Two Buck Chuck drive it forward.

Most important, these three wines reveal something about the powerful forces that continue to shape and reshape the world of wine. So let's uncork . . . er . . . open up these three containers and see what they can tell us about the future of wine.

THE FUTURE'S IN THE BAG (IN THE BOX)

One of my favorite globalization books is *The Box: How the Shipping Container Made the World Smaller and the World Economy Bigger* by Marc Levinson.[1] It is the story of how the invention of the standard shipping container (those 20-foot steel boxes you see on ships, railcars, and truck beds) made international trade much cheaper, more efficient, and more secure. Now it looks like another kind of box is about to shake up the wine world.

I'm talking about box wines or bag-in-box (BIB) wines that feature an airtight wine-filled plastic bladder inside a cardboard box. You use a built-in spigot to get to the wine. They can be found on the bottom shelf of the wine wall and behind the bar and out of sight at your local restaurant. They come in several sizes—3 liter and 5 liter containers are the most common. You can find 10 liter containers in restaurants that sell a lot of wine by the glass or carafe.

Box wines have a bad reputation, at least here in the United States where I live. They first appeared in the 1970s and were filled with generic bulk wines. They were one step *down* from the popular 1.5 liter "magnum" bottles of "Burgundy," "Chabils," and the notorious headache-inducing "Rhine" wine. Box wine was cheap, nasty stuff that acquired a frequently deserved bad rap.

The technology of box wine is very solid. The airtight bladder is a neutral container that is well suited to holding wine for relatively short periods of time. (Don't "cellar" box wine—consume within a year of production— check out the "drink by" date on the box.) The bladder and spigot do in fact protect the wine from oxygen in the short run, so it will last longer once opened (especially if the box is stored in the fridge) than similar leftover wine in bottles.

Bladders are so good at the particular thing that they do that they have become an industry standard technology for bulk imported wines, which are shipped in huge bladders inside steel shipping containers (big bag in big box) and then bottled in the destination market. The box is the standard 20-foot shipping container and the bag is a flexible, seamless, multilayer disposable 24,000 liter wine bladder. (Seriously! Can you imagine it?) Vast quantities of bulk wine can be efficiently shipped by sea to local processing centers in these containers, where they go from big box bladders to smaller ones and then on to their place at the bottom of your friendly wine wall. So you may already be drinking box wine and not know it.

Box wine sales are growing in the United States. Bag-in-box accounted for about 10 percent of off-premises retail wine sales (and rising) at the end of 2009. The total market for box wines rises if we include on-premises sales. Recent data indicate that box wines (served to customers in carafes and by the glass) are strong sellers in casual dining establishments.

The rise of box wine in the U.S. market is part of the trading down effect, clearly, since most box wines fall into the two price categories that experienced the highest growth rates during the recent economic downturn. Does this mean that Americans have traded down all the way to the bottom, back to the nasty box wines of the 1970s? The answer, incredibly, is no. Or at least not necessarily, according to a review in *Wine Spectator*.[2] *Wine Spectator* purchased thirty-nine box wines in packages that ranged from 1 liter to 5 liters. Twenty-seven wines were rated as "good" (a score of 80–84) and ten "very good" (85–89). The names of the two wines that scored below 80 were not reported.

The top box wine, going by the rating numbers, was white: Wine Cube California Chardonnay, sold in Target Stores for $17 per 3 liter box, which is $4.25 per standard bottle equivalent. It earned a very respectable 88 points. Wine Cube is a partnership between Target and Trinchero, the maker of a wide range of wines including Sutter Home.

The best red wine (at 87 points) was the Black Box Cabernet Sauvignon Paso Robles 2006, which cost $20 for 3 liters or $5 per standard bottle equivalent. Black Box is a widely distributed Constellation Brands product.

Some box wine, apparently, is both pretty good and pretty cheap. Perhaps just to show that they really do rate wines "blind," *Wine Spectator* gave a pretty good 84-point score to a nonvintage Carlo Rossi Cabernet Sauvignon

California "Reserve" wine. Five liters for $13, in case you are interested. That's $1.97 per standard bottle equivalent.

How can decent wine be this cheap? One answer, of course, is that you can choose to make the wine itself less expensive by economizing all along the product chain, from vineyard (high yields) to cellar (no costly oak) to store. But to a considerable degree the box itself is responsible for the savings.

The bag-in-box container costs less than $1, according to the *Wine Spectator* article, which automatically saves $4 to $8 compared with a similar quantity of wine in standard glass bottles and the box they come in. Shipping costs are also less since the boxes weigh much less than glass bottles for the same quantity of wine and are less likely to be damaged in transit. There are environmental benefits too, especially in areas where glass bottle recycling is problematic because the sour economy has undermined the market for recycled glass.

Is box wine the future of wine? No, but it is part of the future, especially if environmental concerns become more important. Better wine in better boxes (and with consumers embracing a more relaxed idea of wine) certainly deserves to play a bigger role in the future of wine. Another triumph for The Box!

PUT A CORK IN IT!

The 20-foot steel shipping container replaced a shipping method called break bulk cargo that was the traditional way to transport merchandise until things started to change about fifty years ago. If you've ever seen the classic 1954 Elia Kazan film *On the Waterfront* you know what break bulk cargo is all about.[3] Compared with neat, secure containers crammed tight with traded goods, break bulk shipping is a messy, labor-intensive process that is still used for many types of cargo. Each item—bags, boxes, crates, barrels, drums, bundles, reels, rolls, and individual pieces of machinery, and so on—was sorted, loaded, stacked, unloaded, sorted, and stacked again.

It seems inevitable that something would go wrong—lost, stolen, broken, mixed up—with break bulk shipment. Container shipping has its problems and limitations, but the advantages over the old-fashioned break bulk system are obvious. But it wasn't easy for containers to break through, as Levinson's book makes clear. A lot of interests resisted the box, such as port authorities unwilling to make major investments needed to take advantage of container technology and dock workers who rightly feared job losses from less labor-intensive operations. But the efficiency of the box won out in the end for many types of shipping.

What I'd *like to* say right here is that the traditional glass bottle and natural cork is the break bulk cargo of today's wine world—traditional, accepted, inefficient, and doomed. It would be a good "shocker" way to get your attention. It's not entirely true, although it's not completely false either.

Glass bottles are heavy, awkward, and fragile. Corks are difficult to insert or extract without specialized equipment and can fail to hold a seal or suffer from musty, chemical smelling cork taint (2,4,6-trichloroanisole, or more commonly, TCA). Conventional wisdom holds that 3 to 5 percent of modern cork-sealed glass wine bottles suffer some sort of packaging-related flaw ranging from horrible stench to a subtle dulling of aroma and taste. That's a lot of bad (or sometimes just disappointing) wine!

If bottles and corks are so bad, why are they ubiquitous (or nearly so)? The answer is that cork and bottle were the equivalent of the 20-foot shipping container of their day—imperfect to be sure, but so much better than the alternative. Clay amphorae were used to ship wine before the advent of handmade glass bottles (probably first developed by the Romans). The vigorous wine trade of ancient times accounts for the large number of amphorae that divers turn up when searching for shipwrecks.

Amphorae were OK for shipping wine, but they were too unwieldy to use to serve it, so wine was necessarily decanted into a variety of pottery jars, stoneware jugs, or wooden casks. With relatively open exposure to air, it was unusual, I think, for wine to last very long in these conditions. You would be doing well if this year's vintage was still drinkable by the time next year's vintage was ready.

Commercial production of wine bottles began early in the seventeenth century. A 1636 British law made it illegal to sell wine in bottles because the size and shape of the containers varied considerably and unwary buyers could easily be short-changed. The law was repealed in 1860, by which time the wine bottle had reached its present form: standard bottle sizes, natural cork, label, and protective capsule or "foil."

Although the quality of each of the components of a modern wine bottle has certainly improved in the last 150 years, the basic technology remains the same. It's not really surprising that innovations like bag-in-box wines have appeared to try to do to glass and cork what *they* did to clay amphorae. But traditional packaging is unlikely to entirely release its hold on wine and wine lovers for some time.

Cork and bottle is the best choice for fine age-worthy wines and I see no end in sight for this combination. Fine Bordeaux and Vintage Ports designed to be put down for years or even decades benefit from the neutral quality of glass and the opportunity cork provides for wine to age and develop. The cost of losing 3 to 5 percent of a great vintage to cork taint is, for connoisseurs at least, a small price to pay for the aesthetic heights that great wine in traditional containers can achieve.

THE 70 PERCENT SOLUTION

Glass bottles with cork closures will thus remain at the top of the wine wall. But it is easy to understand why they might gradually fade away. Jean-Charles Boisset argues that using traditional glass containers with cork closures makes little sense—either environmentally or economically—for most of the wine sold today. He observes that at least 70 percent of wine retails for $12 to $10 or less (probably much more than 70 percent, I suspect) and 70 percent is consumed within three hours of purchase. Finally, 70 percent of the production cost of these low-price wines is in the packaging, not the wine itself.

These wines are quotidian pleasures, purchased for quick consumption. Heavy, expensive, "traditional" packaging makes little sense for 70-70-70 wines. Producers, consumers, and their environment would all likely benefit if these wines were packaged and sold in ways that reflect their real consumer product function, not a false elite identity. Wine will have come of age, some argue, when it no longer needs the borrowed prestige of the heavy bottle or a faux-traditional label.

But that borrowed prestige—or perhaps it is the comfort of tradition—will keep bottles and corks (albeit many of them synthetic to reduce the incidence of cork taint) on wine wall shelves for a good long time. The link to tradition is important even (or perhaps especially) for wines that are the most unlikely to benefit from extending bottle aging. Two Buck Chuck is a bottle and cork wine, for example, as are a great many inexpensive wines. It's the Confidence Game once again and I guess the confidence that bottle and cork gives to wine is one thing that unites the people who shop the bottom of the wine wall with those who buy from the top.

SCREWED? OR CORKED?

I am glad that the bottle and cork with their layers of tradition will still be around in fifty years' time (despite its obvious disadvantages), but many of my friends can't imagine anything else. They are appalled at the idea that wine would ever change. They find innovation in wine positively threatening (although many of them embrace innovation in all other parts of their life, scrambling for the newest smart phones, downloading the latest "apps," and proudly displaying new high-tech corkscrews and complicated vortex wine aerators).

Wine is for them a link to the past, to traditional values, to a culture they associate with the Old World. They understandably want to preserve this side of life and of themselves. But change is coming—indeed it has already happened. The third bottle on my table—the third vector in the future of wine—symbolizes innovation. It is a bottle closed with a screw cap.

Noncork closures including screw caps were nearly invisible just ten years ago (with perhaps 1 percent of the bottled wine market), but this is changing quickly. A report in *Meininger's Wine Business International* suggests that about 35 percent of wine bottles—over 2.5 billion units—had noncork closures in 2007, including about 90 percent of New Zealand's wine production.[4] The percentage has surely risen since 2007, due in part by the determination of British supermarkets like Tesco to bottle virtually all their own-brand wines under screw cap. Increasing consumer acceptance is part of the story, too, of course.

Screw caps have long been associated with inexpensive wine, but this too is changing. The August 2008 issue of *Decanter* magazine featured an article titled "50 Reasons to Love Screw Caps." Ten wine critics including Steven Spurrier and Linda Murphy recommend wines for summer drinking and commented on both the products and their screw tops. "The screw cap closure is one of the best things to have happened to wine in my lifetime," according to Spurrier (the organizer of the famous Judgment of Paris tasting).[5]

"Given the choice of the same wine with screw cap or a cork, I'd choose the screw cap every time," writes Joanna Simon, the *Sunday Times* wine writer. It's a pretty enthusiastic endorsement, especially coming from *Decanter*. Economics is behind the move away from cork. Screw caps are not remarkably cheaper than cork in themselves, but they avoid the loss of good wine to cork taint and they are, like the box, efficient and reliable.

The screw cap reminds us that there are many ways to seal a bottle and the traditional natural cork is only one of them. Once in Switzerland I was served a bottle sealed with a crown cap (same as some beer bottles). The waiter whipped out a bottle opener, and "pop" the wine was ready. It was a simple local wine, he said, best drunk as soon as possible. Why bother with a cork? Why bother indeed.

In fact, crown caps like the one on the Swiss wine bottle play an unexpectedly prominent role in the wine world. Champagne (and sparkling wines generally) are traditionally sold to consumers sealed with a mushroom-shaped cork held in place with a metal foil and wire cage. Twist, twist, twist, "pop," and serve. That's the tradition.

But those fancy corks are mainly there for show. During the long years that Champagne matures in the bottle and its bubbles develop, its top is sealed with an ordinary crown cap. The tops are swapped when the bottle is disgorged (the dead yeast cells responsible for the bubbles removed).

Not that the show isn't important, especially with restaurant wines, where the ceremony of revealing the bottle, pulling and inspecting the cork, taking the first taste, and so on is part of the bigger show. I met with a famous New Zealand winemaker a few years ago who had started bottling some of his best wines under screw cap and was worried about the loss of ritual. He had a plan, which he shared with us with glee. The sommelier presents the bottle with a clean towel hiding the screw cap top. Then, with back deftly turned, the twist is made and the bottle opened, and the ritual completed.

In practice, the elaborate ruse was unnecessary. Many restaurants, he reported, found no resistance to screw caps. Those that did reacted by simply putting the wine on the popular and profitable "wines by the glass" menu, where it sold very well *sans* faux cork-pulling ceremony.

The history of the screw cap and the controversial cork closure debate are interesting enough to have spawned at least one well-regarded book, *To Cork or Not to Cork* by George M. Taber.[6] The first application of a screw cap to wine took place in France in 1959, according to the *Oxford Companion to Wine,* using technology already used in the spirits industry. Australian Consolidated Industries bought the rights to manufacture the Stelcap-vin in 1970, renaming it Stelvin, a trade name that has become a generic term for screw caps in the wine industry today.

The rise of the screw cap was driven by winemakers, particularly in Australia and New Zealand, who were tired of seeing their fine wines spoiled by faulty corks. One source suggests that Swiss winemakers played a part, too—their very light wines were especially susceptible to cork taint problems (hence the crown cap I encountered years ago?). What strikes me most about the screw cap is that it is an example of a technical innovation that both improves the quality of wine (which is what winemakers want) and also makes wine more convenient (which is what wine consumers want).

The screw cap is not the last word in wine innovations, of course, even if we are just talking about closures. There are a number of synthetic cork products available that preserve some elements of the romance of wine while removing the threat of cork taint. They're appropriate for "70-percent" wine, I understand, but not for wine that you are going to put down for several years to age. Synthetic corks add a bit of unexpected mystery to wine, I have noticed. It is easy to tell if a wine has a screw cap but almost impossible to know if a non-screw-cap wine is sealed with cork or synthetic—the foil that tops the bottle disguises the closure.

Last year at the International Pinot Noir Celebration we were served an Oregon Pinot sealed under an Alcoa Vino-Seal glass closure. It looked a bit like a small crystal decanter top, dainty and delicate, with a high-tech liner to keep the wine sealed. An interesting technical development and very attractive, too—who knows what will be next?

A RACE TO THE BOTTOM . . . OR THE TOP?

George Taber ends his book with an indirect commentary on wine globalization, which is worth noting here. Finding a solution to the wine closure dilemma is a worldwide problem, and the global market competition is forcing the stopper makers to innovate and make better and better closures and forcing winemakers to get better, too, since they can no longer automatically blame any flaws in their wines on bad corks. "Unfettered competition," he writes, "remains a powerful driving force for good."[7]

You may not share Taber's Adam Smith–like optimism about the benefits of free markets, but we should acknowledge that he has correctly identified the critical issue in this debate: competition. Globalization and Two Buck Chuck are both cause and effect of increased competition in the world of wine. Will increased competition improve wine, as Taber suggests here, or be its downfall?

Globalization is all about a broadening and deepening of competitive forces. Wines from the earth's far corners find their way to your local wine shop or upscale supermarket shelves, where they must fight for space (and attention) in an increasingly competitive environment. Does exposure to a global market and its powerful competitive drive make wine better? This is a complicated question and there is more than one reasonable answer. One thing that I think I've learned is that the opposite of competition—wine protectionism—makes wine very bad, and so trying to stop market forces is unexpectedly dangerous. I have seen this over and over again. We learned about New Zealand's experience in an earlier chapter. Abandoning protectionism and embracing the global market has been the key to their astounding growth. In an earlier book, I wrote about Argentina's parallel story.[8] One hundred percent tariffs kept foreign wines out and locked nasty, sweet, domestic products in. Argentina's spectacular rise as a maker of quality wines owes its origins to market reforms that let better international wine in (along with international investment and winemaking expertise). A protected market encourages least common denominator wines.

Washington State, for example, has a vibrant wine industry today, making wines that sell well and win awards, but it wasn't always like this. Once upon a time Washington wineries made foul wines that had few takers outside the state's protected borders. The key event that pushed Washington wines up the wine wall took place in March 1969. That's when the Washington legislature passed House Bill 100, the California Wine Bill. The California Wine Bill exposed the Washington wine industry to competition from both domestic (California) and international competition and forced winemakers to improve quality or disappear.

Here's the backstory. Many wineries opened or reopened in Washington when Prohibition was repealed in 1933. Almost the first thing they did was to seek protection from the state legislature from out-of-state competition. This protection was provided almost immediately in the form of the Steele Act of 1935, which set up a dual distribution system for wines. "Domestic" Washington wineries could sell directly to wholesalers, but "foreign" out-of-state wines (including wines from California) had to be distributed through the more rigid channels of the state liquor monopoly, the Washington State Liquor Board. "Domestic" wines were relatively easy to purchase and widely available, but "foreign wines," including California products, could only be purchased through state stores with their limited hours and strict controls.

Later legislation provided for minimum prices in order to prevent competition from cheaper California wines.

The result of this protective legislation was exactly what you'd expect. With little competition to keep winemakers honest, quality suffered. The industry focused on the low end of the market, making large quantities of cheap, sweet, fortified wines. There was little incentive for winegrowers to seek quality (although some did) because good grapes and poor ones were all blended together. Although scientists like Dr. Walter Clore were busy developing quality winegrapes in their Prosser labs and test vineyards, Washington's most important grape crop for many years was the Concord grape that went into Welch's juice and Gallo's sweet sparkling Cold Duck.

Rather than thriving behind its protective wall, the Washington wine industry collapsed. There were only eight wineries in Washington in 1969 (down from forty-two in 1937) and, with a few exceptions such as Associated Vintners (now Columbia Winery), their wine was mediocre at best. The paradox is that protecting a wine industry actually destroys it. The only thing that can protect a wine industry is competition, which forces winemakers to become more efficient and to raise quality.

GLOBAL + LOCAL = GLOCAL[9]

But what happens to terroir when the competitive forces of globalization and Two Buck Chuck sweep through? The common assumption is that the global always and everywhere overwhelms the local, although I have my doubts about this. Walmart wasn't able to conquer the German market, for example. Local champion Aldi was too well dug in. Sometimes the local wins out—*viva les terroirists!* More often, however, the result of global plus local is glocal.

Glocal is an awkward word but a very useful one. Glocal is what you get when you marry global with local and it describes a complex process of exchange. Many people see the global and the local only as adversaries, like two football teams. Global market forces are assumed to be fundamentally opposed to local traditions and values. Because there is more money behind the global team, most people assume that the local players (and the values they represent) are doomed. Resistance is futile. In fact, of course, the process is more complicated than this and influences travel both ways. This is obviously true about football, so why should we be surprised that it also applies to wine?

The most valuable local characteristics are not necessarily preserved through isolation, as we have seen, so the choice is not as simple as global *or* local. The global market can destroy, as we are all aware, but protected local markets do not necessarily preserve either. We are left with the reality of glocalism. International influences are imported, with both positive and negative effects, and local practices, products, and values are exported, influencing winemakers and consumers abroad. Producers may feel pressure to make wines to an international standard or to please powerful wine critics, but they also gain from a larger and more diverse market for their products.

Glocal exchange is deeply embedded in the wine industry. A growing number of winemakers now work abroad as well as at home, making wines that are informed by their international experiences but still hopefully a reflection of the particular local terroir. They are at once both global *and* local in differing degrees. Although some focus only on the potentially homogenizing influence of international "flying winemaker" consultants and multinational wine corporations that invest locally to produce wines for the international market, in fact the counterflow of talent and ideas also exists. It is a tradition among winemaking families, for example, for young people to spend time working abroad through informal exchange arrangements, soaking up experiences, trying out new ideas, and making lifelong personal connections. It is an important part of a winemaker's education. I have met these "flying interns" wherever I have traveled in the world of wine. They are a very healthy part of the glocal wine mix.

So how will glocalism turn out for the world's wine industry? It is too soon to tell, of course, but informed speculation is possible. It will not turn out all one way or the other, that's for sure. The global-local mix is seldom the product of a single huge blending vat and it can yield bottles (OK, containers) and wines as diverse as the three that sit here on my desk, all of which are the result of a complex process of global exchange.

Time for our second wine tasting. Then, suitably fortified, we move on to the "revenge of the terroirists," which is the vital third element in wine's future. Globalization and Two Buck Chuck are powerful disruptive forces that threaten many interests and values. It is natural to suppose that a countermovement would arise to oppose and resist these market forces and, as noted above, I am optimistic that they will help prevent the McDonaldization of wine. But it won't be easy because many obstacles stand in their way, including, unexpectedly, the terroirists themselves!

Two Buck Chuck Tasting

For this tasting I'd like you to experience globalization and Two Buck Chuck firsthand. This requires you to taste wines made by a multinational company that sells a portfolio of branded wines designed to please many wine buyer categories at many different price points. Your assignment, if you choose to accept it, is to try to see, through personal sensory analysis, if the personalities of the wines survive the corporate process, or if terroir-free nowhere wines are the result.

Which wines should you sample? The list of "usual suspects" is quite long, but I suggest you seek out wines made by Boisset Family Estates. Jean-Charles Boisset (originator of the 70-70-70 wine rule discussed in this chapter) heads the company. He's French, of course, and so you would expect him to be a terroirist. But don't forget that France is home to many of the most successful consumer goods multinationals and Boisset fits this mold, too. Boisset Family Estates is an interesting example of a winemaker that is at once both Old World and New World. As if to make this point ridiculously obvious, Jean-Charles Boisset is married to Gina Gallo, granddaughter of Julio Gallo and head wine-maker at Gallo Family Vineyards. If there was ever a company that epitomizes the combination of globalization and Two Buck Chuck, it is Boisset.

Based in Burgundy, the terroirist stronghold, Boisset makes and sells wine from France, California, Italy, and Canada. There are twenty-six brands and hundreds of individual wines. Which ones should you taste?

Let's begin with French Rabbit, an example of Boisset's innovative drive. French Rabbit wines come from the South of France, a traditional region, but they don't look very traditional. They come packaged in the 1 liter Tetra Pak packages that I often describe as supersize juice boxes, where the juice in question is Chardonnay or Pinot Noir. They sell for about $10, more expensive than basic bag-in-box products and much costlier than One Buck Chuck Aldi wines, which are packaged much the same way.

French Rabbit is a wine that was invented to fill a demand, which is very New World, I know. The demand was for a quality wine with a much smaller carbon footprint. Green wine. The Tetra Pak container is enormously lighter than a standard glass bottle and is more easily recycled. I would say that it is the ultimate answer to the 70-70-70 problem except that Boisset's Yellow Jersey wine may be even better. Packaged to appeal to Tour de France bicycle race fans, this wine comes in a Stelvin-sealed plastic bottle that, once emptied of its contents of French wine, can be refilled with water and inserted neatly in a bicycle water bottle holder. What could be greener?

French Rabbit and Yellow Jersey show how demand-driven competitive forces can produce innovative wine solutions. Since Boisset is from Burgundy, try to find a French Rabbit Pinot Noir (Burgundy's signature grape) for your tasting. Next I think you should try a wine from the Bouchard Aîné & Fils part of the portfolio. The Bouchard wine tradition in Burgundy dates back to 1750. Bouchard today makes a full range of wines that start at the top shelf with vineyard-designated wines such as a Chambolle-Musigny "Les Cras," then drop down to regional wines such as Bourgogne Pinot Noir before taking the next step down the wine wall to relatively simple Vin de Pays d'Oc Pinot Noir (similar in origin to the wines in the French Rabbit range). I suggest you choose a Bouchard wine as high up on the wine wall as you can reasonably afford to maximize the comparison potential.

Finally, a true New World wine seems in order. Boisset's DeLoach Vineyards is a well-known California Pinot Noir maker so perhaps you should choose a bottle from its lineup, which starts with simple California and Central Coast Pinot blends, moves up to Russian River appellation wines, and tops off with a number of very limited production single-vineyard bottlings. You can choose either upmarket or down here—a more expensive wine to match your glass of Bouchard or a cheaper one to compare more directly with the French Rabbit. Or both, if you're not driving!

Now take your time and taste. At the end of the day I think you will find that you have three (or four?) very different glasses of wine in front of you—I don't think you'll feel they were all drawn from the same global-sized vat. Do they reflect their natural and market terroirs? What do *you* think? Which one is *best*? That's up to you, too—*you* have the opportunity to try these wines and decide for yourself, thanks to the power of globalization and Two Buck Chuck!

Flight Three
REVENGE OF
THE TERROIRISTS

13

Mondovino and the
Revenge of the Terroirists

If you want to understand how globalization is changing the world of wine, a good place to begin is to watch *Mondovino,* the filmmaker Jonathan Nossiter's 2004 documentary about markets, globalization, and wine.

Mondovino is a classic tale of good and evil and the tension that exists between them as these forces exist in the world of wine. Good wine, according to *Mondovino,* is wine that reflects local land, climate, culture, and traditions. It is wine that embodies its *terroir,* to use the unavoidable French term. It is wine with somewhereness.[1]

Evil wine, on the other hand, cannot hide its nowhereness. It is a reflection of the industrial process that produced it and the unselfconsciously commercial motivations of its makers. It may be free of technical imperfection, as precision industrial products often are, but it has no soul. This wine isn't evil in itself, its evilness derives from the economic threat it poses to terroir. *Mondovino* fears that nowhere wine is here to stay but hopes that soulful winemakers, the *terroirists,* can persevere and perhaps even triumph.

Films about *things* are boring, but films about people and places can be fascinating, so *Mondovino* travels through the world of wine (to France, Italy, Britain, America, Argentina, and even to Brazil) to meet people who cast themselves into various roles in this drama. Three famous Americans represent the forces of evil that threaten good wine and its makers: Robert Mondavi, the California corporate winemaker; Robert Parker, the Maryland

167

wine-rating guru; and Michel Rolland, the micro-oxygenating multinational wine consultant (the king of the flying winemakers). Michel Rolland is really French, not American, but he numbers Americans among his more than one hundred global clients and, as an emissary of evil in the film, he thinks and acts like an American is supposed to—talking too loud, dropping names, privileging market values over traditional values, and generally treating wine as processed industrial output rather than a hand-crafted product of sun and soil.[2]

There are many heroes in *Mondovino* and they are mainly French. First among them is bleary-eyed, tweedy old Hubert de Montille, the Burgundian winemaker of ancient tradition, who stands for everything that is good and true and noble about wine—in stark contrast to Mondavi, Parker, and the turncoat Rolland. Bemused, outraged Aimé Guibert, owner of the famous Mas de Daumas Gassac in Aniane, is a *Mondovino* hero too. When Mondavi sought to purchase vineyards in France and set up operations there, Aimé Guibert lead the noble vignerons of Languedoc into battle like a modern-day Astérix the Gaul and repelled the foreign invaders. The wine war between Guibert and Mondavi is immortalized in France as *La guerre des vins: L'affaire Mondavi.*[3]

Everything seems black and white in *Mondovino*, on first viewing at least, even the dogs, who play an unexpectedly important part in the film.[4] Aimé Guibert's dog is good and faithful, as a dog should be, for example. Robert Parker's bulldog, George, farts extravagantly. This is significant, apparently, because according to Nossiter, dogs resemble their masters' wines.[5] Old World wines, like its dogs, are faithful and true while New World wines are enthusiastically vulgar.

Everything about *Mondovino* makes clear the filmmaker's opinion of how globalization and branded wine (the Two Buck Chuck phenomenon) are reshaping the world of wine. New replaces old, tradition is destroyed and taste is debased. Even the noble dog is disgraced. It isn't a simple process—it's not really as black and white as I may have made it seem here. Not all the Americans in the film are evil industrialists, for example, and not all the French are sons and daughters of the soil, but the message comes through pretty clearly. A new world of wine is assaulting the old one and the soul of one of the world's oldest and most revered cultural products is in jeopardy.

I think that *Mondovino* is a terrific film, but is the story that it tells about globalization, Two Buck Chuck, and wine the whole truth? Well, of course not! How could it be? How can anyone explain what is happening to the world of wine today in a 135-minute video?[6] To find out what is really happening you need to dig a little deeper, both into the story that *Mondovino* so effectively tells and into the counterstory as well, because there isn't just one answer, there are many. Each story is like a bottle of wine itself: a mystery, really, until you pull the cork and see, smell, and taste what's inside. Let's pull some corks and see what we find.

GLOBALIZATION AND WINE IN THE LANGUEDOC

The French are suspicious of globalization, just like the rest of us. They are simultaneously pulled by its opulent appeal and appalled by its frightening disruptive potential—just like the rest of us. It is no wonder, then, that the prospect of Robert Mondavi, the human face of global wine, bringing an American idea of wine to France would produce strong reactions, as *Mondovino* made clear. Some, like Andrè Ruiz, the prodevelopment socialist former mayor of Aniane, welcomed the Mondavi investment enthusiastically. Others, like Manuel Diaz, the militant communist mayor, and Aimé Guibert, the outraged winemaker, couldn't wait to drive the Americans out. Many, perhaps most, were simply torn between the two poles, unwilling to commit to one or the other.

Aniane, the location of the drama of *L'affaire Mondavi*, is a wine town in the South of France, a couple of hours' drive southwest of Avignon. It lies in the Languedoc (or Languedoc-Roussillon if we include, as is the custom, the neighboring region), the place that lays claim to the title of world's largest vineyard. It is the largest winegrowing region in the largest winegrowing country on earth. Perhaps as much as a third of all the wine grapes in France come from this arc of land that reaches from Provence to the Spanish border.[7]

Languedoc has had an uncomfortable experience of markets and globalization in its history. Wine markets are to Languedoc, I think, like Lucy and her football are to Charlie Brown in the *Peanuts* cartoon. The market for wine has tantalizingly promised prosperity, and sometimes even delivered it, only to jerk it away again and again. You would have mixed feelings about markets, too, if you made your living from wine in Languedoc.

Wine and wine trade came early to Languedoc, perhaps as early as the sixth century BC when Greek and Etruscan settlers planted vines. Wine became big business, however, with the Roman invasion of Gaul around 125 BC. Wine grapes thrived on the broad alluvial plains of the Roman province of Narbonne in today's Languedoc and soon its wines were being exported to Rome and elsewhere in the empire. The Languedoc vignerons (winegrowers) connected to the "global" market for wine, as it were, and apparently profited greatly from it.

In fact they were too successful for their own good. Rising production from Languedoc threatened the livelihood of Roman winegrowers, so Emperor Domitius issued an edict in 92 AD that ended Languedoc's boom. No more vines were to be planted in the Roman Empire, the order proclaimed, and half of all existing vines in the provinces were to be uprooted. Languedoc's great vineyards were suddenly empty fields. The subsequent collapse of the Roman Empire and its well-organized market for wine effectively finished off what was left of the Languedoc industry—no more demand, no more supply. Kaput! Wine survived on a limited scale mainly due to the influence of the abbeys in the region, which made wine for their own consumption and for religious purposes. The biggest vineyard in the world sat barren because of politics and foreign competition.

The wine industry was revived as a major force in the seventeenth century in response to rising demand in growing north European cities. The Canal du Midi was completed in 1681, connecting the Mediterranean port of Sète with the inland city of Toulouse. Goods could ride the canal northwest from the sea to Toulouse and then move on to the Atlantic via the River Garonne. The Canal du Midi cut a month off of transportation time between southern France and the thriving northern markets in Britain and Holland. A new era of prosperity seemed ready to bloom. But politics and competition got in the way again. Languedoc's main rival for the northern trade was Bordeaux and the River Garonne, the Canal du Midi's natural extension, meets the sea at the port of . . . Bordeaux! Apparently the burghers of Bordeaux, seeing clearly their self-interest in the matter, erected no end of barriers and obstructions to trade, which favored Bordeaux wines over those of the south. Bordeaux protectionism prevailed until 1776, when the "Bordeaux preference" was removed and freer competition prevailed.

Languedoc prospered from 1776 to the middle of the next century. Its wines enjoyed a good reputation—the American oenophile and future president Thomas Jefferson visited in 1787, drawn by the wine's renown—and as wide a market as sea trade would allow.

The fall of Languedoc wines from this high plateau is easy to trace. It is due to an excess of prosperity of the type that only markets can create. To be specific, it was due to the railroad and the effects and reactions that came with it. To an economist, the arrival of the railroad in the nineteenth century is much like globalization and the Internet today—it was a disruptive innovation that lowered costs, shrunk time, and thereby made the world more interconnected. If this analogy holds, then we can say, without doing too much damage to the truth, that the fall of the Languedoc wine industry was due to nineteenth-century globalization.

The railroad reached the Languedoc in about 1845, connecting it with the large and growing urban centers in Paris and Lyon with their thirsty wine-drinking worker populations. Wine could be loaded into huge vats called *tuns* or pumped into specialized tank cars and sent by rail to Paris at lower cost (and with less damage to the wine) than ever before. The railroad vastly expanded the market for Languedoc wine and set in motion a chain of events that transformed the wine market in France over the course of the next seventy-five years.

Urban factory workers were interested in strong cheap wine, and the wines of the south were certainly cheap. In fact, they were cheaper than wines from other parts of France and the first effect of the railroad was on the northern winemakers, whose market had previously been protected by high transportation costs. The advent of cheaper southern wines put many of these winemakers out of business as they could not match the price and strength of the southern wines. The winemakers who remained evolved to fill particular niche markets based on quality or distinctive appeal. If today the Languedoc winemakers are fearful of competition from cheaper New World wines, they are perhaps motivated by the knowledge that once they were that cheaper source themselves.

As late nineteenth-century industrialization gained pace, urban centers grew and the market for cheap wine increased dramatically. You would think this would be music to the ears of the Languedoc vignerons, but in the end it created a problem because of the asymmetrical structure of the wine business. Wine distribution in Paris and Lyon and elsewhere was big business, with efficient large-scale wine wholesalers. They built what I think of as big pipelines that they needed to fill with cheap wine of consistent if not high quality (they weren't real pipelines, of course—wine was delivered in barrels by cart). Wine production, however, was badly fragmented. Most wine was produced by family farms (or by families working on a sort of sharecropping arrangement). There were literally thousands of small producers of uneven quality wine. The structure of supply and the structure of demand just didn't line up. Unless and until the wholesalers could find reliable bulk suppliers, they would not be able to fully exploit their distribution efficiencies.

The solution to this mismatch came in the form of an intermediary called a *négociant*, a merchant who bought up new wine from individual producers, blended and aged it, and filled the pipelines that the urban markets created. The wine blended by a good négociant would necessarily be more consistent than wines from perhaps hundreds of individual small-scale producers and cost less too, once scale economies were taken into account. Négociant wines were also sometimes better because these merchants didn't hesitate to import even stronger wines from Algeria and the south of Italy to beef up their blends and better match their customers' requirements. More to the point, négociant wines had a broad market, since they were supplied in quantities and styles that matched the market structure. The market for a small lot of wine by an individual producer of uncertain reputation was very limited by comparison.

Market power shifted from the individual producers (supply) to the négociants (demand), particularly as the négociants developed brand-like reputations. They used this market power to squeeze the growers, offering lower prices for the new wine and sometimes refusing to buy it at all if it lacked quality or during periods of excess supply. The négociants had what economists call *monopsony* power—the power that comes with control over demand. Demand for Languedoc wine was surging in the cities, but the growers found themselves on the wrong end of the market. The profits increasingly went to the merchants—the négociants.

Cooperatives—or *caves coopératives* as they are called in France—were the producers' response to this imbalance in market power. Groups of growers formed cooperative cellars and signed contracts to supply their grapes (in some cases they committed their entire crop, in other cases the contribution was variable). Large wineries were built, subsidized by the French government (due to the political clout of the winegrowers) and financed with cheap loans from the *Credit Agricole*. New vats and equipment were purchased, and a professional winemaker hired. Winegrowers brought their grapes to the cooperative and were paid according to crop weight, sometimes in cash and in other cases in a share of the wine itself, when it was ready, which they could sell on their own.

Cooperatives in general have a socialist smell, but you would be wrong to think of the Languedoc cooperatives that way. The vignerons were stubbornly independent and did not feel any strong proletarian solidarity. The cooperatives were a defensive measure, a way to gain concentrated market power over supply to match négociants demand power. And it worked. The cooperative wines were more consistent than the wines of individual growers and easier to market, too. It must also be said that the new vats and equipment were generally cleaner and more up to date than the sometimes worn and moldy cellars of the vignerons. The *caves coopératives* were an effective institutional reaction to the new "global" wine market.

Cooperatives remain an unexpectedly important component of the wine business. It is easy to imagine that wine production today is basically cold corporations versus noble family grower, but the cooperatives still dominate in many regions, especially in Europe. More than half the vineyard area in France today is owned by cooperative members and the *caves coopératives* produce more than half of all French wine! Two-thirds of German winegrowers are cooperative members. Over 60 percent of Italian wine is made by their cooperatives, called *cantina sociale*. The cooperatives are similarly strong in Spain and Portugal. Much of the inexpensive bulk wine made in Europe is the product of these cooperative cellars. A few have managed to establish reputations for high quality, however, and charge a premium price. But much of it is mediocre wine—unable to hold a candle to inexpensive wines from Chile, Australia, and elsewhere. Why?

The problem is the age-old trade-off between quantity and quality. The cooperatives were designed to provide consistency, not quality, and individual growers were rewarded based upon the quantity of grapes they delivered, not the quality of the wine that was produced. This created predictably unfortunate incentives that have undermined the cooperative cellar system.

Where growers were not required to sell all of their grapes to the local cooperative, they would naturally reserve the best grapes for themselves, for their own wine production or for sale to quality-conscious buyers—and dump the rest in the cooperative vats. Where growers must sell all of their grapes to the cooperative, their incentive is to produce the greatest possible tonnage of grapes at the lowest possible cost, resulting in weak, characterless wines. I am tempted to call it McWine, since that's the sort of term we usually apply to least common denominator products, which is what the worst of the cooperative wine was and still is, but I don't want to offend French readers any more than I have to!

The choice of quantity over quality even extended to the types of grapes grown. Most wine drinkers are familiar with the names of the famous French grape varieties: Cabernet Sauvignon, Merlot, Chardonnay, and Sauvignon Blanc. These are the names that you see most commonly on labels in the supermarket, so you might reasonably assume that these would be the most commonly grown grape varieties in Languedoc, the world's largest vineyard. But you would be wrong.

Carignan is the typical grape of the Languedoc cooperatives today. Have you heard of it? Since French wines are mainly identified by region rather than grape variety, you may have drunk wine made from Carignan grapes without knowing it. Carignan is the sixth most-planted red grape variety in the world after Cabernet Sauvignon, Merlot, Grenache, Tempranillo, and Syrah. There are about a quarter of a million acres of Carignan vines still in production today, mainly in the South of France, even after a European Union vine pull program that encouraged growers to rip nearly half of them up. Carignan (a.k.a. Carignane) is also planted in California's Central Valley, where it is an integral part of that state's red jug wine industry, and in some parts of Latin America.

The advantage of Carignan is its great productivity, which means that although there are more acres of Cabernet Sauvignon grapes planted around the world, there may be more Carignan wine produced than any other kind. Carignan makes wine that is strong and deeply colored, which has made it useful to French growers in the years since Algerian independence when the supply of blending wine from North Africa dried up, but it is also acidic, bitter, and tannic. It is, according to experts, notable for being too harsh to drink young and not worth aging. A wine connoisseur could never love Carignan (although I have read that wines of real character can be made from old-vine Carignan hillside plantings). Only a merchant could love it—for its low cost. And so the market-driven cooperatives fell in love with bad wine.

The situation of the Languedoc vignerons in the *Mondovino* drama is thus a complicated one. We would like to think that they represent a tradition of good wine, soulful and reflecting a distinctive terroir. This would make their battle against the forces of industrial science (Michel Rolland) and terroir-free multinational corporation (Robert Mondavi) a noble one. Who wouldn't root for them to prevail?

But the situation on the ground is far different. The Languedoc cooperatives are creatures of the market as much as Mondavi—more perhaps, since Mondavi at least can sometimes shape his market to a certain extent, whereas the history of the cooperatives is mainly that they react to the market. Mondavi, and the large-scale commercial winemakers that he represents in *Mondovino*, must make better wines because of competition. Who will buy cheap bad wine when, in today's global market, there is always the option of better, cheaper wine? That's one element of the Two Buck Chuck effect.

The truth is that many of the Languedoc cooperatives are dinosaurs—creatures of a previous era when quality mattered little, quantity counted for a lot, and French wine consumption was high. They are victims of globalization and Two Buck Chuck. In today's world, with per capita wine consumption in a free fall in France and other Old World markets and global competition heating up, the Languedoc cooperatives and the world's largest vineyards are threatened. Does the world really need them and their wines anymore? No. Not unless they change—adapt to changing market conditions.

And some of the cooperatives have indeed adapted, by investing in new techniques and equipment, replanting vineyards with dense rows (to reduce vigor and improve quality) of quality grapes, and hiring one of the flying winemakers like Michel Rolland to introduce modern winemaking techniques. Some would say that the wine that results has been McDonald-ized or Mondavi-ized, since it has more in common with wines from Chile, California, and Australia than it does with the harsh and bitter Carignan-based wines of recent tradition.

But resistance to these changes is strong and it is easy to understand why. At one time the Languedoc vignerons saw a vast market before them, only to find themselves under the thumb of the merchants who controlled access to that market, the négociants. The only way they could escape that dilemma was to form cooperatives, which gave them supply power to match the demand power of the other side. But now that supply power has slipped away again and what are they to do? An alliance with Mondavi would formalize the pressure to change. Better access to global markets, which Mondavi could provide, would come with a loss in power and independence. It would be the railroad story all over again.

And so the real story is revealed. It is not about tradition and terroir. It is about power and autonomy. Having been powerless once, the growers of the Languedoc fear they will become powerless again. So they cling to the false security of their cooperative and hope, falsely again, that mediocre wine will come back into style. They are terroirists in *Mondovino*, but their motivation is less a noble principle than it is power.

ASTÉRIX THE GAUL VERSUS MONDAVI THE AMERICAN

The terroirists' leader is Aimé Guibert. Or so the film suggests. This makes a good story because Guibert is such a colorful character, a sort of winemaking Astérix the Gaul (a popular French cartoon character); he lacks only the extravagant mustache to complete the picture. Except that where Astérix opposes Roman imperialism, Guibert seems to think of himself as leader of the resistance to imperialism of the foreign corporate kind.

This image, which is easy to take from *Mondovino*, is filled with irony. Aimé Guibert is an unlikely terroirist and the enemy that he opposes is not as foreign as it seems. The battle we see in parts of *Mondovino* is less about wine than it is about gloves.

Aimé Guibert's family business wasn't wine, it was gloves. The Guiberts were a major Parisian manufacturer of gloves until globalization in the form of cheaper gloves from Asia put them out of business. The property that is now their wine estate, Mas de Daumas Gassac, was purchased as a vacation retreat with no thought of making wine. This changed when a professor of oenology from the University of Bordeaux who happened to visit recognized the outstanding potential of the soil and site for making fine wine. (I suspect that the site wasn't previously developed as a vineyard because its higher altitude made it unsuitable for high-volume heat-loving Carignan grapes.)

The first vines were planted in 1974, but they weren't the grapes of local tradition, they were high-quality "international" varieties, fitting for an enterprise that aspired to an international reputation. Today the vineyard includes grapes traditionally associated with Bordeaux (Cabernet Sauvignon, Merlot), Burgundy (Pinto Noir, Chardonnay), and the Italian Piedmont (Nebbiolo, Barbera) as well as a number of quality varieties historically associated with the Languedoc. The first vintage was made in 1978 under the supervision of Emile Peynaud. Peynaud was a famous oenologist at the University of Bordeaux and one of the first internationally famous winemaking consultants. The villainous Michel Rolland was his pupil! Peynaud shook up the wine world in the postwar era by putting taste above tradition (demand above supply, to use my terms). He advocated strict control of all elements of winemaking from vine to bottle and introduced many of the vineyard and cellar techniques that are standard practice in quality winemaking today.

Under Peynaud's influence Mas de Daumas Gassac produced really excellent wines that were nothing like the cheap plonk that flooded the Languedoc plains. Of course it was different: different grapes, low yields, stressed vines, no fertilizers, modern winemaking techniques, and an aim to exploit the potential of an exceptional vineyard site. Daumas Gassac wines are built to be aged—decades are required for the wine to achieve its full potential according to Guibert, unlike the ready to drink Chateau Cash Flow wine of the region. The wine expresses its terroir, but I have to think that it does so not because this is natural, but because it is the intentional consequences of cold calculation. Daumas Gassac is often called the "Grand Cru of Languedoc," which is meant as a compliment, comparing the wines to the best of Bordeaux, but the real truth is that they are Bordeaux wines made in Languedoc and therefore selling at lower prices.

Although I am sure that he would object to this comparison, I think you might call Aimé Guibert the Robert Mondavi of the Midi. Mondavi built his famous Napa Valley winery at roughly the same time that Guibert built his. Both operations were driven by a strategy of quality instead of quantity, which ran counter to the prevailing pattern. Both based their best wines on Bordeaux grape varieties. Both were successful but in different ways—Mondavi in the big American way and Guibert in the cunning French way. Of course there are differences, but they only add to the irony. The Mondavi family business was wine, not gloves, for example, and the Mondavi Napa project was an intentional business risk, not the happy accident of a well-placed vacation home. Guibert was a victim of globalization, since global competition ruined his glove business. Mondavi was a victim in a different way. His attempts to harness globalization and expand his business weakened his control of it until finally it was bought up by one of the world's biggest wine producers, Constellation Brands. Probably Guibert fears that the same could happen to him.

It seems to me that Aimé Guibert doesn't really have much in common with the Languedoc vignerons he appears to champion and represent in *Mondovino*. Well, he does share one thing: fear of foreign competition and it is a legitimate concern for anyone at the margin of an industry. Guibert is on the margin in the sense that he cannot really overcome the fact that he is a Languedoc producer and will never be able to get top dollar (or top euro, I suppose) for his wine. If Guibert makes the best wine in Languedoc this will not pay as well (or provide as much prestige, which is important, too) as making, say, the thirtieth best wine in Bordeaux. Guibert's wines sell for less than some of Mondavi's. The Languedoc growers and their cooperatives are on the margin, too, but in a different sense. They need to make better wine, not more wine, and they need to do it in a market where demand is falling and foreign supply is on the rise. They have the largest vineyard in the world, but that doesn't really mean a thing if no one wants to buy their wine.

WE HAVE MET THE ENEMY . . . AND HE IS US!

Who is the enemy? It is easy to say that it is Robert Mondavi, the American invader with the Italian sounding name who is not the enemy himself but represents the enemy, the global wine market and the need for supply to adapt to demand in that market. But, really, I think the greater threat is closer to home. A better symbol of the global market and how to succeed in it, which is what the Languedoc cooperatives must confront, is a Frenchman with an Italian sounding name, Robert Skalli.

Robert Skalli is the founder of what is called today the Skalli Group, a holding company that is one of the largest producers of wines in the Languedoc. The Skalli conglomerate makes branded varietal wines (just like Mondavi) and sells them in France and around the world, just like Mondavi. The latest news is that Skalli is taking its wine to the Indian market.

Skalli's story provides us with a particularly French image of wine and globalization. Robert Skalli's parents were *pied noirs*, French migrants to Algeria. Many pied noirs emigrated to Algeria starting in the 1870s, when phylloxera wiped out vineyards and grower incomes in the Languedoc. The Skallis left

France in the 1930s, presumably in search of greater opportunity in North Africa—and they found it. Robert-Elle Skalli, Robert Skalli's grandfather, built an empire on grain and wine. By the time that Francis Skalli took over from his father after World War II, the family business included a huge grain operation, Rivoire et Carré with a mill in Marseilles; the number two pasta company in France, Lustucru; a vineyard in Corsica; a rice producer, Taureau Aile, and of course vineyards in Algeria. By 1964 the Skalli vineyards in Algeria spread over 600,000 acres, which is nearly as large as all the vineyards in Languedoc today (700,000 acres, which is much less than a few years ago). This was the wine that the French négociants blended with the weaker Languedoc product to make industrial strength *vin du jour* and they made vast quantities of it.

Like many other pied noirs families, the Skalli eventually fled to France as a result of the Algerian war and its independence in 1962. They settled in the Languedoc and went about rebuilding their business. Robert Skalli entered his father's and grandfather's business in the 1970s and, as part of his education, studied and worked (as a flying intern) with winemakers in Australia and the United States. Significantly, according to the official company history, he worked with Robert Mondavi, who introduced him to the idea of branded varietals and opened his eyes to a different vision of the wine business, one based not on the condition of supply (and the traditional practices and regulations governing production) but on demand and the development of vineyard, cellar, and marketing techniques that would provide buyers with wine that they could understand and appreciate, and that they would buy.

Skalli returned to France and began to organize a business to make the clean, consistent, midrange varietal wines that he saw in California and Australia. He established partnerships with growers and cooperatives in the Languedoc, providing financing for the process of pulling out their tough old vines and replanting with market-friendly varieties like Merlot and Chardonnay. Replanting is expensive, both in direct outlays and in lost production while the vines mature. I suppose having the backing of the profitable Skalli grain business was useful in this transformation process.

The main Skalli brand, Fortant de France, was established in 1983 to produce and market these wines both in France and in twenty-five foreign countries. Kobrand distributes these wines in the United States. The Cabernet Sauvignon sells for about $6. There is a cheaper brand, Couleurs Du Sud, sold mainly in European hypermarkets. There is also a kosher wine line.

A premium brand called simply F. (for Francis Skalli, Robert's father) is a Languedoc wine that "dares" to approach Bordeaux "Grand Cru perfection," according to the marketing literature. It is made from the best grapes from the best sites in the Skalli portfolio, blended under the watchful eye of Michel Rolland and sells for about the same as Aimé Guibert's Daumas Gassac, the other famous Bordeaux wine made in the Languedoc.

The Skalli family now concentrates on wine—the grain and pasta businesses have been sold or spun off. They have wine interests in Languedoc, the Rhone Valley, in Corsica, where they own the largest private vineyard, and in California. Skalli bought what is now the St. Supery winery in Napa Valley in 1982. St. Supery is best known for its Sauvignon Blanc and Cabernet Sauvignon, which sell in the $20–$30 range. Skalli credits Mondavi with helping him make this investment. And in return, Skalli supported Mondavi's aborted attempt to invest in the Languedoc on the logic, I believe, that Mondavi would draw favorable attention to the Languedoc, which would benefit both family businesses.

Robert Skalli owns vineyards, of course, but he's not a vigneron. He is really a négociant. Most of his wines are made from grapes supplied under long-term contract and subject to strict control. Some of the wine is made by local winegrowers and cooperatives, too, also under tight control. The resulting wines are frequently criticized for being soulless—for lacking terroir. But I can't help but observe that this is a good thing, in the case of the Languedoc, where the wines of recent memory have been acidic, bitter, and thin and often produced in such excess supply that they end up being distilled to make industrial alcohol.

I can also appreciate how Skalli's success must feel to many of the local growers and cooperatives who are not part of his network. The battle in the twentieth century was cooperatives versus négociants—supply versus demand—and the suppliers were able to hold their own, or so it seemed. And now the twenty-first century seems already to belong to Skalli (a pied noir!) and his like and this means that power has shifted to them and the French cooperatives have lost. Mondavi's arrival in Languedoc would not have changed the balance between supply and demand. The balance has already shifted. Mondavi was only a symbol of the change and, because he was an American, a useful target in a country that loves to bash America even as it embraces all things American.

SHARP EDGES AND THE TASTE OF PLACE

As I was revising a draft of this chapter I came into possession of a new book by Jonathan Nossiter, *Mondovino*'s creator.[8] Although *Liquid Memories: Why Wine Matters* is not intended to be a supplement to or continuation of *Mondovino*, I certainly learned quite a bit about the making of the film and its characters and about Nossiter, too. Indeed, the book is really about Nossiter and how wine inspires his memories and provokes his emotions just as a small cake, a madeleine, famously provoked Marcel Proust. It's not my favorite book because I guess I'm not that interested in Nossiter's memories, or at least not as interested as he is, but I did find things to like in it.

In one of my favorite scenes from the book, Nossiter and a filmmaking colleague are driving back from a day of *Mondovino* preshoot research in Burgundy and they talk about why they are so attracted to terroir—why they have become terroirists in the way that I use the word. Members of a somewhat rootless transnational artistic class, they recognize that perhaps terroir is so precious to them because it is something they feel they have lost. Nossiter, the American raised in Paris, now lives in Brazil; well, you can see how he would feel nostalgic for the authentic home terroir he maybe never had. That's an emotion many of us can appreciate.

Another passage subtly probes this same feeling in a different context. Why is terroir and regional identity so important now? Because sharp divisions have caused so much pain and hardship in the past (think Europe and the two world wars). Suppressing differences and rounding off sharp corners to create a more peaceful whole has been the agenda of the last fifty years. Now we find that universalism has gone pretty far, creating the terroir-free transnational world of the European Union and we start to value what we have lost. Sharp edges seem pretty desirable now that we've lost them, even if they sometimes bruise or cut.

I tasted both sides of this problem when we visited Friuli in the Italian northeast a few years ago. We stayed outside of Cormons with the Venica family at their winery estate and visited the Sirk family at La Subida. The land and people of this area were brutalized by the two wars and so, when postwar peace appeared, they gathered grape varieties from around the world and planted them all together in one serene vineyard. The wine from these grapes, *Vino Della Pace* (wine of peace), isn't especially distinctive on the palate as I recall, but is memorable nonetheless for its optimistic symbolism.

We longed for the taste of peace when we didn't have it. Now that we do, we find it a little bland. So we seek out terroir, even if it threatens to divide us once again. Interesting, isn't it? Even in Friuli it is the intensely distinctive local wine of long memory—Pignolo, Schioppettino, Ribolla Gialla—that attracts our attention today, not the wine of peace.

Although Nossiter's book is about cultural politics (if you believe the French title *Le Goût et le Pouvoir*—Taste and Power) and social philosophy (if you consider the American one), it seems to me that a great deal of space is actually given over to wine economics. The business of wine with its commercial pressures, and especially the ethics of wine pricing, gets a great deal of space.

"It occurs to me," Nossiter writes, "that it is impossible to talk about wine without talking about money"; I think he is right. "Wine is inextricably linked to money like all objects of desire in a capital-driven world." He continues,

> Though a given bottle's price varies even more peculiarly than the price of fine arts, a given bottle's price is supposed to be a reflection of its intrinsic values. Whether it is the producer who sets the initial price, or the importer, distributor, or end seller, each time the price of the wine is set an ethical decision has been made in relation to the wine's origins and contents.[9]

Nossiter is disgusted by the religion of money, but in this passage he seems instead to be seduced by it, to accept the premise that market prices are moral judgments even as he protests their verdict. I think the premise is wrong and that intrinsic worth is measured by a different scale. It isn't easy being a terroirist!

TASTING NOTES

Changing Places: The globalization of wine continues, and in late 2011 most of the wine assets of the Skalli empire (see page 178) were purchased by the Boisset family (see page 161). This transaction broadens Boisset's wine footprint in France at the same time that Jean-Charles Boisset has been expanding its presence in California with the acquisition of Raymond Vineyards and the historic Buena Vista Winery.

Twin Peaks: Jean-Charles Boisset and Gina Gallo are now the happy parents of twin daughters. The family recently purchased the former Napa Valley residence of Robert and Margrit Mondavi. There is a *Mondovino* sequel here somewhere, I think!

14

The War on Terroir

The crime was typically French, an *assemblage* of politics, viticulture, and vigilante violence.

> On March 6, [2006] more than 120 masked men armed with crowbars descended on the Mediterranean port city of Sète in France's Languedoc region. They targeted two wine merchants' warehouses, dumping thousands of gallons of wine onto the ground.[1]

The masked men, fashionably dressed in black with balaclavas disguising their identity, were not anarchist protestors of the sort who typically attack McDonald's restaurants and Starbucks stores at meetings of the World Trade Organization. Nor were they the radical Arab terrorists who inhabit the nightmares of paranoid National Front voters in the South of France. Some of them drove tractors.

> More *vignerons* formed a roadblock on the highway between Montpellier and Béziers, blocking traffic and setting a police car on fire. When the police arrested nine of the men and brought them to trial, the court simply released them. Charges were dropped against five, while four received suspended one-month jail terms.

It was easy to tell who was behind the attack. A press photo shows "CRAV" scrawled on the wall next to a now-empty wine tank that was previously full of cheap Spanish wine destined for French supermarket shelves. CRAV terroirists fight fire with fire. Each bottle of New World wine is a "bomb targeted at the heart of our rich European culture."[2] No wonder they feel it necessary to respond in kind, with explosives and guerrilla raids.

And no wonder their destructive acts are tolerated, apparently even by the courts. They are the resistance, like during German occupation, not criminals. They resist the occupation of France by the unsophisticated wines (and cultures) of Mondavi's world.

CRAV stands for Comité Régional d'Action Viticole (the Regional Committee for Viticultural Action), a group of about a thousand protesters and activists who are outraged at . . . at what? Well, at everything, really. Everything that threatens their idea of *terroir*, their notion of French wine. So they are mad at the hypermarkets, who sell cheap imported wine in cardboard Tetra Paks for a euro a liter, undercutting French producers. They are mad at the European Union for kicking the Common Agricultural Policy (CAP) subsidy stool out from under them and forcing them to compete with foreign producers in a game increasingly played by international, not French, rules. They are mad at their fellow Frenchmen and women, too, for seemingly abandoning wine as the beverage of choice and drinking more beer, soda, and water.

CRAV has a lot to be angry about and it all got worse in 2009 as the continuing effects of the economic crisis added to the pressures facing Languedoc vignerons. No wonder they threatened that "blood will flow" if French president Nicolas Sarkozy did not find a way to push French wine prices higher.[3] CRAV struck again, vandalizing equipment and burning barrels at a négociant facility near Beziers and at a cooperative in Clermont l'Herault. The war goes on; the resistance will not yield.

THE WAR ON TERROIR

Terroirists have an important role to play in the future of wine, even the black-clad activists of CRAV (although I admit that I don't see them as *especially* important, not unless Jonathan Nossiter decides to make *Mondovino 2: CRAV Strikes Back*).

Globalization and Two Buck Chuck are agents of change and change is very disruptive. It threatens vested interests and imbedded values. You can't expect such change to go unopposed. Two of my favorite political economists explained how and why.

Joseph Schumpeter[4] was perhaps the first political economist after Marx to take change seriously as an economic force. He compared the economy to a living organism with two interdependent types of systems. One, which you can compare to the circulatory system, was meant to sustain the organism while a second governed growth and development. The sustaining system needed to be constant and consistent, but the growth system operated in fits and starts—we call them "growth spurts" in young people. Both systems need to work well to sustain people through their lives and societies over time.

Growth spurts and the punctuated equilibria of personal development are disruptive—you surely know this lesson if you have ever had to buy shoes for or give relationship advice to a teenager. Schumpeter coined the term *creative destruction* for periods of disruptive economic change. New products, processes, and opportunities are created but they threaten or replace older elements of the economy. Schumpeter was thinking about the first industrial revolution (change due to the introduction of steam power) and the second industrial revolution (electrical and chemical innovations), but his ideas apply pretty well to the information-driven postindustrial revolution of today as well.

Karl Polanyi[5] went beyond Schumpeter and created the theory of the "double movement." Creative destruction does more than open some doors and close others, disrupting profits, income, and investment opportunities; it also challenges fundamental values and shreds the fabric of social relations. You cannot expect society to sit quietly while this destruction takes place. So a dialectic is unleashed, which is the heart of the double movement. Economic change (the first movement) provokes social reaction (the second movement) and it is the combination of the two that pushes economy and society forward. The future is not just one movement but both in a continuing dynamic interaction.

I first thought seriously about the double movement when I was asked to edit a book about globalization in the twentieth century for a series the *New York Times* was putting out.[6] I was given one hundred years of the *Times* to work with—all the news articles, book reviews, editorials and op-eds, obituaries, photos, and cartoons—and asked to tell the story of the rise of the global economy. I think the publisher expected me to tell a simple story of globalization's rise and rise, but that's not how I read the history. Instead I drew on Schumpeter and Polanyi and found articles in the *Times* that underlined the disruptive nature of globalization (easy to do, especially with the financial crises of the late twentieth century) and the social and political reactions (easy to do, both in the 1930s and at the end of the century, with the anti-WTO protests in Seattle).

You can't understand the history of the past without taking into account both disruptive change and the political and social reactions to it. You can't understand the future without taking both forces into account either. The future of wine will be the story of globalization, which brings new products, producers, and consumers into the market, the rationalizing and commercializing force that I associate with Two Buck Chuck, and the reaction of those whose interests and values are threatened—the revenge of the terroirists.

A RIESLING RENDEZVOUS

It is easy to think that the New World is the source of creative destruction and the Old World has the terroirists, but as we saw in the last chapter, the wine world is not as simple as that. Change is everywhere—it is as French or Italian as it is Australian or American. And resistance is widely diffused as well, both the fashionable French kind and less dramatic but possibly more useful forms found elsewhere.

These facts were driven home with particular force when I attended the Riesling Rendezvous meetings sponsored by Chateau Ste. Michelle and Dr. Loosen, a famous producer from Germany's Mosel region. Chateau Ste. Michelle is America's largest Riesling producer; it makes a wine called Eroica in cooperation with Dr. Loosen. Riesling producers from around the world came to the conference.

The Riesling Rendezvous was a chance to see the future of wine developing right before my eyes. I think that I have literally never been in a room with more terroirists at once! Riesling is thought to be a wine that most particularly captures the essence of the time and place. It is (or can be, at least) a true somewhere wine. I certainly felt a sense of somewhere, particularly during an unexpectedly intense tasting of German and Austrian wines led by *über-terroirist* Terry Theise.

The key to these wines was the fact that they were local, not global, and made to exacting personal standards, not commercial market norms. The intensity of the feelings these producers held was explained in part by their personal motivations—no one becomes a Riesling winemaker because it seems like an easy way to get rich. Rieslings are the great underappreciated wine. Like Rodney Dangerfield, Rieslings "can't get no respect," or at least not the respect that their proponents (me included) think they deserve.

But I think there was more to it than this. Riesling makers everywhere have had a particularly unfortunate experience of the globalization and Two Buck Chuck phenomena before. They were the victims, you see, of the Curse of the Blue Nun, which tainted the markets for their products for years. That's why they are the Rodney Dangerfield of wines.

Destructive market forces pushed them into a corner, with their backs to the wall, defending their territory, their terroir. But they didn't want to turn their back on those forces, exactly, because they really need them. Globalization . . . well, that's a given for producers who have gathered in the United States from their homes in France, Germany, Austria, Canada, Australia, and New Zealand, and six American wine regions (California, Oregon, Washington, Idaho, Michigan, and New York). Globalization is what they were, terroir is what they had and, well, Two Buck Chuck was the thing that they either had to master—to bend to serve their needs—or destroy. And, CRAV aside, it didn't seem likely that they would destroy it.

So much of the conversation was very constructive—the sort of discussions that I see as an important part of the future of wine. The world of Two Buck Chuck is a world of brands. Quality Riesling is a brand, of sorts, but not a very successful brand. Why? And what can be done about it? There were obviously many opinions and I don't think a unanimous response was possible, but an International Riesling Foundation was formed to try to make progress on common issues (a terroirist foundation!)

THE LEMON WINE PROBLEM AGAIN

Although I don't think any of the winemakers would put it this way, I think they settled on the "lemon wine" problem, which I discussed in an earlier chapter, as an area where progress could be made. Wine is an experience good—you don't know if you will like a particular wine until you try it. If the particular qualities of a kind of wine are not very obvious, you may run into several "lemons"—wines that don't suit your taste (no matter how good they might be in their own way)—on your way to a wine you really like. The higher the risk of lemons, the less likely consumers are to continue to make purchases.

Brands are of course one solution to the lemon wine problem. Consumers who couldn't make sense of indecipherable German wine labels could trust the lady in the blue dress (in the blue bottle). They might not have bought the best German wines, but they avoided purchasing ones that they didn't like.

Rieslings are complex wines (or can be) but the lemon wine problem comes down to a question of sweetness. Rieslings can be very dry or very sweet or anything in between. Consumers looking for one kind of Riesling find it difficult to avoid the other, hence the lemon problem and low wine sales. The International Riesling Foundation came up with a solution, albeit a partial one—a uniform voluntary dry/sweet Riesling Tasting Profile scale that many producers have adopted. The hope is that it will make Rieslings more transparent to buyers and, like a brand, give them more confidence. But without the negative associations that brands carry and without in any way interfering with the pursuit of distinctive terroir.

In the future I think that the Two Buck Chucks of the wine world will try to emulate the terroirists as they seek to hold on to consumers who start out in the lower half of the wine wall and, for reasons of their own, slowly work their way to the top. And I think that terroirists like the Riesling producers I met will borrow some of the tools and techniques of branded goods to create a global market for their distinctly local wines. I am too hard-headed to believe that it is always a win-win situation when opposing groups meet, but I am romantic enough to think that at least sometimes good things can happen.

I suppose my optimistic attitude is based on my earlier research into the Slow Food movement.[7] Slow Food doesn't so much wish to oppose fast food and the fast world as seek to offer an alternative to it. Significantly, like some of the Riesling terroirists I met, they use the tools of the enemy to try to defeat it. That, not CRAV's terrorist *terroirism*, is a key part of the future of wine.

SECOND THOUGHTS ABOUT TERROIR

I'm an optimist that thoughtful terroirists will complete the double movement and prevent globalization and Two Buck Chuck from evolving into the sort of destructive competition that terrorist *terroirists* fear, but I admit that it isn't a sure thing. Wine lovers like to sniff and swirl (and sometimes spit!) as they rhapsodize about the local characteristics that they find in their glass, but the fact is that terroir is a contested idea. Not everyone takes terroir as seriously as the terroirists themselves do.

And it is easy to see why. Most products and services we buy and use today are pretty terroir-free—they could come from anywhere and go to anywhere. When the particular local attributes of a product—its somewhereness—are stressed, we wonder if it is real or just hype. I see this all the time on restaurant menus, where it seems like each additional adjective pushes the cost up a few bucks. A grilled chicken breast is usually a good deal cheaper than a grilled free-range product from a particular farm and region. Is it real or just marketing hype? Some of both, I suppose.

Voices are heard inside the wine business that argue that it is possible to make great wine almost anywhere if the right choices are made in the vineyard and the cellar. Michel Rolland, the devil in *Mondovino*, is often linked with this view—a fair association, I suppose, since he makes wine on several continents. Is terroir just an excuse for bad wine? Sometimes, I think, it is!

Sometimes attacks on terroir come from unexpected sources. In his 2008 book *Bordeaux/Burgundy: A Vintage Rivalry*, French cultural critic Jean-Robert Pitte argues that, although terroir is real, the character of fine wine is often much more determined by other factors.[8] One argument is that the association between terroir and great wine is a self-sustaining virtuous cycle.

If your wine was identified as great in the famous Bordeaux Classification of 1855, for example, then it is natural that the vineyards and winemaking have received enormous attention and investment over the years, and that this extra effort alone may be responsible for its exceptional quality (as compared to a wine that was omitted in the 1855 rankings and so has languished in terms of both input and output all these years). I'm sure that the idea of virtuous and vicious cycles in wine is true to at least some extent. Wine becomes great because it is said to be great just as some celebrities are famous for being famous. The fact that the Classification of 1855 was based on market prices not critical assessment reinforces the argument.

Pitte also asserts the market terroir is as important as vineyard qualities. Wine evolves, he argues, to suit the tastes and requirements of the people who buy it. So Burgundy, for example, is different from Bordeaux not just because of climate and geography but also because historically Burgundy was the wine of the French court and Bordeaux was the wine of British aristocracy. Since these two groups were so different in many ways (and shipping the wine to them involved such different challenges), it is unsurprising that the wines themselves are so different.

I appreciate the importance of market terroir. It is hard to make a living selling bad wine to a sophisticated clientele and perhaps even harder to profit selling good wine to undemanding customers. The former won't buy if they have better choices while the latter will balk at the required price. Great art requires both great artists and an appreciative (and hopefully affluent) audience. Supply and demand.

TROUBLE IN TERROIR-DISE

CRAV terrorists threaten local winemakers in the Languedoc who forsake Old World ways, but bigger forces threaten proponents of terroirism in general. I'm not talking about critics like Robert Parker or big multinationals like Gallo and Constellation Brands . . . or even intellectuals like Jean-Robert Pitte. The biggest threat is more fundamental and forceful. It strikes at the root of the very concept of terroir. It is huge, bigger than any vineyard or wine region. It is everywhere and it is coming forward with surprising speed.

I'm talking about global climate change. The whole notion of terroir is built on the idea that through decades of trial and error it is possible to understand the relationship between wine, vine, and society. CRAV's black-clad activists protest threats to this balance. But global climate change threatens to sweep this all away, or at least to alter it fundamentally.

Wine is the canary in the coal mine in terms of global climate change. Although we think of vines as robust plants, sending out new shoots every year, in fact they are quite delicate, like roses in a way, sensitive to natural threats and climate and weather changes. (If you have visited a vineyard you might have seen roses planted at the ends of the vine rows. Roses and vines suffer from some of the same plant diseases and the roses are there not just because they are pretty but also as an early warning indicator of trouble.)

Different grape varieties perform best in quite specific climate conditions and global climate change threatens to change growing conditions in all the major wine-producing countries and regions—some more than others, but all are affected.

I know that many people are skeptical about the idea of climate change, but the evidence from the vineyard (as summarized in an article in *Decanter* magazine) is very persuasive.[9] Average vineyard temperatures rose between 1950 and 1999 by more than 1.5 degrees Celsius in California's Napa Valley, Washington's Columbia Valley, and Italy's Chianti region, for example. Bordeaux, Burgundy, the Rhone Valley, Oregon's wine-producing areas, and Rioja warmed up almost as much. Even the regions least affected by higher temperatures—the Mosel Valley, Alsace, Champagne, South Africa, and the Barossa Valley—experienced significantly higher temperatures. Conservative forecasts suggest that warming will continue and in fact accelerate between 2000 and 2049, with further temperature increases ranging from less than one degree Celsius in South Africa to more than two degrees Celsius in a number of regions including Portugal, Bordeaux, Burgundy, Barolo, and the Loire, Rhone, Barossa, Napa, and Columbia Valleys.

These temperature increases will potentially transform the accepted terroir of many important wine regions.[10] Pinot Noir, for example, is a cool climate grape that produces quality in the 14 to 16 degrees Celsius temperature band. Some regions that were great Pinot Noir zones in 1950 will be outside this range (or on the threatened edge) in 2050 if the predictions hold. Warm zones, suitable for Merlot and Cabernet Sauvignon will become hot zones, where Zinfandel and Nebbiolo do best. Hot zones will become too hot for quality wine grapes at all, with Zinfandel yielding to table grapes or raisins or perhaps other types of crops altogether.

It is estimated that that climate change is likely to push today's terroir toward the poles by between 280 and 500 km (about 200 to 300 miles) by 2050.[11] The impact of climate change won't be as simple as just moving north, but it will be just as disruptive—perhaps even more so, since rising temperatures (and shifting latitudes) are not the whole story. Climate change also brings increasingly unstable weather patterns and longer growing seasons (more days between the last front of spring and the first one of winter). One study indicates that the frost-free period for the North Coast region of California increased by sixty-eight days between 1949 and 2002. That is an incredible change. (The average increase for all winegrowing areas studied was thirty-four days—one whole month!) The number of very hot days has increased in many areas while the threat of deep freeze has diminished.[12] These factors change the terroir equation just as much as warmer weather.

Climate change has the potential to alter many of the common assumptions about wine today and its future, too. As winemakers and sellers adapt, globalization and Two Buck Chuck's creative destruction will be compounded by nature's own. We don't have to wait for forty years to see this, however. Grapes are mainly water (water plus magic, I suppose) and in terms of water the climate change future is now.

DROUGHT AND WATER FOOTPRINTS

The Bible tells us that Jesus turned water into wine (John 2:1–11)—a miracle! Given the amount of water used in making wine today I think the miracle isn't so much the conversion itself (no sacrilege intended) as the efficiency with which it was accomplished. Jesus didn't waste a drop. Improving water use in winemaking is a serious issue today and it is an early symptom of the climate change problem.

Droughts and increasing water scarcity in wine-producing areas are perhaps the most visible and immediate indicators that precious terroir is slipping away. The supply of water for wine production is limited by nature, of course; and climate change, by magnifying weather extremes, makes the problem worse. All agriculture suffers when water becomes scarce and drought conditions force both a general reduction in farm output and also a shift away from the most water-intensive crops to those that use water more sparingly. In Australia, for example, we have seen a decline in grape production in some areas due to drought and a shift from rice to grapes in other areas.

Water use in wine grape production varies considerably. Irrigation isn't always necessary or even desirable, but high-volume production is very water dependent. It takes 75 gallons of water in the vineyard to grow the grapes for one gallon of wine in the California North Coast area. That seems pretty inefficient until you compare it with Central Valley production, where the ratio is 430 gallons in the vineyard to one gallon of wine! Water is also used in some areas for frost protection, which adds to the total water bill.

Water use doesn't end once the grapes have been harvested. On average it takes about 6 gallons of water in the cellar to make a gallon of wine. Barrel washing and tank cleaning account for much of the water use, but everything in a wine cellar needs to be as clean as possible, and water is often the most convenient tool. The trick, as many wineries have discovered, is to conserve and recycle. High pressure/low flow nozzles and barrel-cleaning rigs can do more with less. Waste water can be collected and filtered for many uses from irrigation to flushing the toilets. Erath Winery in Oregon employs a filtration process that allows it to reuse 97 percent of winery processing water in one way or another. (Local ryegrass farmers use the rest as fertilizer.) Snoqualmie Vineyards uses just 2.9 gallons of water in the cellar per gallon of wine, an indication of the sort of savings that are possible.

It's only a matter of time, I think, until we start worrying about our *water footprint* as well as our *carbon footprint*. You can learn more about the water footprint concept at www.WaterFootprint.org. Here are some estimates of water costs associated with various products as reported on their website.

- One cup of tea: 30 liters
- One slice of bread: 40 liters
- One apple: 70 liters
- One glass of beer: 75 liters
- One glass of wine: 120 liters
- One cup of coffee: 140 liters
- One glass of milk: 200 liters
- One liter of wine: 960 liters
- One hamburger: 2,400 liters

I have seen reports that a Big Mac's water footprint is 5,000 liters, a huge number but understandable when you consider that the production of beef and cheese are both very water intensive (particularly when the cattle are raised on diets of irrigated grains instead of natural grasses). I guess a kilo of beef requires 15,500 liters of water. Amazing!

These figures are estimates of the total water use, including transportation and packaging, which is why the wine figures are so high. I'm sure that it takes a lot of water to produce and clean wine bottles. The labels (paper), closures, and shipping boxes add to the water footprint. It all adds up, for wine as for other products. It's a problem now that will only get worse as climate change progresses.

HITTING THE RESET BUTTON

As I read the studies, it seems to me that global climate change threatens a giant "reset" for the world of wine. I think everyone (or nearly everyone) is going to have to rethink which wines they make, where, and how.

What can be done? Some winemakers, like terroirist John Williams of Napa Valley's famous Frog's Leap Cellars, take the big perspective. Global climate change isn't a wine problem, it's a global human problem and the best way to respond is by doing everything possible to address its causes. "I worry about global warming, but I worry about it at the humanity scale, not the vineyard scale," he says.[13] Williams has a great deal at stake since his Napa Valley vineyards are not just organic but dry farmed (no irrigation).

I find it interesting that so little attention has been paid to climate change effects on wine so far. Many of the stories I've read focus on alcohol levels and English wine. The alcohol story is fairly simple: longer, warmer growing seasons produce riper grapes and the extra sugar becomes extra alcohol during fermentation. Even with a good deal of wine undergoing partial dealcoholization, alcohol levels have crept up by as much as two percentage points in some regions. My favorite California Zinfandels had about 12 percent alcohol in the 1970s, but it is hard to find one with less than 14 percent today. Wines with too much alcohol can be unbalanced and there are certainly negative health effects to consider.

The story of English wine gets a lot of attention, too. For years English wine was a joke. London is at about the same latitude as Calgary, Canada, which seems ridiculously far north to produce quality wines. But English wines today are gaining respect, especially the sparkling wines. The reason: higher temperatures, longer growing seasons, and, in some areas, the same chalky soil that gives Champagne's sparkling wines their distinctive style. It is no joke to consider that Champagne producers may one day jump the English Channel in hot pursuit of their runaway terroir.

But there's little attention given to the bigger problem. Perhaps that's because climate change creeps up a little at a time, not all at once like a hurricane or tsunami. Adjustments like gradual alterations in the vineyard and winemaking cycle and even the advent of dealcoholization bring about incremental adjustments that only seem significant in retrospect. The climate change issue is lost in the jumble of daily events.

But perhaps there's a bigger reason climate change has been ignored. So far, we like it! So far the warmer temperatures and longer growing seasons have actually improved the quality of wine in most regions. If wines are riper and more alcoholic, well this seems to suit the tastes of many consumers, especially those who prefer New World wine styles. But the world may be approaching the tipping point, where the factors that have made wine better and more widely produced become the ones that make future vintages worse and slowly erode the edges of precious terroir.

I've written a lot about financial crises and I know that it is hard to get anyone's attention during the upswing of a boom market. Bubbles feel great right up until the moment they explode. Even when all the facts and figures point to only one thing—collapse!—that boom market high is simply irresistible. I admit that it's probably an overstatement, but maybe it is not unfair to propose that climate change has been driving a global wine boom that is unsustainable if the vineyards keep getting warmer, the seasons longer, and weather patterns more unstable.

And so this is where I feel the terroirists will play an especially useful role in the future of wine. Globalization makes it possible to ignore climate change until it is too late—you can always source your wines from somewhere else, or so it might seem at least for a while. Is Champagne too hot for sparkling wine? Well, go to England, then Scotland, then Norway. The Two Buck Chuck effect of branded wine could compound this problem. If brands based upon terroir are weakened, then commercial brands become more important and that critical natural connection is lost. The role of the terroirist is to remind, resist, and sometimes, I suppose, even to revolt like the black-clad partisans of CRAV.

I'm counting on the terroirists to come through and temper the excesses that global markets and corporate commercialization can sometimes create. But it's not going to be easy if they have to defend themselves on so many fronts at once. How will it turn out? Well, in wine tasting you learn that sometimes it can be helpful to tilt your glass at an angle and look at the edge of the wine. Sometimes this "sideways" view provides information about the past and clues to the future. It's time to take a sideways look at the future of wine.

15

The China Syndrome

My first taste of Chinese wine was exactly what I expected and quite a shock at the same time. Odd combination of reactions, but sometimes, you know what you are in for but just can't believe that it could be true.

It was a 1999 Changyu Cabernet Sauvignon that Brian West brought back from his semester abroad in Beijing. Changyu is China's oldest winery (and one of the biggest); it was a good example of a midmarket Chinese red wine. I knew what to expect because I'd found a video review of this wine on the Internet that described the wine as being all about ashtray and coffee ground flavors with aromas of urinal crust. Hard to imagine that wine could taste this way (or that a critic would be so familiar with urinal smells). Until you taste it, that is. The description was right on the money. We passed the bottle around so that everyone could get a little taste. A taste of what? The future? Gosh, I hope not!

A Berry Bros. & Rudd report on the future of wine thinks that China might one day make wines to rival Bordeaux. Based on the Changyu, I'd say they have a long way to go, but I wouldn't completely rule it out. Fifty years ago I don't think that anyone would have predicted that New Zealand would make great wines or that the United States would become a leading wine market. Although it is impossible to know for sure, I think that China will be a serious player in the future of wine.

But that bottle of Changyu suggests that much will need to change in China. Although almost everything about wine in China is different (some of it, I'm told, is so fake that it isn't even made from grapes!), I believe that the future of Chinese wine will be shaped by the same forces as elsewhere: globalization, Two Buck Chuck, and the revenge of the terroirists. Turning the wine world "sideways" and taking a good look at this far edge just might tell us something about the future of wine generally. Or at least that's the premise of this chapter. Let's get started.

CHINA DREAMS . . . AND NIGHTMARES

One of the things I uncovered as I studied the history of world trade during the twentieth century for a book on globalization in a *New York Times* series[1] was what I call the China syndrome. The China syndrome is both the dream that China will buy all the goods we try to sell her and the fear that she will turn the tables and take over our markets. The *Times* was full of China syndrome stories a hundred years ago. History buffs might want to look up an article called "The Future of Our Trade with China" that promoted the dream on April 13, 1900, and an early suggestion of the nightmare in "Japan and China Find a Ready Market Here" published on September 3, 1905. Both are reprinted in my *NYT* volume.

The same dreams and nightmares are commonplace today.

I was reminded of this while reading the *Grape Wall of China* blog,[2] a reliable source for China wine news and views. An article by Jim Boyce (a.k.a. Beijing Boyce) caught my eye: "No Worries: Australia Targeting China Wine Market at Every Level."[3] The article tells of Australia's dreams for Chinese wine sales.

The Australian wine industry is dreaming about a Chinese future because its present reality is an emerging nightmare. Australian wine has been battered by a number of factors, both natural and market driven. Although there are many distinctive and delicious Australian wines, "Brand Australia" is pretty much defined by relatively one-dimensional Yellow Tail–class Shiraz and Chardonnay, both of which seem to have fallen from consumer favor. The "brand" was easy to understand and promote, but it didn't have legs, as they say. Many consumers seem to have moved on and there are plenty of options for them to choose from. The recent recession only makes things worse. Too much globalization and Two Buck Chuck—not enough attention to the terroirists' message.

Australia has adopted a new marketing plan called Landmark Australia[4] meant to highlight the quality and diversity of its terroir. It's a good idea but a difficult one to put into practice—hard to un-ring the Yellow Tail bell, if you know what I mean. Beijing Boyce reports that Australia is promoting its new image pretty vigorously in China and by 2009 had risen to number two in bottled wine imports after France. The French have 40 percent of the fine wine market to Australia's 20–22 percent. The United States, Italy, and Chile trail far behind. So perhaps Australia will be successful in redefining itself in a new market and realize its China dream.

But Australia's China dream has become its China nightmare. Foster's, the big Australian beer and wine group, announced in 2010 that they were splitting their profitable beer business away from the loss-making multinational wine group. Rumors immediately began to circulate—who would buy Foster's diversified portfolio of wine brands from France, Italy, Australia, Argentina, New Zealand, and the United States given global overcapacity?

The whispered answer—unconfirmed when this was written—was China! That's the nightmare part of the China syndrome: the fear that China will start out by buying up your distressed wines at low prices, then buy up your distressed wine brands at low prices, and then . . . well, sell them back to you at premium prices!

ALL THE WINE IN CHINA

Many people are surprised to learn that China is an important wine nation. Tea? Yes, of course. Wine? Really! Well, wine has a long history in China, reaching back more than two thousand years to the first wine imported from Ferghana in what is now Uzbekistan. It wasn't until the nineteenth century, however, that more than a trickle of wine was produced or consumed. Western missionaries brought grapes and wine to China along with their bibles as they did in so many other countries. The real roots of today's industry were planted in the late 1800s, however, when Changyu and other wineries were founded, mainly to produce wines for the foreign communities in the commercial centers.

The communist government expanded wine production after the 1949 revolution. Wine was promoted as a form of alcohol made from abundant fruit (grapes, both *vitis vinifera* and indigenous varieties, and other fruits) in order to reduce use of precious food grains for alcohol production. Wine was meant to replace beer or grain spirits in the diet. Wine was typically made from a combination of grapes and other fruits. I understand that it is still sometimes necessary to specify *grape wine* in China, since generic *wine* may be made out of any number of fruits. It is probably not surprising that Chinese who were brought up on these mixed-fruit wines might today mix dry grape wine with fruit juice or Coke to get a more familiar flavor.

China's vineyards are indeed vast, totaling 6 percent of the world total. There are 453,000 hectares of vineyards in China, which is roughly equal to the U.S. total (380,000 hectares) plus Germany (98,000 hectares) or just over half the vineyard area of France. But 80 percent of the grapes are grown as fruit for the table grape market. About 10 percent of the grapes are dried to make raisins. The remaining 10 percent are winegrapes. China's wine production is relatively small but growing—730 million liters in 2005 compared with 2,546 million liters for the United States and 898 million liters for Germany. China produces about as much wine as Moldova and Romania combined—a lot of wine, but still just 2.6 percent of the global total according to *The Global Wine Statistical Compendium.*

Comparative wine production statistics for China are a bit problematic because much of the wine produced is not pure grape wine but may be mixed-fruit wine and the rules on what can be labeled Chinese wine are quite, er, flexible. Grape wine needs to be only 50 percent grape wine (the rest can be made from other fruits) and Chinese wine needs to be only 50 percent from Chinese-produced juice. This means that a great deal of the bad wine that tourists report being served is not really grape wine and may be a blend of a little Chinese grape wine and a lot of imported bulk wine of undetermined origin. Rules get bent and outright fraud is not uncommon, I understand. The standards don't encourage quality production, but remember that they are the legacy of a system where wine was valued most as a nongrain source of alcohol.

China had about 450 wine producers at last count, which is fewer than in Washington State. The industry is highly concentrated with four wineries accounting for 60 percent of domestic production and sales. The big four are Great Wall, Dragon Seal, Changyu, and Huadong. Foreign partnerships are common, giving Chinese winemakers access to international technology and expertise. The French multinational Pernod Ricard helped create Dragon Seal in 1987, for example, and Seagram's and Remy Martin have also been involved in joint ventures.

If the quality of the large-scale wineries is disappointing, as many tourists report and my Changyu tasting confirms, the reason can be found in the supply chain. Wine is only as good as the grapes that go into it, or so growers tell me, and the grape supply situation in China is difficult. Most of the winegrapes are grown by families that lease about an acre of land from their local agricultural commune. That acre is typically divided into four or five small plots that are planted with different crops so as to minimize risk. One or perhaps two of the plots may be winegrapes in the vineyard regions. So vineyard scale is impossibly small—smaller even than in the South of France.

These small growers insist on calling the shots, which is natural since they are so dependent upon the success of their tiny farms. The wine producers have little or no control over what these thousands of microvineyards produce, how they are cropped, and when the grapes are picked. Researchers suggest that the grapes are chosen and grown to maximize quantity not quality and that the grapes are picked as soon as possible to minimize risk of poor weather that could destroy the crop. So small crops of flavorful, fully ripe grapes—the winemaker's dream—this is not going to happen in a typical Chinese vineyard.

Grapes sell for as little as $80 a ton, an indication of their poor quality. The rule of thumb in winemaking is that the per-ton price divided by 100 gives you the per-bottle price of the finished wine. So Pinot Noir grapes can sell for $3000 per ton if they have the quality to produce a wine that consumers will pay $30 a bottle for. If the wine isn't good enough to earn $30 per bottle, buying the grapes for $3000 per ton is a money losing deal. Chinese grapes at $80 per ton? Well, if the 1/100 rule translates accurately into Chinese, it means that they are only good enough for 80-cent per bottle (or a dollar per liter) wine.

There is not much incentive for individual growers to sacrifice quantity for quality because their grapes are sold by weight to agents who lump together fruit from dozens or hundreds of individual growers. Good fruit would quickly get mixed with inferior fruit, so why pay more? The local agents often then resell the fruit to regional agents who sell again to the large winemakers. You can just imagine the condition of the fruit by the time it finally gets to the winemaking facility having passed through so many hands. This system is worse than even the most uncompetitive European cooperatives (and I didn't think anything could be worse than that).

Wine is sold in all sorts of ways. The Changyu website offers to let me buy wine by the barrel, which is perhaps what I would do if I owned a restaurant or a village drinks shop where I could decant the wine into bottles, jugs, or any other available container. Economists who study the Chinese wine market are increasingly focusing on supermarkets as a growing distribution vector. Partly I think this is because grocery store sales of wine are increasing, but also I think because these economists are interested in the potential for foreign wine imports. I don't think relatively expensive French or California wines have much chance of penetrating the traditional bulk distribution system where a lot of Chinese wine goes, so supermarkets and restaurants are their best bet. Supermarkets may also eventually play an important role in educating Chinese consumers about wine in general and foreign wine in particular.

The bottom line is that the future of wine in China is difficult to predict. Surely wine consumption will grow as China gets richer and Chinese adopt more Western consumption habits. Wine production will grow, too, and quality will rise as better technology is adopted. But it will be interesting to see how quickly Chinese consumers accept dry Western grape wines after their long experience with mixed-fruit wines. And it will be interesting to see how quickly the quality of grapes can be raised.

It seems to me that the biggest barriers to quality wine are not in the stores or even in the habit of mixing red wine and Coke. The biggest problem remains the sorry state of rural Chinese agriculture—a good reminder that wine is fundamentally a product of the soil.

CRACKING THE CHINESE MARKET

Everyone looks hungrily at China with its growing economy and expanding consumer base. But it is hard to break in. Bulk wine imports (to be blended into "Chinese" wine) are substantial, but at unsustainably low prices. No future there.

France and Spain have had better luck. The French have been able to leverage their reputation and the prestige of their finest producers to carve out an attractive niche market for Bordeaux and Champagne as luxury products. The Spanish achieved success through old-fashioned hard work. They have partnered with Chinese wine producers in both production and distribution. If Chinese wines are improving in quality (and I understand they are) then this is at least in part due to technical improvements facilitated by joint ventures.

Australia is obviously not the only wine-producing country with China on its mind and I was pleased to receive an invitation from ViniPortugal to participate in a recent China seminar program and tasting of Portuguese wines. Sixteen winemakers flew from Lisbon to Beijing to present and promote their wines. This would be a good chance to observe this Old World wine country's China strategy in action. Beijing is a long way to go for an afternoon tasting, so I was represented by my crack China wine research team, Matt Ferchen, who teaches international relations at Tsinghua University, and Steve Burckhalter, who then worked as a translator for the Chinese public relations firm BlueFocus. Matt and Steve, former students of mine at the University of Puget Sound, are not wine experts but they are keen observers of rapidly changing Chinese markets.

Matt said that he was impressed with the wines he tasted.[5]

The first wines I tasted, and the ones I ended up liking the best, were from a cooperative called Adega Coop. de Borba. A couple of the wineries were family owned and there was a kind of earthiness to the wines that I really enjoyed. I was especially impressed with the Portuguese whites, which were all very crisp and I think would go very well with spicy Chinese food.

I find that most of the wines available in Beijing, both foreign and Chinese, are expensive and mediocre or cheap and bad. Across the board the price to quality ratio was just excellent and I really hope that some of these wineries can find distributors here . . . [but] . . . there was only one of the wineries that had any presence in Beijing.

So the product is good and a good value. But that doesn't necessarily solve the Chinese market puzzle.

Most of the representatives seemed rather disappointed that the turnout at the tasting was quite small and that many of those who were in attendance weren't in the wine business (i.e., they didn't see many prospects for finding distributors even if they found possible retail customers). I was asking some of the representatives why Portugal seemed so far behind Spain in terms of entering the Chinese market, especially given what seemed to me the outstanding quality of their product. The answer mostly just seemed to me a question of focus, that somehow the Spanish wine organization was just more aggressive about getting Spanish wines to China and advertising.

Steve also commented on quality and value—and the problem of focus and establishing reputation.

> The[seminar] speaker, who I believe was a Chinese man from Macau, noted the long history of winemaking in Portugal, the long time presence and popularity in Macau ("We drink this all the time in Macau"), the diversity of wines they are able to grow thanks to the wide range of different climates in Portugal, wines unique to Portugal—such as a "green wine" they grow in the North, which he reasoned would do well in China, being 'fruity and sweet'—and finally he also stressed that "Nearly all Portuguese wines are reasonably priced. It's hard to find any in excess of 200 RMB."
>
> He also expounded on why Chinese outside of the Southeast regions don't care for white wines, which I found interesting. As for the growers and the distributors, there was some diversity to be found in "Brand Portugal." Interestingly, some were insistent on showing tasters how they straddled both New and Old World winemaking (actually, the speaker also touched on this, going on about a vineyard that had invited Australian winemakers to teach them in the ways of new world wine). Others, however, were insistent that they were exclusively Old World—"Portugal is Old World. How can it be New World— that's not us."
>
> In response to how they were looking to position their wines, one of the winery reps said that they were looking to focus on promoting, above all, their grapes: the varieties, why they grow so well in Portugal, etc. And their other edge (which I heard from several people) is in pricing, "what you get for X RMB in a Portuguese wine is better than what you get for X RMB in a French wine." That tended to be the dual answer whenever someone brought up how Chinese people generally went straight for French or Italian wines.

Based on Matt's and Steve's reports you can be either an optimist or a pessimist regarding Portuguese wines in China. The upside is that there are many potential advantages, cost being one of them. It is obvious that Portuguese winemakers would like to be seen as a "value" fine wine and avoid the cheap and anonymous bulk wine trap. Good thinking. But then there is a bit of an identity crisis. Old World or New? Well, both—a harder sell. Focus on regions or grapes (or both)? That requires a substantial sustained education program.

Even the most basic question is problematic: red or white? Westerners know that crisp whites like *Vinho Verde* taste great with Asian foods—great to Westerners, anyway. But, as has often been said, the first duty of wine in Asia is to be red.

I'm cautiously optimistic about Portuguese wines in China, especially if they can settle on the right focus and sustain the education/marketing efforts. But they have a long way to go. Steve reports that "I noticed at a store (targeting Western tastes) last night the only Portuguese wines (out of hundreds and hundreds) were four Ports. Haven't been to Carrefour in a while, but I bet it's the same deal."

Good luck to Portugal—and to Australian and American winemakers, too, of course. China is a key market for the future. But scaling the Great Wall is a real challenge and many will be frustrated in the attempt.

THE PAPILLON EFFECT

There is one area where China's wine market power is already being felt: the auction market for iconic wines, especially the first-growth Bordeaux wines that oenophiles and status seekers treasure. The center of the highly publicized market for these wines is shifting to Hong Kong, to be closer to where the money is. Hong Kong abolished its tariff on wine imports in 2008 to facilitate this shift. The tariff on wine was an incredible 80 percent until a few years ago, when it fell to a still hefty 40 percent. So the drop to a zero rate and the price reductions that followed were welcome news indeed for wine drinkers in this prosperous Asian hub.

The world auction market for wine is large and growing. London (with annual wine auction sales of $1.2 billion) and New York are at the traditional centers of this market, but as much as 40 percent of the expensive auction wine is sold to Hong Kong residents. The high taxes on wine discouraged Hong Kong buyers from bringing auction purchases home to drink or to resell, so the wine was held in foreign warehouses (or sometimes in bonded warehouses in Hong Kong).

The impact of Hong Kong's auctions is likely to be felt well beyond Asia and well outside the gilded halls of the auction houses. Have you heard of the butterfly effect? It is the idea that small changes in complex interconnected systems can sometimes produce large effects. The name, coined by Edward Lorenz in 1961, comes from the idea that a butterfly beating its wings in Brazil, by disturbing air flows in ways that compound and multiply, can theoretically cause a hurricane in Texas. It is a famous concept in the field of nonlinear dynamics.

Natural systems are obviously complex and interdependent and sensitive to initial conditions. Tipping points, butterfly effects, and the like are both theoretically possible and empirically observable. Economic systems can have these same properties.[6] This is perhaps especially true for complex global markets, like the market for wine.

The shift in the wine market to Hong Kong should have fairly significant effects on wine flows and prices—especially for trophy French and particularly Bordeaux wines, the object of much London and now Hong Kong auction activity. So I'm calling the effect of the Hong Kong wine tax cut the papillon effect (*papillon* is French for butterfly—if the Hong Kong buyers were focused on Italian wines it would be the farfalla effect). It will be interesting to see just how much market turbulence the Hong Kong tax change creates when all the effects are finally felt.

Will the Hong Kong butterfly's wings cause a tornado in Bordeaux? Prices are already staggeringly high for the most famous and highly rated products. But the really interesting question concerns the side effects in other markets. How will surging Bordeaux prices affect the rest of the wine world? Will the object of speculation remain fairly narrowly focused or will the boom's domain expand to include investment-grade wines from around the world? How far will the papillon effect extend?

And then there is the question of stability. The clear message of the butterfly effect is that the compound effects of small changes may not be sustainable—they can be disruptive and even explosive, like a tornado. Will the Hong Kong tax changes merely shift the wine market centers and expand demand and supply, or will it blow up a bubble, as often happens in financial markets?

China's rising global influence was already clear in 2010 as the peculiar and highly ritualized Bordeaux *en primeur* market enfolded. Most wine is sold on what a financial economist would call a spot market. You pay your money and you take your wine. The exchanges of money and goods are concluded at the same essential moment. The *en primeur* Bordeaux market is more of a futures market. You pay now for wine that will be delivered on release a year or more later. It is a way for some people to lock in delivery before the wine hits the open market and for others to, well, speculate that the market price when the wine is released will be higher than its *en primeur* cost. The producers get their money up front, rather than waiting several years for the wine's release.

One of the things that makes the Bordeaux *en primeur* market unique is that buyers don't really know what they are getting. Bordeaux 2009 was tasted in spring 2010, for example, with the wines only a few months in the barrel and the final choices for blending the wines still months away. Buyers and critics tasted blended barrel samples that might or might not bear much resemblance to the finished product. This matters a lot for those who purchase to drink, but the only thing that matters to speculators is the critics' opinions, since they are likely to influence auction prices.

The 2009 *en primeur* market will go down in history as the first one dominated by Asian (and especially Chinese) buyers. American buyers were pretty much absent from the market, I'm told, mainly for economic reasons. Lots of wines from previous vintages still unsold and prices falling. No need to rush out to get more. But Chinese buyers more than filled the gap. *Decanter*, the self-proclaimed "world's best wine magazine," published its first Chinese language (simplified Chinese, I think) *en primeur* market guide. As wine futurologist, Bob Dylan might have said, you don't need a weatherman to know which way the wine blows!

The emergence of China as an important buyer of investment-grade French wines is a good thing, I suppose. Good for the French sellers, anyway. But it serves to reinforce the problem that Matt Ferchen identified above. Apart from trophy wines that collectors seek out, wine in China tends to be expensive and mediocre (second class imports trading on the prestige of investment wines) or cheap and bad (cursed by that dismal supply chain and mixed with surplus bulk wine from around the world). China won't play an important part in the future of wine—except indirectly through the papillon effect—until something happens to shake things up.

SEVENTY-TWO BUCK CHUCK

Good wine is a matter of balance—take any single feature of wine to the extreme and you spoil it. Too many tannins? Too much acidity? Too much alcohol? Too much sugar? Too much oak? Too much of anything is . . . well, too much. Poor China (or at least poor Chinese wine!) suffers from too much globalization and too much Two Buck Chuck.

At the top end, wine in China is too much about the global wine markets for trophy wines and the emergence of Hong Kong as a leading auction center will only encourage this tendency. The focus on trophy wines that only a few can afford to purchase and even fewer will actually drink distorts much of the market, at least for now, by drawing attention toward the small number of auction-worthy wines and regions and away from other sources of very good wines, like the Portuguese wines that may struggle for a time to find an Asian market.

Down at the bottom of the wine wall, China has taken Two Buck Chuck to an unhealthy extreme, although it is perhaps an understandable exaggeration given wine's particular history in China. German wine drinkers seem to value low price over distinctive quality in their Aldi-brand quotidian wine, but Aldi's wines and their Trader Joe's American relations are at least competent mass-market products. They may not be wines of great distinction, but they aren't really revolting, either.

Chinese mass-market wines are, or at least can be, much worse, and as we've seen, it is the result of both an unsophisticated demand and unreliable supply. If, as I suggested earlier, America's wine culture is still recovering from Prohibition, Chinese wine is still haunted by the specter of communism that redefined the role of wine and left the legacy of small peasant plots that is such a barrier to quality winegrape production.

A 2010 *Wall Street Journal* article on China's wines included tasting notes by a panel of local experts.[7] The nonvintage Changyu Cabernet Sauvignon they sampled sold for the equivalent of $5.40 and reminded them of dirty sweat socks and cleaning fluid—possibly a step up from the one I tasted. At the other extreme, a 1998 Cab from Great Wall was apparently really quite good—"deep colored, full bodied, tannic, but with a lot of fruit." Price? The equivalent of $72. Seventy-two Buck Chuck! Yikes.

The value choice was a $2.87 "dry red wine" from Great Wall. "Clean and pleasant if light and simple, reminding me of the Charles Shaw 'Two Buck Chuck' wines in the U.S." That doesn't sound like high praise, but I think it is. The optimist in me is thinking that the folks at Great Wall have found a way to master that awful grape supply chain and to make decent if unexceptional wine. That would be a big step forward for wine in China. My pessimistic side (after all, I am a "dismal scientist") is pretty sure that bottle was full of cheap bulk wine, probably from Australia, and has more to do with global oversupply than it does with any actual improvement in winemaking in China.

LOST IN TRANSLATION

Recently a group of us tasted the hopeful future of Chinese fine wine, a bottle of 2003 Grace Vineyards Tasya's Reserve Cabernet Franc. Grace Vineyards is often cited as the most promising winemaker in China and the contrast between this bottle and the Changyu was night and day. The attention to detail in the winemaking was evident and the use of estate grapes (rather than the unreliable supply chain cited above) was apparent, too. The contrast between the two wines was stunning, mainly because the Changyu was so very bad, of course, but that didn't stop me from finding out more about Grace Vineyards—I wanted to understand how they could make good wine in such unfavorable circumstances.

Here, briefly, is what I learned. Hong Kong businessman C. K. Chan invested $7 million to build a French-style chateau in Shanxi Province. Most people who see pictures of the winery are fascinated by the chateau building and the paradox of such an ornate structure in the middle of China. I'm more interested in the vineyards, which look just great. I don't know how Judy Leissner, Mr. Chan's daughter, managed to get the resources to plant an estate vineyard, but somehow she did. A reliable source of first quality grapes is an obvious advantage if you are trying to produce quality wine.

Grace also draws upon international connections. A Bordeaux flying winemaker got the project started and an Australian makes the wine today. Torres, the Spanish giant, handles distribution within China (one of its many successful partnerships). International networks come naturally to Ms. Leissner, who is a graduate of the University of Michigan and a veteran of international investment banking at Goldman Sachs.

Grace Vineyards is expanding its production to forty thousand cases and gets lots of attention from the international press. Just as Mondavi was the benchmark when French wine enthusiasts thought about California wine back in the 1970s, Grace is the Chinese standard today.

How does it taste? Well, the *Wall Street Journal's* panel tasted three Grace wines. The 2008 Cabernet ($10) was described as thin, without much character. A 2001 Merlot ($28) was over the hill—on the road to vinegar-ville.

A $42 Bordeaux blend was well balanced and flavorful, the panel said, but lacking depth.

Our Grace Vineyards Cabernet Franc was a solid effort, we thought, but nothing special—a bit light compared with American wines of this type. Writing in *The Wine Economist*, I noted a distinctive "green" taste I associate with wine made from underripe Cab Franc grapes. A problem in the vineyard, I speculated. Maybe the climate's just too contrary to fully ripen these grapes.

A day later one of my readers lobbed in a counterargument.[8] Maybe, he said, that green flavor is intentional. He had heard that this particular flavor is familiar to Chinese consumers and that some Chinese wineries harvest grapes a bit earlier in order to achieve it. It wasn't a flaw in the wine, he suggested, but a feature. Something that makes it Chinese wine, not a Chinese imitation of someone else's wine. It's the Chinese market terroir, if you will. Maybe the thinness that the critics note is another reflection of local taste?

A little research turned up more evidence that the judgments of Western critics might be unfair to Chinese wines. Jeannie Cho Lee, Korea's first Master of Wine, argues that Asian food and wine traditions prime consumers to think about wine differently and to appreciate different qualities in it.[9] Why don't Chinese wine drinkers appreciate that a crisp Pinot Gris pairs nicely with their cuisine? Well, Ms. Lee explains, many Asian cultures do not consume beverages (apart from savory soups) with their meals—they drink them before and after. White wines are generally chilled, of course, and most Asian drinks are warm or room temperature. And the sweetness of a Pinot Gris can seem unrefined to palates that are used to more complex sweet-sour flavor profiles.

Why such a fascination with Bordeaux? It could be the tannins, Ms. Lee argues, which are appealing to wine drinkers from cultures with a tradition of consuming very tannic teas. Even the basic flavor reference points are different, she explains. Westerners think of Pinot Noir in terms of raspberries and strawberries, for example, but the Asian descriptors would be *yangmei* (bayberries), dried wolfberries, and dried bonito flakes! An Asian description of Sauvignon Blanc would start with pandan leaves and longan and move on to mangosteen—not a familiar flavor or aroma vocabulary for me. But I can relate a bit better to her description of Riesling: Thai white blossoms, lemongrass, and green mangoes.

Wouldn't it be great if the most important qualities of Chinese wines—the ones that Westerners reject—turn out to have been lost in translation and that a true indigenous Chinese wine culture evolves, one that reflects China's history, cuisine, and palate. I hope so because it would support my theory of the future of wine. Suffering just now from the excesses of globalization and Two Buck Chuck, China needs to unlock its inner terroirist soul!

As you can tell, I'm cautiously optimistic that China will find a way to shape its wines and wine cultures successfully. But what about the rest of us? Are my "grape expectations" justified? Turn the page to see if you agree.

TASTING NOTES

Beer versus Wine: The Chinese did not buy the Foster's wine portfolio, as I speculated in this chapter. Instead Foster's "de-mergered" its wine and beer operations. The international wine business is now a stand-alone company called Treasury Wine Estates. Multinational giant SABMiller purchased the beer business.

Not Greek to Me: Interest in the Chinese wine market continues to intensify. The American wine magazine *Wine Enthusiast* launched a Mandarin language edition in 2012.

Location, Location, Location: Not satisfied with buying up first-growth Bordeaux wines, Chinese investors have reportedly starting buying the chateau estates themselves.

World Class: The wine community was stunned to learn that a Chinese wine had received a top prize in the 2011 Decanter World Wine Awards competition. The International Trophy for best Red Bordeaux varietal over £10 (about $16) was revealed to be winery He Lan Qing Xue's Jia Bei Lan 2009 Cabernet blend. Maybe now the French will start buying Chinese vineyards!

The Best of Wines or the Worst of Wines?

This book is a record of the journey that wine has made over the last fifty years, from the dismal post-Prohibition wine wall of the 1960s to the rather extravagant, highly globalized, heavily branded wine wall of today. The wine wars have changed wine—for the better on the whole, I think—and will continue to transform it in the future.

Writing this book has also been a personal journey for me. My life as a wine economist, as I explained briefly in the first chapter, began thirty years ago in a dark wine cellar on the Silverado Trail just north of Napa, California. That's where a winemaker taught me (through his probing questions) that wine is a product of its economic *terroir* almost as much as its natural environment and I began to think seriously about some of the ideas and themes that run through this book.

I don't know if it was chance or fate, but as I was in the final stages of writing *Wine Wars* I received an invitation to attend a series of wine events on that same stretch of highway. It gave me an unexpected opportunity to quite literally close the circle on this journey and to consider my ideas about the future of wine in terms of a particular time and place. And so, thirty years later, I found myself driving north out of Napa once again on the Silverado Trail.

RETURN TO STAGS / STAGS' / STAG'S LEAP

The invitation came from the Stags Leap District Winegrowers Association, to take part in their annual Vineyard to Vintner program, attend seminars, meet winemakers, and sample their signature Cabernet Sauvignon. The Stags Leap District didn't exist when I drove this road thirty years ago. Winemaking in this Napa Valley nook was just getting started then, although the place was already on the world wine map. The much-proclaimed red wine winner of the 1976 Judgment of Paris Old World versus New World wine tasting was a 1973 Cabernet Sauvignon from Stag's Leap Wine Cellars. It earned a total of 127.5 points on the French judges' scorecards, narrowly edging out Chateau Mouton Rothschild 1970 (126 points), Chateau Haut Brion 1970 (125.5 points), and Chateau Montrose 1970 (122 points).[1] That was enough to focus global attention on this patch of vineyard land.

The first stage of my research to prepare for the Stags Leap trip took an unexpected turn that reminded me of Warren Zevon's song "Lawyers, Guns and Money" or at least the lawyer and money parts. Most stories of famous wine regions are about places, faces, and then finally, the wine. They start with places (the *terroir),* then move to faces (of the famous winemakers who helped establish the region's reputation), and end with the wines themselves. But the Stags Leap region's story is a bit different—it really is a war story.

Stags Leap District AVA (American Viticultural Area) certainly has the terroir. The district, about six miles north of Napa on the Silverado Trail, is marked by a 1,200-foot vertical basalt palisade that is both landmark and a source of the particular soil and microclimate that helps define the district. The growing season is longer in Stags Leap than in other parts of Napa Valley, with bud break coming two weeks earlier. The grapes ripen more slowly during their longer time on the vine, which seems to have a positive effect.

Stags Leap has it famous wine faces, too. The most notable is Warren Winiarski of Stag's Leap Wine Cellars. A former lecturer in Greek at the University of Chicago School of Social Thought, he was one of the early movers in Stags Leap. The prize-winning 1973 Cab was just his second vintage. Incredibly, the winning wine was made with grapes from three-year-old vines—infants! Unfortunately, according to my sources here, the vineyard was not in the Stags Leap District but rather farther north in Napa Valley. In any case, it established the winery's and the region's reputations at once. There is even a hallmark Stags Leap style—"perfumey fruit" according to one expert, although not every wine is made in a way that highlights this.

So where do the lawyers come in? Well, the first thing I did when I started this project was to grab my copy of James Halliday's classic *Wine Atlas of California*.[2] Halliday devotes seven pages to Stags Leap places and faces and its distinctive Cabernet Sauvignon wines, but he begins his report with the most controversial part of the AVA's history: its name and the legal battle over the valuable intellectual property rights (IPRs) associated with it.

The area takes its name from the legend of a prodigious jump that a stag (or maybe several stags) took on the palisade while fleeing hunters. Warren Winiarski naturally included this colorful reference in the name of his winery, Stag's Leap Wine Cellars, when he founded the operation in 1972.

But so did Carl Dounami, who started Stags' Leap Winery just up the road, also in 1972. Two wineries, two strong personalities—they battled for years over the right to the Stag's/Stags' Leap name. More than an apostrophe separated them, of course, although any grammarian can tell you that where the apostrophe is placed makes all the difference. The right to label your wine with some variation of Stag's/Stags' Leap had obvious economic advantages and both winemakers wanted clear title to the designation. The IPR battle reemerged and intensified when the AVA was formed and its geographic lines drawn.

Clashing economic interests made the process of choosing a name and drawing AVA lines particularly contentious, according to Halliday. Although everyone agreed that the wines were distinctive, they could not agree on much else, including where the district lines should be drawn or what the resulting area should be called. "Anyone reading the testimony and the BATF[3] ruling may well wonder how any Viticultural Area can be legitimately defined, and indeed how any atlas such as this can be logically justified," Halliday reports. "For the experts could agree neither on the climate nor the soils of this tiny area, and the subsequent commentators and writers are unsure whether it is the climate or the soil (however each is defined) which makes Stags Leap District such an exceptional—and distinctive—producer of Cabernet Sauvignon."

The compromise name—Stags Leap (no apostrophe anywhere, purely plural, nowhere possessive) settled the legal squabble, leaving the real task clear: making great wine. It was hard to know how Stags Leap and its wines would develop when I first opened the door thirty years ago. There were a lot of indications that the area might turn into what some critics say the whole of Napa Valley has become—the overcommercialized Disneyland of wine.

STAGS LEAP BECOMES A GLOBAL BRAND

The combination of fine wine and global recognition made Stags Leap more than just a great terroir—it is a valuable brand, hence the squabble over intellectual property rights instead of (or perhaps in addition to) water rights, land title, and so on. The rush to invest in Stags Leap District wineries, already under way, intensified and even globalized in a way that will surprise readers who foster romantic visions of Napa Valley winemaking.

Clos du Val (first vintage in 1972) was the result of a collaboration between American businessman and wine industry investor John Goelet and Bordeaux winemaker Bernard Porter. Chimney Rock Winery (1980) looks like a South African Cape Dutch estate because its founder Sheldon "Hack" Wilson made his money selling Pepsi-Cola in South Africa. He was the largest volume Pepsi bottler in the world at one point, according to Halliday. Silverado Vineyards (1981)—a beautiful winery with a beautiful view—unintentionally reinforces the Disneyland theme because the family of Walt Disney built it, starting with a vineyard purchase in 1976 and continuing today.

It was easy to imagine thirty years ago that this trend would continue—and the wines would suffer—as more global money flooded into the tiny Stags Leap area. But some of the early Stags Leap investors were the sort of people I have labeled terroirists who value wine for its somewhereness. I suppose that Dick Steltzner would fit into this group. An experienced viticulturalist, he planted what might have been the first vineyard at the base of the Stags Leap palisade in 1965, finally making his own wine at Steltzner Vineyards in 1977.

Warren Winiarski, the guy who won the red wine competition in the 1976 Paris tasting with his Stag's Leap Wine Cellars Cabernet Sauvignon, strikes me as a terroirist, too, although perhaps he is just a stubborn, philosophical wine perfectionist. So all the pieces were in place for a battle for the soul of Stags Leap wine.

Looking back to my first visit, it seems like the Stags Leap wine war could have gone either way. Globalization, money, and media creating Coca-Cola wine . . . or the revenge of the terroirists, preserving the distinctive quality of Stags Leap.

FOLLOW THE MONEY

The big money certainly arrived and you can see it today in the deluxe facilities that the wineries have created.

Stag's Leap Wine Cellars was a tiny one-building operation when I visited thirty years ago. Now that original structure with its oak doors is Building 1 on an expanded campus of facilities that includes a network of tunnels for barrel storage and entertaining. Everything is sleek and custom-made for entertaining clients and visitors as well as making wine. The barrel room at Stag's Leap Wine Cellars is gently curved like a barrel stave. The barrels are stacked five deep.

Warren Winiarski is responsible for these changes, but he doesn't own Stag's Leap any more. He sold out in 2007 to Tuscany's Antinori family. I've read that he figured he could trust them to uphold his vision of wine. The Antinori in turn partnered with Ste. Michelle Wine Estates (SMWE) of Washington State, who *they* trusted because of their successful joint venture on Red Mountain, Col Solare. (SMWE, to continue the "reveal," is owned by Altria, a corporation that also owns Philip Morris and U.S. Smokeless Tobacco.)

Stag's Leap Wine Cellars is not the only winery in the district to be acquired by big business. Stags' Leap Winery, its rival in the apostrophe wars, has roots that go back a long way. The original vineyard was planted in 1893 although it did not become a prominent winery until Carl Doumani acquired the property in 1971, about the same time that Winiarski arrived on the scene. Stags' Leap was purchased in 1997 by Beringer Wine Estates, which was in turn acquired by Foster's Wine Group, the wine arm of the big Australian brewer, in 2000.

Chimney Rock is now owned by the Terlato Wine Group, a company that owns several notable U.S. wineries and is a major force in wine distribution (they represent Gaja and Santa Margherita wines from Italy, for example). Pine Ridge Winery, which produced its first vintage in 1978, was acquired by the Leucadia National Corporation in 1991, which also owns Archery Summit in Oregon and is best understood as a diversified holding company investing in manufacturing, telecommunications, oil and gas drilling, gaming, entertainment, and real estate activities.

So the big money did in fact come to Stags Leap and many of the wineries they created are rather grand—far from the simple cellar that I visited thirty years ago, as can be imagined. Economics dictated the large scale and luxurious feel of many of today's Stags Leap District wineries. Winemaking is capital intensive, so it is important to produce in volume. Stags Leap District AVA Cabernet Sauvignon (necessarily limited in supply by the AVA's tiny size) is often therefore produced alongside higher volume "Napa Valley" wines, for example, and Chardonnays from Carneros grapes in order to get volumes up to an economic level. Nothing wrong with that.

The plush feel of the wineries themselves, with plenty of space for entertaining, events, and on-site culinary staff, is a product of the practicalities of distribution. Direct sales—to cellar visitors and wine club members—can, if managed correctly, yield more revenue than restaurant and retail sales that must make their way through the tortuous and costly three-tier distribution system. It is important to build and establish direct-sale personal relationships and to provide appropriate winery facilities. One winery's wine club manager told me that nearly 70 percent of sales came through this direct channel. Wow! That's a lot of revenue and worth a substantial investment. So it is important to both make good wine and to create a memorable winery experience. Understandable.

But what happens to the wine in the process? Is there so much focus on image and marketing that the wines themselves are an afterthought?

My answer, based on an intense weekend in Stags Leap, is that it ain't necessarily so. Sure, we tasted a couple of wines (I won't name the makers) that seemed like they were made to catch the attention of critics more than to capture a sense of place, but for the most part the wines we sampled seemed to be authentic variations on a Stags Leap theme. And the winemakers we talked to spoke with conviction of wine made in the vineyard, not the advertising agency.

Can big multinational money coexist with an authentic idea of wine? Yes, at least in Stags Leap. (Robert Parker goes further—he seems to think that the Antinori/Ste. Michelle money and technical attention might actually restore the faded, according to him, glory of Stag's Leap Wine Cellars.)

So the way I framed my question—money, business, and globalization versus terroir—was plain wrong. Money, marketing, and multinationals don't guarantee good wine, but they don't make it impossible, either. Wine is too complicated for that. The pessimistic *Mondovino* hypothesis that the wine business inevitably destroys wine itself doesn't always hold. I'm not saying this is true everywhere, but elements of the somewhereness of Stags Leap has survived these thirty years and seems likely to persist for years to come.

GLOBALIZATION AND ITS DISCONTENTS

I've told the story of my journey in terms of three large forces that I call globalization, Two Buck Chuck, and the revenge of the terroirists. I think that wine's recent past and its probable future owe much to theses forces and the way that they combine and interact. I am optimistic that the wine world they are creating is a good one. Let me bring together the main points of the book to explain why.

It is difficult to underestimate the influence of globalization both in terms of its ability to bring a world of wines to our doorsteps and also the way it has pushed wine into unexpected corners of the world (like China, for example, and India). Globalization means more choice for those of us who live in traditional wine-drinking nations and it means new choices for "emerging" wine market buyers. Economists like me are biased in favor of choice. More choices are better than fewer choices, at least up to a point.

But more choice and new choices also present problems. Wine can be confusing if you haven't mastered the DaVino Code (and most of the new consumers have not). Choices are most efficient when markets are transparent—the qualities of products clearly displayed, the value of alternative choices readily apparent. Wine, for all its physical brilliance, is one of the least transparent products on earth. Globalization has magnified wine's confusing properties just as it magnifies so much else, creating a sort of Tower of Babel and an urgent need for some way to break through the cacophony so that wine enthusiasts can make their purchases with confidence.

Brands like Two Buck Chuck are an obvious solution to this problem, so it is no surprise that branded wines have become more important. Brands (like Robert Mondavi, Antinori, or Mouton Cadet) simplify wine, winning the Confidence Game, even if they also threaten to oversimplify it, dumbing down the idea of wine.

So simplification is one effect of the expanding market, but not the only one. As the wine wall gets bigger and more cluttered, its top and bottom extremities are exaggerated, too. The bottom shelf becomes a battle zone with wines from many countries competing for the bargain-hungry buyer. As I was writing this chapter, for example, I received reports of new discount wines in unlikely places. Walmart is rolling out its Two Buck Chuck–class wine in Japan, for example. Its own-brand Oak Leaf wine will sell for about $4 per bottle, a new low for the Japanese market.[4] British wine buyers like bargains, too, and a hard-discount chain called 99p Stores (where everything presumably sells for 99 pence or about $1.50 at today's exchange rate) announced plans for 99p wine.[5] That's not a low price compared to the basement wines in the German Aldi stores, but it is about half the cost of the next lowest-priced wine in Britain. Wine snobs are appalled and antialcohol advocates outraged, but it seems like a sign of the times. The global market is awash in cheap surplus wine and some of it is likely to come ashore at the discount store near you.

The global market also magnifies things at the top of the wine wall where the trophy wines reside. Here we have a worldwide market that focuses on the very best (or, if it is hard to tell what is best, then the most famous or the highest rated). Superstar wines that earn superstar prices (as I am writing this a case of Chateau Mouton Rothschild 1982 has sold at auction for over £14,000 or around $20,000). The only way to explain these high prices is the truth: they are what happens in a winner-take-all market when global attention is focused (like a magnifying glass focuses light) on a tiny object. Sometimes the result is simple exaggeration, occasionally it's destructive combustion. We can be happy, I think, that for all the attention that trophy wines get, they represent such a small part of the actual world of wine.

THE FUTURE OF WINE

So what about the future? Trophy wines will become even more ridiculously expensive and that's fine. Let the people who want to pay that much to own them enjoy the opportunity. It's a big wine world and there's plenty to go around.

Basic wines will be globally sourced. They may become generic in the Two Buck Chuck mold, with reliable if not exceptional quality, good enough to satisfy many at a price they are willing to pay. Remember that for most of the world (and especially the Old World, where wine consumption is in steep decline), basic wine doesn't compete with fine wine or trophy wine. Wine competes with beer, soda, juice, and water. It will succeed in this competition—creating the foundation for a durable "Wagnerian" wine culture—when everyday wine is as reliably good as these other products.

And so this leaves the vast middle ground of today's wine wall up in the air. Which way will it go? Back to the bad old Thunderbird days that I described at the start of the book? Unlikely.

Terroirists fear that the rationalizing force of the market will oversimplify wine—dumbing it down, and I acknowledge this possibility. But just as Stags Leap (wherever you put the apostrophe) was able to be both Disneyland and its opposite, I think the wine wall will become both simpler and more complex.

The simplicity that I associate with the rise of New World wine markets gives consumers confidence to buy wine and that is very important. Although some will suffer "arrested development" and never move beyond the Two Buck Chuck stage, I am confident that many will seek out the great diversity of wines that exists between the top shelf and the bottom of the wine wall and will master the intricacies of the DaVino Code. Egged on by terroirists, I think they will create a rich and diverse market for wines of every sort.

The future of wine will be much better than its past, although not all of it will be to your taste. So you see, I really do have Grape Expectations.

TASTING NOTES

The Long Finish: Now that you've finished the book (except for the final wine tasting), what do you think? I find the wine world as fascinating as when I started thinking about it thirty years ago. And although my opinions have changed a lot along the way, one thing remains the same: I still have grape expectations.

Grape Expectations Tasting

I tasted the future of wine—or at least one vision of that future—as I was writing this chapter and I invite you to celebrate reaching the end of this book by organizing your own version of this tasting.

We jumped into our rented Hyundai Sonata and corkscrewed our way on Highway 128 from Davis, where I was speaking at a wine economics conference, to Rutherford in the Napa Valley. We had three stops to make that are symbols of three ideas of the future of wine.

The first stop was at Arger-Martucci winery, a small (for Napa) five thousand case operation. The winemaker, Kosta Arger, is a Reno-based cardiologist with a passion for wine. We sipped his Petite Syrah, sourced from 140-year-old vines in Calistoga, and thought about the past of wine and how family wineries like Arger-Martucci connect that past to the present and the future. Who could have guessed back in 1870 that the vines they planted then would be producing wine today?

There are many Arger-Martuccis in the wine world today. Less than a mile away, for example, is Tres Sabores, where our friends Julie Johnson and Jon Engelskirger make authentic wines that balance the "three flavors" provided by the winemaker, the location, and the grape variety.

The third and final stop of the day was at the Robert Mondavi winery, which is about as far removed from Arger-Martucci or Tres Sabores as you can imagine given that fewer than five highway miles actually separate them.

Where Arger-Martucci (and similar modest operations) evolved as time, money, and luck allowed, Mondavi was designed with flair and style to make a statement and build a brand. And it worked, of course, making the Mondavi name one of the most widely recognized trademarks in the wine world.

Mondavi's name was actually everywhere at my conference, too. I attended a symposium at the Robert Mondavi Institute for Wine and Food Science and went to a reception and dinner at the Robert Mondavi Performing Arts Center, both on the UC Davis campus. The conference banquet took place at the winery (overlooking the To Kalon vineyards) and the postconference tour visited Opus One, the Mondavi-Rothschild trophy wine operation across the street. Mondavi was the face of American wine, especially to my European colleagues, and it presents a powerful, positive, carefully programmed image. Everyone enjoyed the Mondavi wines and great food we were served with cruise-ship class efficiency.

Although the founder's widow Margrit Mondavi hosted the dinner, the Mondavi family doesn't run Robert Mondavi winery any more. Constellation Brands, then the world's largest wine company, bought it in 2005 and manages it as part of its global portfolio. Constellation doesn't mess with the winemaking, I was told, but all the business operations have been streamlined to improve efficiency. At two hundred thousand cases, the Mondavi winery was much larger than nearby Arger-Martucci or Tres Sabores, but it is dwarfed by its own offspring, the Mondavi Woodbridge winery, which makes more than eight million cases of value-priced wines each year in its giant Lodi-area plant.

Sandwiched between the small and the big was the second stop on our itinerary, Frog's Leap. Frog's Leap is related to Stag's Leap by an inside joke. When the winery was just getting started, John Williams and his winemaking partner Larry Turley worked part-time out of an old building that had once been used as a frog farm. Williams's day job was at Stag's Leap Wine Cellars, where he helped blend and bottle the famous Judgment of Paris Cabernet Sauvignon. Since Williams had one foot on the frog farm and another at Stag's Leap, Frog's Leap seemed like a good name.

Frog's Leap is much bigger than Arger-Martucci—about sixty thousand case production compared with five thousand—but enormously smaller than Mondavi, especially if the Woodbridge wines from Lodi are included in the count. It also occupies a middle ground in another way. No one would accuse the boutique family wineries of being brands like Mondavi, but Frog's Leap really is a brand—it stands for something. The wines, the name, the elegant label, and even John Williams himself have brand recognition in the wine world.

John Williams is a terroirist whose organic vineyards are dry farmed in stubborn opposition to the conventional wisdom that favors irrigation and chemical intervention. His famous Zinfandel is a "field blend" in the style of the old Italian American winemakers. Frog's Leap success, both in the United States and internationally, confirms my optimistic view of the future of wine.

Globalization (think Mondavi) will produce lots of perfectly good but somewhere-free wines (think Two Buck Chuck) that will satisfy the needs of many consumers. But I don't think these wines will crowd out or kill off the diversity of wine that is the key to its greatness because there will always be terroirists who will have their own idea of wine and there will always be people who appreciate the differences.

Your assignment for the grape expectations tasting is to try to re-create my day in the Napa Valley by pouring three glasses: a global brand like Mondavi or Antinori (or Gallo or Two Buck Chuck) to give a sense of the high standard of wines available nearly everywhere. Then move to a wine from a very small producer like Tres Sabores or Arger-Martucci. Stop to appreciate that these two types of wines complement each other more than they compete, giving breadth as well as depth to the idea of wine.

Finally, seek out the wines of a terroirist like John Williams and consider the *tension* in the glass because terroirist wines like Frog's Leap use the techniques of globalization and Two Buck Chuck (international markets, brand power) to resist the negative effects of this system. Globalization brings the world to you, Two Buck Chuck makes it understandable and gives you the confidence to buy, but we need terroirists so that we don't forget that wine is a beautiful product of nature, not a commoditized manufactured good.

A toast: to the terroirists' revenge!

Notes

CHAPTER 1: A TALE OF TWO GLASSES

1. See Adam Smith, *The Wealth of Nations* (New York: Modern Library, 1937), 144–74.

CHAPTER 2: OLD BOTTLES, NEW WINE

1. "Berry Bros. & Rudd Future of Wine Report," tdh46.typepad.com/mondosapore/files/BerryBrosReportFutureWine.pdf (accessed November 25, 2009).

2. Data in this section taken from Glyn Wittwer and Jeremy Rothfield, *The Global Wine Statistical Compendium 1961–2005* (Adelaide: Australian Wine and Brandy Corporation, 2007), www.wineaustralia.com.

3. Hilaire Belloc, "Advice," in *History in a Glass: Sixty Years of Wine Writing from Gourmet*, ed. Ruth Reichl (New York: Modern Library, 2006), 193–94.

4. André L. Simon, *Wines of the World* (New York: McGraw Hill, 1967).

5. Simon, *Wines of the World*, 144.

6. Simon, *Wines of the World*, 607.

7. Frederick S. Wildman, Jr. "Fine Wines of California," in *History in a Glass*, 162–76.

8. Hugh Johnson, "The Wines of California," in *History in a Glass*, 155–61.

9. E. Frank Henriques, *The Signet Encyclopedia of Wine* (New York: New American Library, 1975).

10. The Ridge White Zin *was* good, apparently. Culinary maven Florence Fabricant recommended it as an aperitif in her 1986 book *Pleasures of the Table* (New York: Galahad Books, 1986).

11. See his book, George M. Taber, *Judgment of Paris: California vs. France and the Historic 1976 Paris Tasting that Revolutionized Wine* (New York: Simon & Schuster, 2005).

12. Slow Food Editore, *Guida ai Vini del Mondo* (Bra, Italy: Arcigola Slow Food Editore, 1992).

13. Data in this section is taken from Omer Gokcekus and Andrew Fargnoli, "Is Globalization Good for Wine Drinkers in the United States?" *Journal of Wine Economics* 2:2 (Fall 2007): 187–95.

CHAPTER 3: THE DAVINO CODE

1. Italy, Switzerland, and Argentina are other Syrah-producing countries. I've even tasted Canadian Syrah, too.

CHAPTER 4: MISSIONARIES, MIGRANTS, AND MARKET REFORMS

1. I've written about McDonald's and globalization in my books *Globaloney* (2005) and *Globaloney 2.0* (2010).

2. I have sampled "Alaskan" wine made far north of the 50th parallel, which seems to violate the rule, and it was tasty, too. It was technically Alaskan, according to state regulations, made using grapes from Washington State combined with a small amount of local huckleberry juice.

3. For a fine history of winemaking in New Zealand see Michael Cooper's *Wine Atlas of New Zealand*, 2nd ed. (Auckland: Hodder Moa, 2008).

4. *Montana* is Croatian for mountain—a good name for wines but confusing here in the United States, where they are marketed under the Brancott Estate brand.

CHAPTER 5: THE MASTERS OF WINE

1. Much of the information in this section is based on Sally Stening, Kaus Kilov, Larry Lockshin, and Tony Spawton, "The United Kingdom," in *The World's Wine Markets: Globalization at Work*, ed. Kym Anderson (Northampton, MA: Edward Elgar, 2004), 127–32.

2. John V. C. Nye, *War, Wine, and Taxes: The Political Economy of Anglo-French Trade, 1689–1900* (Princeton: Princeton University Press, 2007).

3. This section is based on John Burnett, *A Social History of Drinks in Modern Britain* (New York: Routledge, 1999), 155–56.

4. See Stening, Kilov, Lockshin, and Spawton, "The United Kingdom."

5. Alas, as this chapter was written in 2010 there were indications that the poor economy was forcing Tesco to pull back its ambitious plans for the more expensive house brand lines.

CHAPTER 6: CURSE OF THE BLUE NUN

1. Arend Hejibroek, *Winning Strategies in the Wine Industry* (Rabobank International, 2006), 11.

2. The Zollverein is a favorite topic of economic historians. You can think of it as one of the very oldest ancestors of today's European Union.

3. Black Tower was actually created in 1965, but it is a good example of the kind of brands that came out of this period. It remains Germany's largest export wine brand. Reh Kendermann, the producer, began producing wines of this sort in the 1920s under Carl Reh's guidance, first as négociant and then as wine producer.

4. The ad copy says it is from the "sunny Palantine region," which sounds Italian but isn't. The geographical designation is Pfalz, Germany. I'm sure it is quite good as Pinot Grigio goes.

5. Karl Storchmann and Günter Schamel, "Germany," in *The World's Wine Markets*, ed. Kym Anderson (Northampton, MA: Edward Elgar, 2004), 121.

6. The Albrecht brothers are listed as cochairmen of the Aldi firm but operate the two arms of the company separately, although based upon the same business model. Feuding brothers is not a unique story in German business history. When the Dassler brothers Adi and Rudolf of Herzogenaurach, Germany, couldn't agree about how to run their athletic shoe business, it too broke in half. One part is Adidas and the other is Puma.

7. Think about Trader Joe's and Aldi and you will appreciate the California chain's German DNA. Trader Joe's sells mainly own-brands, just like Aldi, and many of the food products are actually sourced from Europe.

CHAPTER 7: AMERICA'S HANGOVER

1. The actual figure was 8.5 liters per person of wine (and rising) as of 2005. There are nine liters of wine in a standard case of twelve 750 ml bottles.

2. See Thomas Pinney, *A History of Wine in America: From Prohibition to the Present* (University of California Press, 2005) for the most comprehensive analysis of American's Prohibition problem and the continuing hangover.

3. Assuming that wine bottles held four-fifths of a quart.

4. Now reorganized as the TTB—Alcohol and Tobacco Tax and Trade Bureau.

5. I'm using Robert Mondavi as a symbol of the rising fine wine movement in America starting in the 1970s in the same way that I used Gallo as a symbol of the post-Prohibition rebirth. Obviously there were many more winemakers involved. See Pinney's *A History of Wine in America* for a more complete account.

6. The markup on Kirkland Signature wines is 15 percent.

CHAPTER 8: MARTIANS VERSUS WAGNERIANS

1. Thomas Pinney, *A History of Wine in America: From Prohibition to the Present* (Berkeley: University of California Press, 2005), 367.

2. Pinney, *History*, 367.

3. Pinney, *History*, 367.

4. Pinney, *History*, 368.

5. See "Project Genome Home & Habits" at www.nccommerce .com/NR/rdonlyres/1DF163EE-22E2-40D7-8599-49463BF0A20C/0/ ConstellationWinesGenomeHomeandHabits.pdf (accessed May 19, 2010).

6. An English translation is available online at www.onemanga.com/Kami_no_ Shizuku/1/00-cover/. (Note: click on the images to move to the next page. Don't worry if it appears to be in Japanese—the English shows up once the story begins. Read the story panels from right to left on each page the way the Japanese do.)

CHAPTER 9: THEY ALWAYS BUY THE TEN CENT WINE

1. "Top 30 U.S. Wine Companies—Profiles," *Wine Business Monthly* (February 15, 2009), www.winebusiness.com/wbm/?go=getArticle&dataId=62893 (accessed May 24, 2010).

2. The wine is officially called "Charles Shaw Wine." Charles Shaw was a Napa Valley fine wine producer that experienced business reversals some years ago. Franzia bought up the well-regarded brand, which he repurposed as an extreme value product.

3. Rabobank Food & Agriculture Research, "New Perspectives: Wine and Marketing," presentation, Utrecht, Netherlands, October 2, 2006.

4. "Pleasure Experience of Wine Goes Up with Price," *Medical News Today* (January 15, 2008), www.medicalnewstoday.com/articles/93947.php (accessed May 24, 2010).

5. Johan Almenberg and Anna Dreber, "When Does the Price Affect the Taste? Results from a Wine Experiment," *American Association of Wine Economists Working Paper 35* (April 2009), wine-economics.org/workingpapers/AAWE_WP35.pdf (accessed May 24, 2009).

6. There is now a Charles Shaw International brand that sources wine from outside the United States. I purchased a Shiraz from southeastern Australian, which is Yellow Tale territory.

7. George A. Akerlof, "The Market for Lemons: Quality Uncertainty and the Market Mechanism," *Quarterly Journal of Economics* 84:3 (1970), 488–500.

CHAPTER 10: EVERYONE'S A CRITIC

1. See Sophie Kevany, "Jancis Robinson: Critics Should Show More Humility," *Decanter.com* (April 21, 2008), www.decanter.com/news/253184.html (accessed May 25, 2010).

2. Elin McCoy, *The Emperor of Wine: The Rise of Robert M. Parker, Jr. and the Reign of American Taste* (New York: HarperPerennial, 2006).

3. No offense intended to *Wine Enthusiast* and *Wine & Spirits.*

4. In a comment on *The Wine Economist* blog, *Wine Spectator* editor Tom Matthews suggested that it was problematic to judge his publication by its advertisers—a fair criticism.

5. George M. Taber, *The Judgment of Paris: California vs. France and the Historic 1976 Paris Tasting That Revolutionized Wine* (New York: Scribner, 2005).

6. Dennis V. Lindley, "Analysis of a Wine Tasting," *Journal of Wine Economics* 1:1 (May 2006), 33–41.

CHAPTER 11: THE MCWINE CONSPIRACY

1. Data are from a study reported in *Restaurant Wine,* #131 (2009), www
.restaurantwine.com/newsletter/issue.php?issueID=130 (accessed May 26, 2010).

2. "Yellow Tail Wines Buck Industry Trends," Yellow Tail press release (August
17, 2009), assets1.casellawines.com.au/assets/KBeqnj7C2eQ568q/yellow-tail-
buc%E2%80%A6ds-aug-09.pdf (accessed May 26, 2010).

3. Yellow Tail data are taken from Felicity Carter, "Casellas at the Crossroads,"
Meininger's Wine Business International (October 10, 2007), www.wine-business-
international.com/Company_Profiles_Casella_at_the_crossroads.html (accessed
May 26, 2010).

4. See Chan Kim and Renee Mauborgne, "Creating a Blue Ocean of Profit,"
The Chief Executive (March 2005), findarticles.com/p/articles/mi_m4070/is_206/
ai_n13471106/ (accessed May 26, 2010).

5. See "Sideways Meets Bridget Jones," *The Wine Economist* (May 29, 2008), wine
economist.com/2008/05/29/sideways-meets-bridget-jones/ (accessed May 26, 2010).

6. Terry Theise, "The Matter of Globalization" (July 2005), www.skurnikwines.com/
msw/globalization.html (accessed May 27, 2010).

7. Theise, "The Matter of Globalization."

CHAPTER 12: THE FUTURE OF WINE IN THREE BOTTLES

1. Marc Levinson, *The Box: How the Shipping Container Made the World Smaller
and the World Economy Bigger* (Princeton: Princeton University Press, 2008).

2. Augustus Weed, "Outside the Box," *Wine Spectator* (October 15, 2009), www
.winespectator.com/magazine/show/id/40580 (accessed May 31, 2010).

3. A great film with a dynamite cast: Marlon Brando, Karl Malden, Rod Steiger,
Lee J. Cobb, and Eva Marie Saint.

4. Joel B. Payne, "Bottles under Cork Account for Less Than Half of All Wine Sold,"
Meininger's Wine Business International (July 22, 2008), http://www.wine-business-
international.com/News_Bottles_under_cork_account_for_less_than_half_of_all_
wine_sold.html (accessed June 1, 2010).

5. Quotes are from "50 Reasons to Love Screw Caps," *Decanter* (August 2008), 32.

6. George M. Taber, *To Cork or Not to Cork: Tradition, Romance, Science and the Battle for the Wine Bottle* (New York: Scribner, 2007).

7. Taber, *To Cork or Not to Cork*, 265.

8. See Michael Veseth, *Globaloney: Unraveling the Myths of Globalization* (Lanham, MD: Rowman & Littlefield, 2005), 161.

9. This section is based on a short article I wrote for WineSur.com, a website that reports on the Argentinian wine industry. See "Glocalism and the Future of Argentina's Wine Industry," *WineSur* (August 15, 2008), www.winesur.com/news/glocalism-and-the-future-of-argentina%C2%B4s-wine-industry (accessed June 2, 2010).

CHAPTER 13: *MONDOVINO* AND THE REVENGE OF THE TERROIRISTS

1. Matt Kramer of *Wine Spectator* is frequently credited with the "somewhereness" definition of terroir.

2. Jonathan Nossiter, on the other hand, is an American who comes across as French in the film: soft-spoken, multilingual, wearing distinctively continental clothing. He is the son of author and journalist Bernard Nossiter and grew up in France, Italy, and other countries. Ironically, Nossiter is in some ways to film what Rolland is to wine—a flying entrepreneur.

3. This is the original French title of Olivier Torrès's excellent book *The Wine Wars: The Mondavi Affair, Globalization and 'Terroir'* (New York: Palgrave Macmillan, 2006).

4. Dogs are featured prominently throughout the film. *Mondovino* did not win the prestigious Palme d'Or at the Cannes Film Festival, but it did win the Palme Dog, for best dog film. Seriously.

5. This is taken from a comment Nossiter makes in the director's narration to *Mondovino*.

6. Even Nossiter says this in his director's commentary on the DVD of the film.

7. The province of Roussillon, with which Languedoc if frequently linked, completes the arc.

8. Jonathan Nossiter, *Liquid Memory: Why Wine Matters* (New York: Farrar, Straus and Giroux, 2009). Original French edition published as *Le Goût et le Pousoir* [Taste and Power] (Paris: Bernard Grasset, 2007).

9. These quotes are taken from Nossiter, *Liquid Memory*, 103.

CHAPTER 14: THE WAR ON TERROIR

1. The quotes in this section are from an article by Mitch Frank, "When Winemakers Attack," *Wine Spectator Online* (May 26, 2009), www.winespectator. com/webfeature/show/id/When-Winemakers-Attack_3080 (accessed June 45, 2010).

2. "Unleash the War on Terroir," *Economist* (December 19, 2007).

3. See Carolyn Wyatt, "French Wine-Growers Go Guerrilla," *BBC News* (June 17, 2007), news.bbc.co.uk/2/hi/6759953.stm (acesssed June 4, 2010). You can view a video of CRAV activists making the threat here.

4. Joseph Schumpeter (1883–1950). His best-known book on creative destruction is *The Theory of Economic Development*, first published in German in 1911. The English translation appeared in 1934.

5. Karl Polanyi (1886–1960). His best-known work is *The Great Transformation* (1944).

6. *The New York Times Twentieth Century in Review: The Rise of the Global Economy* (New York: Routledge, 2002).

7. See my *Globaloney 2.0* (Rowman & Littlefield, 2010). Chapter 7 on "Slow-Balization: Using Globalization to Fight Globalization" tells the Slow Food movement's story.

8. Jean-Robert Pitte, *Bordeaux/Burgundy: A Vintage Rivalry*, trans. M. B. DeBevoise (Berkeley: University of California Press, 2008).

9. Beverly Blanning, "Hot Topic," *Decanter* (August 2008), 58–62.

10. Gregory Jones, "Climate Change and Wine: Observations, Impacts and Future Implications," *Wine Industry Journal* (July/August 2006), 21–26.

11. Notes taken at a talk given by Greg Jones and Hans Schultz at Riesling Rendezvous 2010.

12. Gregory V. Jones, "Climate Change in the Western United States Grape Growing Regions," *Acta Horticulturae* (2005), www.sou.edu/geography/jones/Publications/GJones-ActaHorticulturae05.pdf (accessed June 9, 2010).

13. Mark Hertsgaard, "What Climate Change Means for the Wine Industry," *Mother Jones* (April 26, 2010) motherjones.com/environment/2010/04/climate-desk-wine-climate-change-mark-hertsgaard (accessed on June 9, 2010).

CHAPTER 15: THE CHINA SYNDROME

1. Michael Veseth, *The New York Times Twentieth Century in Review: The Rise of the Global Economy* (New York: Routledge, 2002).

2. The *Grape Wall of China: A China Wine Blog*, www.grapewallofchina.com.

3. See the *Grape Wall of China*, www.grapewallofchina.com/2009/09/30/no-worries-australia-targeting-china-wine-market-at-every-level/ (accessed June 11, 2010).

4. See *Wine Australia*, www.wineaustralia.com/usa/Default.aspx?tabid=5348 (accessed June 11, 2010).

5. The quotations here are taken from "Cracking the Chinese Wine Market," *The Wine Economist* (May 23, 2010), wineeconomist.com/2010/05/23/cracking-the-chinese-wine-market/ (accessed June 15, 2010).

6. My 1998 book, *Selling Globalization: The Myth of the Global Economy* (Boulder: Lynne Rienner, 1998), discusses the economic applications of chaos theory.

7. Stan Sesser, "Giddy Times for Chinese Wines," *Wall Street Journal* (March 26, 2010), online.wsj.com/article/SB10001424052748704207504575130192071419922 .html (accessed June 15, 2010).

8. Thanks to Bob Calvert for this insight.

9. Jeannie Cho Lee, "Language of Taste," *Decanter* (July 2009), 78–79.

CHAPTER 16: THE BEST OF WINES OR THE WORST OF WINES?

1. Data are from George M. Taber, *The Judgment of Paris* (New York: Scribner, 2006), 305. Eleven judges rated the wines on the European standard 20-point scale. The winner was named by summing the scores. For an interesting alternative interpretation, see Dennis V. Lindley, "Anatomy of a Wine Tasting," *Journal of Wine Economics* 1:1 (May 2006), 33–41.

2. James Halliday, *Wine Atlas of California* (New York: Viking/Penguin, 1993). The Stags Leap District is discussed on pages 105–15. The quotes are all from this section of Halliday's book.

3. BATF stands for the Bureau of Alcohol, Tobacco and Firearms—the agency that authorized the original AVA. The regulatory agency today is called TTB for the Alcohol and Tobacco Tax and Trade Bureau of the U.S. Treasury.

4. "Japan's $4 Wine, Courtesy of Wal-Mart," *Wall Street Journal* (June 18, 2010), blogs.wsj.com/wine/2010/06/18/japans-4-wine-courtesy-of-wal-mart/ (accessed June 22, 2010).

5. "Ultra-Cheap Wine Mooted for UK Store," *Decanter.com* (June 21, 2010), www.decanter.com/news/299401.html?aff=rss (accessed June 22, 2010).

Acknowledgments

It's been a long journey from that first conversation on the Silverado Trail to the book you have in your hands today. There are almost too many people to thank for their expertise, encouragement, and support, but here goes. I hope the people I've inadvertently left out will forgive me.

Thanks to these wine industry professionals who made time to help me understand what they do and why: Mike and Karen Wade (Fielding Hills Winery); Tom Hedges (Hedges Family Estate); David Rosenthal, Kirsten Elliott, and Lynda Eller (Chateau Ste. Michelle); Chuck and Tracy Reininger (Reininger Cellars); Michael and Lauri Corliss (Corliss Estates); Jeremy Soine (Gallo); Patrick Egan (Boisset); Julie Johnson and Jon Engelskirger (Tres Sabores); John Williams (Frog's Leap); William Hatcher (A to Z Wineworks); Stewart Boedecker and Athena Pappas (Boedecker); Brennan Leighton (Efeste); Allen Shoup, Michael Williamson, and Gilles Nicault (Long Shadows); Charlie Hoppes (Fidélitas); Mark Smith and Jim Duane (Stag's Leap Wine Cellars); Russell Weis (Silverado); Neal Ibbotson (Saint Clair Family Estate); Jane Hunter (Hunter's Wines); Steve Smith (Craggy Range); Robbie and Sheryl Bird (Wishart Winery); Richard Arnold and Shilah Salmon (Robert Mondavi); Norm and Eric McKibben (Pepper Bridge); Annette Alvarez-Peters (Costco); Paul Gregutt and Steve Heimoff (wine critics); Karl Storchman (wine economics guru); Tyler Colman (Dr. Vino); Cynthia Nims (wine and food writer); Patrick Emmons (wine wall expert); Ken Avedisian

(Cordon Selections); Amy Mumma (World Wine Program, Central Washington University); Steve Emery (Earth2o); and Don and Carole McCrone (McCrone Vineyard).

Special thanks to my crack team of "research assistants" (friends and colleagues who keep me supplied with breaking news, crazy ideas, and thoughtful observations): Michael and Nancy Morrell; Bonnie Main and Richard Pichler; David and Anne Seago; Pierre Ly and Cynthia Howson; Ron and Mary Thomas; Ken and Rosemary Willman; Pamela and Michel Rocchi; Kristi Veseth; Mike and Gert Trbovich; Matt Ferchen; Steve Burckhalter; Kylor Williams; Diana Phibbs; Allan Sapp; Sasha Issenberg; David Severn; Devin Visciano; Scott Hogman; Janice Brevik; and Dorothy and Lowell Dann.

This book did not make itself. I appreciate the expertise and support of the professionals at Rowman & Littlefield: editorial director Susan McEachern, production editor Alden Perkins, and copyeditor Cheryl Brubaker.

And finally the biggest thanks of all to my Number One research assistant, Sue Veseth.

Selected References

Akerlof, George A. "The Market for Lemons: Quality Uncertainty and the Market Mechanism." *Quarterly Journal of Economics* 84:3 (1970), 488–500.

Almenberg, Johan, and Anna Dreber. "When Does the Price Affect the Taste? Results from a Wine Experiment." *American Association of Wine Economists Working Paper 35* (April 2009).

Anderson, Kym, ed. *The World's Wine Markets: Globalization at Work.* Northampton, MA: Edward Elgar, 2004.

Berry Bros. & Rudd. "Berry Bros. & Rudd Future of Wine Report." tdh46.typepad. com/mondosapore/files/BerryBrosReportFutureWine.pdf (accessed November 25, 2009).

Blanning, Beverly. "Hot Topic." *Decanter* (August 2008), 58–62.

Burnett, John. *A Social History of Drinks in Modern Britain.* New York: Routledge, 1999.

Cernilli, Daniele, and Gigi Piumatti, eds. *Italian Wines 2004.* New York: Gambero Rosso, 2004.

Constellation Brands. *Annual Report* (various years).

Cooper, Michael. *Wine Atlas of New Zealand,* 2nd ed. Auckland: Hodder Moa Beckett, 2008.

Gokcekus, Omer, and Andrew Fargnoli. "Is Globalization Good for Wine Drinkers in the United States?" *Journal of Wine Economics* (Fall 2007), 187–95.

Gopnik, Adam. "Through a Glass Darkly: What Do We Talk About When We Talk About Wine?" *New Yorker* (September 6, 2004), 156–62.

Halliday, James. *Wine Atlas of California.* New York: Viking/Penguin, 1993.

Heijbroek, Arend. *Winning Strategies in the Wine Industry: Growth Opportunities in a Competitive Market.* Rabobank International, 2006.

Henriques, E. Frank. *The Signet Encyclopedia of Wine.* New York: New American Library, 1975.

Johnson, Hugh. *Vintage: The Story of Wine.* New York: Simon & Schuster, 1989.

Jones, Gregory V. "Climate Change and Wine: Observations, Impacts and Future Implications." *Wine Industry Journal* (July/August 2006), 21–26.

Lee, Jeannie Cho. "Language of Taste," *Decanter* (July 2009), 78–79.

Levinson, Marc. *The Box: How the Shipping Container Made the World Smaller and the World Economy Bigger.* Princeton: Princeton University Press, 2008.

Lindley, Dennis V. "Analysis of a Wine Tasting." *Journal of Wine Economics* 1:1 (May 2006), 33–41.

McCoy, Elin. *The Emperor of Wine: The Rise of Robert M. Parker, Jr. and the Reign of American Taste.* New York: Ecco, 2005.

Nossiter, Jonathan. *Liquid Memory: Why Wine Matters.* New York: FSG, 2009.

———. *Mondovino.* DVD. 2004.

Pinney, Thomas. *A History of Wine in America: From Prohibition to the Present.* Berkeley: University of California Press, 2005.

Pitte, Jean-Robert. *Bordeaux/Burgundy: A Vintage Rivalry* (translated by M. B. DeBevoise). Berkeley: University of California Press, 2008.

Quandt, Richard E. "Measurement and Inference in Wine Tasting." *Journal of Wine Economics* 1:1 (May 2006), 7–30.

Rabobank Food & Agriculture Research. "New Perspectives: Wine and Marketing" (October 2, 2006).

Reichl, Ruth, ed. *History in a Glass: Sixty Years of Wine Writing from* Gourmet. New York: Modern Library, 2006.

Sesser, Stan. "Giddy Times for Chinese Wines." *Wall Street Journal* (March 26, 2010).

Simon, André L. *Wines of the World*. New York: McGraw Hill, 1967.

Slow Food Editore. *Guida ai Vini del Mondo*. Bra, Italy: Arcigola Slow Food Editore, 1992.

Smith, Adam. *The Wealth of Nations*. New York: Modern Library, 1937 (1776).

Taber, George M. *Judgment of Paris: California vs. France and the Historic 1976 Paris Tasting That Revolutionized Wine*. New York: Scribner, 2005.

———. *To Cork or Not to Cork: Tradition, Romance, Science and the Battle for the Wine Bottle*. New York: Scribner, 2007.

Theise, Terry. "The Matter of Globalization" (July 2005). www.skurnikwines.com/msw/globalization.html (accessed May 27, 2010).

Torrés, Olivier (with the collaboration of Dorothée Yaouanc). *The Wine Wars: The Mondavi Affair, Globalization and 'Terroir'* (translated by Kirsty Snaith). London: Palgrave Macmillan, 2006.

Veseth, Michael. *Globaloney: Unraveling the Myths of the Global Economy*. Lanham, MD: Rowman & Littlefield, 2005.

———. *Globaloney 2.0: The Crash of 2008 and the Future of Globalization*. Lanham, MD: Rowman & Littlefield, 2010.

———. *The New York Times Twentieth Century in Review: The Rise of the Global Economy*. New York: Routledge, 2002.

———. *The Wine Economist*. WineEconomist.com.

Week, Augustus. "Outside the Box." *Wine Spectator* (October 20, 2009).

Wittwer, Glyn, and Jeremy Rothfield. *The Global Wine Statistical Compendium 1961–2005*. Adelaide: Australian Wine and Brandy Corporation, 2009.

Index

About the Author

Mike Veseth is an authority on global wine markets. He is the author of *The Wine Economist*, a leading wine industry blog, and teaches a popular class on the Idea of Wine at the University of Puget Sound, where he is Robert G. Albertson Professor of International Political Economy.

Recipient of many honors and awards, Mike was named Washington Professor of the Year by the Carnegie Foundation for the Advancement of Teaching in 2010. Mike is the author of a dozen books including *Globaloney* (named a Best Business Book by *Library Journal*) and *Globaloney 2.0*. He is currently writing a book on "extreme wine" that will explore the far edges of the wine universe to uncover the best, worst, cheapest, most expensive, and most unexpected wines.